...eorge Clapp Vaillant was born in Boston, Massachusetts, in 1901. He was educated at Harvard, where in 1922 he received the degree of Ph.D., and later he taught at Harvard, Yale, Columbia University, and New York University. His special subject was the early civilization of Mexico and Central America, and he was considered the foremost authority in these fields. His field studies included numerous expeditions to North Mexico and Arizona, and also to Yucatan and Egypt. He was an active member of many archaeological societies in America and in Europe, the author of a large number of pamphlets and articles, and for several years curator of Mexican archaeology at the American Museum of Natural History. He died in 1945. This new edition has been revised by his widow, Suzannah B. Vaillant.

George C. Vaillant

Aztecs of Mexico

*origin, rise, and fall of
the Aztec Nation*

Revised by Suzannah B. Vaillant

Penguin Books

Penguin Books Ltd, Harmondsworth, Middlesex, England
Penguin Books Inc., 3300 Clipper Mill Road, Baltimore 11, Md, U.S.A.
Penguin Books Pty Ltd, Ringwood, Victoria, Australia

First published in the U.S.A. by Doubleday, Doran and Co. Inc. 1944
First published in Pelican Books 1950
Reprinted 1951, 1953, 1955, 1956, 1960, 1961
Second Edition first published by Doubleday 1962
Published in Pelican Books 1965
Reprinted 1968

This edition published 1966 by
arrangement with Doubleday & Company, Inc.

Printed in the United States of America

For Our Children

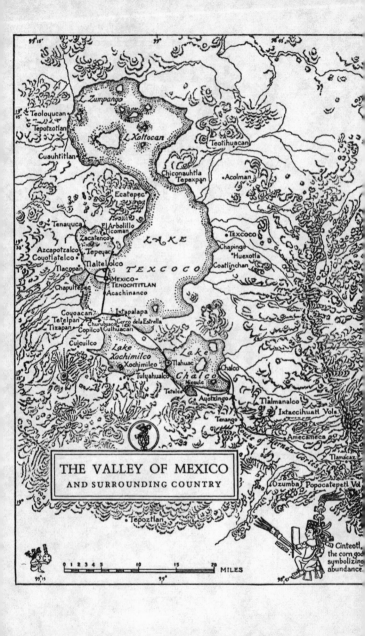

THE VALLEY OF MEXICO
AND SURROUNDING COUNTRY

Cinteotl,
the corn god
symbolizing
abundance.

0 1 2 3 4 5   10   15   20   MILES

Contents

List of Tables

List of Text Illustrations

List of Text Illustrations

List of Plates
and Acknowledgement of
Sources of Plates, Photographs,
and Originals

The writer acknowledges his deep obligation to the American Museum of Natural History for allowing him to use the blocks illustrating articles in the museum magazine, *Natural History*, and other publication series of this institution. In some cases plates in other publications were copied, following general scientific procedure. The list below designates the source of the illustrations taken from such published material and later used in the magazine or guide-leaflet series. Where the photograph was made directly from a museum original for the journal the term *Natural History* is used. Unless otherwise designated the originals are all in the Middle American collection of the American Museum. The writer, therefore, wishes to express his thanks to those scholars whose illustrations are copied here.

The reviser likewise wishes to acknowledge with thanks permission to use original photographs, for which in each case credit is given, as well as photographs from the files of the Hon. Robert Woods Bliss, the National Geographic Society, the Peabody Museum, the Cleveland Museum of Art, and the Instituto Nacional de Antropología e Historia, whose initials, I.N.A.H., will be used in giving credit.

List of Plates

Foreword to the Revised Edition

It is twenty years since publication of the first edition, and in that time new excavations and new studies and the advent of radiocarbon dating* have solved some old problems and posed some new. It is logical that I should attempt the revision that has for some time seemed necessary, not so much because I shared in the work that led to the writing of the original volume, as because it seems essential to me that its text be interfered with as little as possible. So much of the classic quality of this work lies in the author's very personal creative imagination, that to make all the changes that a wiser scholar than myself might have wished, would result in a new book.[1]

Many such will and should be written. My own aim, however, has been to delete entirely, or to bring up to date, only such statements in the original as are no longer accepted by contemporary workers in the field, without altering a single felicitous phrase. There has been no attempt to include new archaeological material or to bring into line with modern sociological thought the chapters on Aztec life. The chapter on the Toltecs has been divided into two, one on Teotihuacan and the other on Tula. The discussion of the 'Olmecs' has been slightly expanded, a few new plates have been included and a few alterations made in the advice to tourists at the end of the book. It is hoped that these changes will be enough for the average reader. For the student I have considerably emended the tables, and added to each chapter notes which will be found at the back of the volume among the bibliographical references. My own bibliography has been incorporated into

* See Notes, beginning on p. 280

the author's, but it may be assumed that all the titles dated before 1941 are his and the subsequent ones mine.

In deciding which changes should be made I have had the advice of C. A. Burland, whose own *postscripta* to the first Penguin edition (1950) and to the Italian edition (1957) have added so much, and of John Paddock, whose *Notes* (1956) were published to help students to make better use of the original edition. Gordon Ekholm, who would have preferred a more drastic revision, spent long hours working on the problem and gave me the benefit of his labours. Due to the generosity of James Griffin in Ann Arbor, and the staff of the Peabody Museum Library at Harvard, I had access to all recent publications. Many scholars too numerous to mention, both in Mexico and in this country, took time to answer my letters, or to talk to me about the problems that faced me. Gordon Willey and Eduardo Noguera saved me numberless hours of bibliographical research, and to them my debt is enormous. Ignacio Bernal gave valuable assistance in the selection of plates. The graciousness of old friends like Robert Wauchope, Samuel Lothrop, A. V. Kidder, Alfonso Caso, William D. Howells, Linton Satterthwaite, Daniel Rubin de la Borbolla, Stephan Borhegyi, and Philip Phillips was matched by the interest of a new, Suzanna Miles.

Ellis Settle, Joanna Vaillant Settle, and Natalie Stoddard helped in the preparation of the manuscript. William Brudon prepared a new map and four new drawings. Robert T. Hatt gave me advice, practical help, and moral support, without which I would not have had the courage to proceed. Clara Claasen of Doubleday & Company was patient with my many vacillations. To all these people I extend grateful appreciation. Where this revision proves valuable the credit is theirs, but where it fails, the responsibility must be all my own.

SUZANNAH B. VAILLANT

Foreword to the First Edition

This book is a history of the Indians of the Valley of Mexico and the civilizations which they wrought. It was a hard book to write. It will be a hard book to read. There are two reasons for this unfortunate circumstance. First, the Indians did not have the same goals in life which we have, so that their pattern of life is different from our own and difficult to understand. Second, Indian history has to be reconstructed from what we can find, so that much of the material, like techniques of making household implements, does not fall within the scope of our usual historical reading. The first five chapters deal with such reconstruction, and the reader is warned in advance that the going will be very difficult. These pages may be skipped if he is not particularly interested in such a historical background.

The remaining chapters are based on contemporary observations made by the conquering Spaniards and by the Aztecs themselves. They deal with people who were seen alive, their culture functioning. We can form an impression of what the Aztecs were like, and this makes easier reading, since we can envisage people in terms of what they did, not in terms of the objects which they made. Even so, this will not be a crystal-clear process, for their customs, habits, and motives differed from ours. However, I hope that I shall be able to show that it was a perfectly good way of life, and the result of considerable experience. Our Western civilization, on the social side, is nothing to boast of today, so we need not be scornful of the Aztecs.

I want here to express my thanks to some of the many people who helped me write this book: to the authorities of the American Museum of Natural History for providing me with the sinews of research and the time to exercise them, to the authorities of the Mexican government for their consistent courtesy and cooperation in making my work possible, to my colleagues in my own and other lands, who by their friendship, counsel, and collaboration make one proud to be an Americanist. To my wife I owe especial thanks for her unfailing aid and comfort during the long hours spent in the field and laboratory and in the preparation of this book.

To Colonel Theodore Roosevelt, Mr A. P. Tedesco, and Mrs Mary Slavin of Doubleday, Doran I am grateful for stimulation and counsel. To Dr Edward Weyer I am under deep obligation for permission to incorporate illustrations and articles from *Natural History*. I wish to thank Miss D. Levett Bradley for her excellent sheet map of Aztec Mexico and, last, but by no means least, Miss Frances Jay for her unflagging patience and judgement in preparing this manuscript and smoothing the path of the reader who traverses the ill-marked trail of this aspect of Indian history.

To Mr Clarence L. Hay I am deeply indebted for collaboration in field and laboratory as well as for supporting much of my research, and to Mr Willard Carr for underwriting our last field season, which brought this book into being.

One of the strangest feelings left to us by prehistory is the sensation of omen. It will always exist. It is like an eternal proof of the *non sequitur* of the universe. The first man must have seen omens everywhere, he must have shuddered at each step.

Giorgio de Chirico

MESOAMERICA —
SOME ARCHAEOLOGICAL SITES

Panuco
Tajín
Tula
Chupicuaro
El Opeño
Teotihuacan
Tenochtitlan
Cholula
Malinalco
Gualupita
Xochicalco
Chalcatzingo
Remojadas
Cempoala
Cerro de las Mesas
Tres Zapotes
Tuxtla
La Venta
Monte Alban
Mitla
Chiapa de Corzo
Bonampak
Kaminaljuyú
Uaxactun
Tikal
Chichen Itza
Labnah
Uxmal

Chapter 1

The Historical and Cultural Background of Aztec Civilization

A somewhat speculative summary of the social and economic factors which directed the rise of Indian civilization

The history of the Americas records the colonization and settlement of a great continent. We take a just pride in our European ancestors, who, from the Vikings down to the most recent political exiles, set forth to find a new life in the changing conditions of a new land. Our histories and traditions describe the evolution of these colonies into the present group of American republics, and it is a remarkable episode in the story of mankind. Yet the European settlement of the Americas, for all its modern political significance, is just a late phase of the history of man on the American continent. The Asiatic colonization of the New World, which preceded the European infiltration by many centuries, has its own proud place in the annals of Continental America.

This immigration from Asia produced the American Indian. Without his preliminary development of the resources of the continent it is dubious whether the European occupation would have succeeded as it did. The great Indian civilizations of the Aztecs and the Incas challenged the European imagination and opened a rich life for their military conquerors. The humble farming skill of the tribesmen of North America's eastern seaboard sustained religious exiles until they could live off the land and create their own type of commonwealth. The Indian and his culture were soon ploughed under, but they enriched a soil which otherwise would never have produced the lavish harvest of Pan-American civilization.

The most violent clash between the Indians and the Europeans took place in the Valley of Mexico during the early

25

summer of 1520, when Cortés and his Spaniards achieved the Conquest of Mexico and overthrew the Aztec civilization, the most advanced Indian culture at that time. Cortés's success was the loadstone which drew to the Americas the iron might of Europe. Stone could not withstand steel, and the days of the Indian were numbered. The history of the Aztecs and their forebears is a synopsis of the rise of Indian civilization and its doom.

The Aztecs were a concentrated population of independent groups living in the Valley of Mexico and later welded into an empire, whose authority reached out to dominate much of central and southern Mexico. Their history and social customs are better known than their neighbours because their conquest had such a far-reaching significance for the European world. Spanish observers of military, priestly, and civil status wrote careful accounts of the Aztec life and history, and Indian authors a generation later augmented these records, drawing on the tribal lore still only thinly veneered by Christianity. A few pictographic records, either prepared before the Conquest or copied afterwards, are precious additions to the Aztec annals. However, our chief data on Indian history come from archaeology, that branch of research which recovers social history through the study of the surviving remains of human handiwork in ages past.

Most of the American Indians had not developed writing, so that archaeology is the one available medium for reconstructing their past; and the Aztec records reveal only a few centuries in the life of a single group. To sketch the broad background of Aztec culture before we turn our attention to the people themselves, we should realize that the earth must be our archive, the shovel our reading glass, and that nature, eternally destroying to create anew, has scattered our materials over mountain, plain, and forest, from Greenland to Tierra del Fuego. Aztec history, like that of the American republics, begins with the discovery of this continent. (See Plate 1.)

Long before the Aztecs existed the ice sheets began to retreat northwards, as the last glacial era was ending. Those animals accustomed to cool climates gradually moved north, and small nomadic bands of hunters followed the game on which their lives depended. Some of these groups moved up through Siberia and reached the shores of the Bering Strait. With so much water held in suspension by the ice sheet, the sea level was probably lower than now, so that the islands were larger and the extent of water between them less. In winter the sea was doubtless choked with ice, and, crossing over this ice, hunters and hunted could reach Alaska. Thus man discovered America and made his first settlements there.[1]

Other hunters may have constructed rafts and boats and passed from island to island until their ceaseless search for game led them to the mainland. The process must have been slow and the migrating units small. We can reconstruct conditions from what we know of modern hunting tribes, who, as social fossils, still pursue a precarious existence in the old, old way. The primitive hunting group moved on foot and had no effective beasts of burden. Therefore they carried little in the way of food or equipment. Their progress was no faster than that of the oldest man or woman, or youngest walking child. Food had to be secured even on the march, and hunting was a slow and arduous process. Such conditions necessarily kept the group units small, for a large cluster of people, when on the march, besides requiring food in quantity, must also scare away the very game on which its nourishment depends.[2]

This nomadic hunting life had its effect on language and physical type. The tendency for hunting groups to split into smaller units whenever their numbers threatened the balance between consumption and available food supply, encouraged the establishment of isolated bands. This loss of contact with other groups intensified mannerisms of speech and thought, so that profound dialectic differences resulted after several generations. Inbreeding also followed, and strains of physical type became established. Such conditions, already existent in the Asiatic life and continued under American conditions, probably account both for the linguistic diversity among the Indian groups and also for their great physical variation within a more or less homogeneous frame of dark eyes, straight or wavy black hair, and a yellowish skin colour.[3]

When this infiltration took place, or how long it continued, has yet to be expressed in exact dates. No tools of a lower paleolithic type have been uncovered in the Americas, but excavations on the campus of the University of Alaska have turned up tools like those found in neolithic stations on the Gobi Desert. Other stone implements, defined by archaeologists as Folsom culture, occur in association with the remains of extinct bison at sites in Colorado and New Mexico. Far to the south, in a cave on the southern tip of the Argentine, the dung of an extinct sloth is mixed with the tools and refuse of men who hunted and ate an extinct type of American horse. Sloth dung also seals in the remains of Nevada hunters.

The discovery in 1947 of 'Tepexpan Man' in possible association with mammoth remains and an obsidian chip, and the subsequent finds, in 1952 and 1954, of the bones of mammoth unquestionably killed or butchered with artifacts of flint and obsidian, suggest that Paleo-Indians lived and hunted in the swampy lands that surrounded the lakes as long ago as 10,000 to 9000 B.C. There is some possibility that the skeletal remains of a woman uncovered in Midland, Texas, antedates Tepexpan man by five thousand years. Radiocarbon test results on buried campfires have run as far back as 35,000 B.C. It would seem, then, that the first man came to America during the late Pleistocene, probably the middle of the fourth glacial period.[4]

Hunting techniques have thus been established as an early form of Indian life in America. Some of the first hunters fished with net and line and gathered shellfish as their chief nourishment. Deep accumulations of discarded shells are found along the coasts of the Atlantic and Pacific and along some of the great inland rivers of North America. In one such heap in Tennessee the earliest layer disclosed bone implements, and no stone tools appeared until very much later. Man, from his earliest beginnings, must have used these rich and relatively stable sources of food.[5]

Another primitive livelihood is disclosed along the shores of dried-up lakes in California and Texas. Mortars and grinding stones found here indicate that the early people ground nuts and seeds into flour, while a lack of well-made stone points suggests that they found the gathering of vegetable foods a more reliable way to fill their larders than the hunting of game. These desert cultures are highly important since they provide early evidence of an economy which led eventually to the development of agriculture.[6]

These three early ways of life – hunting, fishing, and gathering – were often combined in whole or in part. There is no hunting group in the Americas which does not take advantage of vegetable products to some extent, and in North America the properties of four hundred species were known and utilized. Some tribes found their hunting economy so satisfactory that they never abandoned it. Other peoples, like the Eskimos, were so situated geographically that they had to hunt or starve. The Plains tribes, when they acquired the domesticated horse from the Spanish colonies, turned from a successful if drab farming life to a highly dramatic existence, living off the wandering buffalo herds and exalting masculine virtues in war and the chase. Fishing groups, like the tribes of the Northwest coast, were able to live in sedentary villages and create an elaborate social and material culture on the rich abundance yielded by forest, stream, and ocean. In California one of the densest populations in the Americas maintained itself by gathering wild nuts and fruits, supplementing this diet with shellfish and game. Yet in spite of these successful primitive techniques the Indian would have never attained really high cultures without the domestication of plants.[7]

In the New World there were two centres of intense agricultural development, Mesoamerica[8] and the Andean region, which likewise represent the peaks of Indian social and material culture. There is considerable discussion among botanists as to which area first had domesticated plants, but the problem is not yet resolved. Perhaps the answer to this question may have a botanical rather than a social significance, since there are several other areas where plants not cultivated in Mexico and Peru are agricultural staples. The presence, early in the history of America, of peoples who lived largely by gathering must have led almost inevitably to the independent development of several different types of agriculture, based on the food plants common to particular regions.[9]

The great staple of Brazil, for example, was manioc or cassava. Before the introduction of corn in eastern North America, sunflowers, the giant ragweed, and other plants of prairie and savanna were cultivated for their seeds. The highlands of Peru yielded the white potato, but at the time of the Conquest the great basic American foods, corn and beans, were diffused over most of agricultural America. Radiocarbon datings indicate that beans were being cultivated in Huaca Prieta, Peru, in 3000 B.C. and in Mexico in 5000 B.C.; that corn made its appearance in Mexico as early as 3000 B.C. and had reached Huaca Prieta by 1500 B.C. True maize pollen has been found in the Valley of Mexico at levels beneath all evidence of human occupation; and the ancestors of modern corn have been discovered and studied genetically.[10] However, the great principle to bear in mind is that no plant cultivated by the American Indians was known to Asia, Europe, or Africa prior to the white settlement of America. The introduction of these plants more than doubled the available food supply of the older continents.

The development of agriculture accomplished, in America as elsewhere, the liberation of man from the constant search for food. A permanent food supply which could be enlarged by bringing fresh land under cultivation allowed the population to grow. The precarious equilibrium maintained by nature between population and food supply became more stable, and man had leisure to invent techniques and to develop rules for societal behaviour. It became possible to support aggregations of people large enough for the individual to specialize according to his skill and for the community to carry out public projects like irrigation systems and temples.

The successful growth of agriculture was not paralleled in the raising of animals. True, the dog, which may well have come in with the immigrants from Asia, was almost universally domesticated. In the north it was a beast of burden; in Mexico, an article of diet. The Mexican and Pueblo tribes tamed the turkey. The Peruvians ate guinea pigs and raised llamas and alpacas for wool and transport; bees were kept for honey in Mesoamerica and north-west Brazil; some southern Mexican tribes raised cochineal for dye. But the native horse, which might have proved as useful here as in the Old World, became extinct early in America; the cow and sheep were unknown, and the caribou and bison, which, if domesticated, might have taken their place, had their chief range in regions occupied by primitive groups who were content merely to hunt them.[11]

This lack of suitable domestic animals prevented man's migration on an extensive scale, comparable to that of the great hordes from Asia which beat against the walls of Rome. At first the nomadic groups in the Americas were too small to threaten seriously the sedentary groups, and the question of population pressure, so often an indirect cause for war in the Old World, was virtually non-existent in Indian America. War techniques in consequence were little developed in the Indian cultures, and the killing and rapine which took place during the white colonization did not have its origin in the usual Indian political attitudes.

The invention of agriculture accentuated rather than

changed the basic structure of Indian social organization. Those groups which gradually shifted their economic reliance from hunting to farming were in thinly populated country. As their population increased they could enlarge their fields without infringing on the rights of previous inhabitants. A growing population scared away game, forcing neighbouring hunting groups to withdraw to regions where wild life was more plentiful. If the available arable land became insufficient for the community a number of people drifted away to found a new settlement.

According to the environment, be it forested or semi-arid and consequently open, there tend to be two types of settlement. In dry open country the minerals which plants need remain near the surface, so that fields can be farmed over and over again. The people, therefore, can maintain a permanent village. Forest country, on the other hand, presents a serious problem to Stone Age people. To clear ground for planting, trees must be girdled and, after they die, burned. The soil, therefore, rapidly becomes exhausted and incapable of supporting crops. The Indians met this situation in two main ways: by moving the entire village, or by allowing each family group sufficient land so that crop rotation would permit exhausted fields to recover by lying fallow. This last method tended to decentralize the population except in very small communities.[12]

The social implications of these two methods of life are highly important for reconstructing the genesis of American Indian culture. The food plants used by the higher civilizations in the Americas seem largely derived from highland, open-country species, emanating from the kind of region permitting the maintenance of a permanent village. In a community where the village street was a forum, technical school and social centre interests were pooled and techniques improved by emulation and inherited experience. The opportunity to store accumulated equipment, as opposed to the bare

broadly, concentrated on the material technique of supporting life; the Mesoamerican on spiritual or, more accurately, supernatural methods. In the Andes, especially in the coastal valleys of Peru, enormous cities were built and vast irrigation systems watered the fields. Weaving was developed to a point unequalled by man in the whole course of human history, and pottery in excellence of construction and richness of design had no peer in the Americas. This civilization culminated in the Inca Empire, the original benevolent, monolithic state, which combined territorial expansion with the amalgamation of conquered peoples into a social whole.

In Mesoamerica, however, the ceremonial life dominated the civil structure, and the remains of temples rather than cities gauge the splendour of the past. Excavations at Teotihuacan and other sites have shown that there came to be, as necessary support for these centres, a very complex urbanization in highland areas before the time of the Conquest. But the early Classic empires of Mexico were loosely held together by peaceful trade relations and common gods. Even the 'militaristic' Post-classic peoples waged war as much for ceremonial as for political reasons. The cause or causes for this difference are shrouded in the past, but the more primitive North American scene suggests that here again agricultural conditions played a part.

The Indians of the arid South-west built permanent towns but did not devise an imposing ceremonial architecture. In the south-eastern United States the more sophisticated tribes reared great earthen platforms to support their temples and the houses of their chiefs, and to serve as centres at which the community membership might congregate at specified times. The demands of a forest agriculture did not permit the occu-

---

civilizations that flowered at about the same time in many other areas. We call Post-classic the militaristic period that followed the first influx of Nahua-speaking peoples into the Valley and culminated in the great Aztec Empire which the Spaniards found at the time of the Conquest.

pancy of permanent towns like those of the Pueblo country, since the south-eastern tribes had to move their villages, whenever the soil of their farm clearings was exhausted. A good part of the year saw the able-bodied men and women virtually abandon the villages to hunt and gather wild food. But they all united for tribal rites at the ceremonial centres and thus strengthened the bonds of social solidarity, loosened and frayed by the conditions of their ecology. The ceremonial centre occurs late in the history of the South-east and bears the earmarks of a trait imported from Mexico.[14] Yet it answered a very definite need for maintaining social unity in the growing population of a forest area.

Therefore it seems reasonable to suppose that some such ideas germinated centuries before in the lowland forests[15] of Mesoamerica, since the elaboration of this social and ceremonial requirement became a dominant theme in Mesoamerican civilization. There is nothing strange in this practice which characterizes the earlier culture patterns in the development of western Europe and the colonial United States. The great cathedrals of the Middle Ages loomed massively out of a countryside wherein miserable villages, set in tiny clearings, made a violent contrast between the poverty of man's individual material existence and the rich glory of his corporate spiritual life. In New England communities still survive where the church, the store, and the town hall are the social centre for people scattered in isolated farms over the forested hills. The master artists who covered the miles of sculptured temple walls in Cambodia lived in flimsy towns now totally consumed by the jungle. Both the act and the fact of ceremonial building coalesce into a tangible expression the relationships of man to society and of society to the universe; so it is not surprising that different peoples have independently adopted this practice which, in the modern United States, we follow in structures like libraries, hospitals, colleges, and governmental buildings, used primarily for the public benefit.

perform and direct the elaborate ritual, to build the ceremonial structures and to develop the arts and crafts which gave the religion its outward expression.

The Mayas of Guatemala, Yucatan, south-eastern Mexico and western Honduras attained the greatest eminence in the elaboration of this cult. Their temples and priestly dwellings were built of masonry and roofed by means of the corbel or false arch. The sculpture in stone and plaster adorning these buildings has the elaborate sophistication of a matured art. Their carefully pondered delineation of their gods and goddesses reflects theological maturity. Their writing is set forth in conventionalized hieroglyphs, of which only the calendric texts can be deciphered. It is this calendar which particularly excites the admiration of our Western civilization, for it is based on a highly evolved mathematical and astronomical system.[20] (See Plates 6–8.)

The Maya calendar should be a great aid in reconstructing history, but opinions differ as to how it should be correlated with Christian dates. There are several calculations designed to reconcile the Maya with the Christian calendar, but each correlation involves a difference of some two hundred and sixty years in the expression of Maya dates in Christian terms. This lack of agreement has led to quite divergent interpretations of Maya history, although the main trends are well established.[21]

The complexity and elaboration of the Maya civilization, barely touched on here,[22] have challenged the imagination of explorers and students. Extravagant theories have been woven by seers and visionaries as to the origin of the Mayas in lost continents like Atlantis or Mu. Soberer judges see them as American in origin and credit them with carrying to a higher degree, without implication of greater antiquity, a civilization shared by their neighbours.

The excavation and study of remains in Mesoamerican sites disclose a symmetrical cultural development which began at the Pre-classic plane and passed through a long period of highly stylized local development, only to be cut short by a sudden decline and the intrusion of cult practices from Central Mexico (Table 1). In the Maya area even the Pre-classic plane is not uniform at the several sites where it is represented. Pottery and figurines differ so strongly in style and ware as to suggest their manufacture by unrelated groups.

In the last millennium B.C. these Pre-classic forms became more sophisticated as the people began to build temples, to erect stone time-markers and to develop a mature religious art. The differences in style observable earlier became strongly marked as the Classic cultures unfolded, but pottery vessels made at one site have been found as trade objects in another, so we assume that the local cultures were in a broad sense contemporary. We think now that this flowering began just before the Christian era and continued for perhaps a thousand years, and we know from traditional sources that about the tenth century A.D. tribes of Nahua stock moved into the Maya country, where they founded various local dynasties. This movement is reflected in the archaeological remains which show influences from the Toltec culture.[23] (See Plate 27.)

The Maya region, prior to the tenth-century infiltration from Mexico, contained peoples speaking different dialects and having distinctive regional styles in their material culture. Their religion and calendar, however, were essentially the same throughout the area. On the mainland of Mexico we find that the regional populations had not only distinctive arts but also different theological conceptions. Yet these Mexican civilizations, like that of the Maya, had their roots in the Pre-classic cultures and succumbed at the end to Toltec influences.

The recent discoveries of the so-called 'Olmec' culture in southern Vera Cruz and Tabasco suggest a tantalizing explanation for the origin of Mesoamerican civilization. At the sites of Tres Zapotes, La Venta, and San Lorenzo great

Fig. 1. Original drawing by William Brudon of a laughing head from Central Vera Cruz in the collections of the Universidad Autónoma de México.

Fig. 2. Original drawing by William Brudon from a figure in a private collection from the Remojadas area. The similarity to Teotihuacan is no coincidence.

of 'Olmec' art to adorn their buildings. Hieroglyphs accompanied some of them, suggesting further connexion with Vera Cruz; and two 'Olmec' divinities, the infantile god and the tiger god, were represented in ceremonial vases of the period. But a later phase showed a gradual shift away from 'Olmec' influence. Stones were inscribed in a distinctive writing, and calendric calculations were set forth, not in the elaborate long count of the Mayas, but in an abbreviated system which fixed a date in terms of a fifty-two-year cycle.

The third and fourth stages of Monte Alban were of long duration. The Zapotecs grew less susceptible to foreign influence and developed a strongly regional theology and art. (See Plates 5, 9, 10.) At the close of this era they appeared to be in contact with northern peoples, like the Teotihuacanos of Central Mexico, and their culture underwent a transformation in its fifth and final period. The development of the Mixtec[30] of western Oaxaca, who occupied Monte Alban in the Post-classic period, seems to parallel that of the Zapotec. Whether they came into the Valley of Oaxaca at this time and brought with them new gods, a new art, and a new type of calendar and writing, is not yet determined.

Certainly a religious civilization was spreading into the Maya country, carried by members of a totally different linguistic stock, the Nahua, and it reached its zenith among the Aztecs of Central Mexico. Research has not progressed to the point where we can identify the formulators of this civilization. Its place of origin seems definitely to centre in the lands of the Mixtecs in northern Oaxaca and in the territory of Nahua tribes in Puebla. Thus to call the civilization Mixteca-Puebla and to identify its latest carriers under their tribal name, when this is known, seem the best ways to reconcile cultural with political history. In much the same way we use the term Western civilization to cover those culture elements shared by the nations of Europe and the Americas. (See Plate 30.)

In Central Mexico, at the north-western frontier of the

Table I.32 PRINCIPAL CULTURE SEQUENCES IN THE AMERICAS

Approximate dates	NORTH AMERICA		MESOAMERICA								SOUTH AMERICA	
	U.S. south-east	U.S. south-west	Valley of Mexico	Puebla & Morelos	Oaxaca	Vera Cruz & Tabasco	Lowland Maya	Highland Maya	Huastec	Chiapas	Peru North Coast	Peru, South Highlands
1600		Pueblo 5										Late Ica
1500			Tenochtitlan Tlaltelolco	Cholula 5							Inca	Inca
1400		Pueblo 4	Texcoco	Cholula 4	Monte Alban 5	Zempoala			Panuco 6	Chiapa 12	Chimu	Late Ica
1300		Pueblo 3	Tenayuca									
1200			Culhuacan				Mayapan	Chinautla				Middle Ica
1100	Late Mississippi	Pueblo 2		Cholula 3 / Historic Olmecs / Xochicalco 4 / Gualupita 3	M. Alban 4 / Mitla	Tajin 3 / Upper Cerro de las Mesas	Toltec-Chichen		Panuco 5	Chiapa 11		
1000								Ayampuc			N.C.	Pacheco
900			Tula								Tiahuanaco	
800		Pueblo 1						Pamplona				
700	Early Mississippi	Modified Basket Maker	Ahuizola Amantla			Tajin 2 / Upper Remojadas 2	Puuc Tepeu	Amatle	Panuco 4	Chiapa 10		
600												
500								Esperanza				
400	Woodland Cultures	Basket Maker	Xolalpan Tlamimilolpa	Xochicalco 3	M. Alban 3B	Tres Zapotes 3 / Tajin 1	Tzakol	Aurora		Chiapa 9		
300					M. Alban 3A	Lower Cerro de las Mesas 2 / Upper Remojadas 1			Panuco 3			Nazca
200				Xochicalco 2							Mochica	
100	Hopewell		Miccaotli	Cholula 1				Santa Clara		Chiapa 7		
0												

Post-classic Period (upper portion); Classic Period (lower portion)

Pre-classic Period

Date	Paracas / Salinar / Chavín (Peru)	Pánuco (Huasteca)	Holmul / Chiapa (Maya)	Guatemala Highlands	Veracruz / Olmec	Oaxaca (Monte Albán)	Central Mexico Highland	Valley of Mexico	Southwest	East (Adena)
100								Tracualli, El Tepalcate, Tlapacoya, Ticoman, Cuicuilco		
200	Salinar — — —; Paracas — — —	Pánuco 2, El Prisco					Chalcatzingo, Gualupita 2			Adena — — — —
300			Holmul 1; Chiapa 4	Arenal	Lower Cerro de las Mesas, Tres Zapotes 2	M. Albán 2				
400		Pánuco 1, Chila	Chicanel				Xochicalco			
500		Aguilar		Miraflores, Providencia, Majadas						
600	Chavín — — — —				La Venta, Lower Remojadas, Tres Zapotes 1	M. Negro, M. Albán 1	Cholula I, Chalcatzingo, Gualupita I	Tlatilco, Copilco, Mid Zacatenco, El Arbolillo		
700			Mamom	Las Charcas					San Pedro	
800		Ponce	Chiapa 3		Trapiche					
900			Chiapa 2							
1000							Yanhuitlan?			
1200		Pavon	Chiapa 1	Arevalo				Early Zacatenco, El Arbolillo I		
1400								Chalco		
1600								Tepexpan	Chiricahua	
3000									Cochise	
5000									Folsom	
10000	Huaca Prieta									
15000										

reeds, attracted a teeming abundance of wild fowl. On the wooded mountain slopes deer abounded. During the rainy season thick alluvial deposits, ideal for primitive agriculture, were washed down along the lake shore.

As village sites, the Pre-classic peoples selected points along the lake where they could take the greatest advantage of the natural resources of lake and forest, and cultivate most easily their crops of corn, cotton, and other plants. Once located in a suitable spot, they stayed there for a long, long time, enough for twenty-five feet of refuse to accumulate at the site of El Arbolillo, and fifteen at Zacatenco.

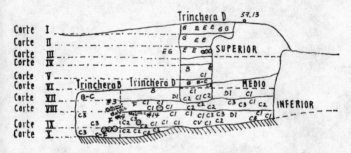

Fig. 3. Section through refuse heap at Zacatenco, with figurine types noted.

Their homes were impermanent affairs which left no remnants of foundations, floors, or fire pits. Little fragments of burned clay, impressed with stick marks, suggest that the dwellings were of wattle, daubed with mud and covered by a thatched roof, like the homes of modern Indian communities in this very Valley. The inhabitants were not troubled by ideals of sanitation or civic neatness, and threw their refuse on their own doorsteps. Broken pottery, animal bones, all the nameless trash that man rejects, found their way to the dump heap, but its most conspicuous element was corn shocks which, in the absence of domestic animals, had no possible use. This vegetable matter, disintegrating into earth, caused the middens to accumulate rapidly and, indirectly, has aided archaeological research, for an object dropped into this mess was as lost as the proverbial needle in a haystack. Even the dead found their way into the middens, not, however, because of their survivors' lack of respect, but because graves were dug more easily with wooden tools in the soft, churned earth of the refuse heaps than in undisturbed soil.

Mexican myths and annals give no clue to the identity of these men or the language they spoke. The study of their skeletal remains reveals a people of medium height, composed of several physical strains; but not enough material has been amassed to trace these affiliations precisely. The middens, however, filthy and fly-blown as they may have been, are real historical documents. Laid down gradually through the years, the successive layers disclose the different types and styles of the people's tools and utensils.[2]

Archaeological research refers to these Lower Pre-classic remains in the Valley of Mexico as the Copilco-Zacatenco culture, named from the sites where the material was first studied. The stylistic sequences also receive their names from the places where they were first determined. Specimens of the entire period were referred to as Archaic until 1917, when the first real excavation defining the Lower Pre-classic material was made under the lava quarry of Copilco. In the winter of 1928–9 excavations at Zacatenco showed that the Copilco remains were a late stage in the history of the Lower occupation of the Valley. Two years later the excavation of El Arbolillo produced deep beds of Early Zacatenco material enabling us to detect three stages of which the earliest, El Arbolillo I, preceded Early Zacatenco.[3] (See Plate 1.)

Thus archaeology works with two sets of factors, peoples in the past and their material remains; the terms used in distinguishing the one do not always apply justly to the other. A style of pottery may be very useful and important in defining

period they gave this practice up, changed the vessel shape and, after the bowl was fired, took a piece of obsidian and etched a running pattern that had the same relation to the previous stiff geometric design that script has to block lettering. (See Figures 4, 5.)

Painted decoration was not very popular. At one village, Zacatenco, in the early period, there was a fashion of painting white geometric designs on red clay. Later on this style shifted to spreading white slip on vessels and adding a simple solid design in red. There was some further experimentation in trying out different types of slip, but the most conspicuous change was the shape of the bowls which, in the later period, differed markedly from the earlier forms.

This impression of smug competence, uninspired by artistic yearnings, is borne out by the little baked-clay images which the people made in abundance. They were usually female and may have represented a mother goddess, symbolizing growth and fertility, a conception common among the religious ideas

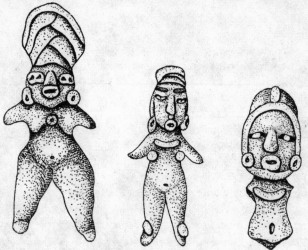

Fig. 6. Lower Pre-classic figurines, types C3, C 1–2, B–C.

of mankind. The figures were not valued in themselves, as they are almost always found broken and discarded in the refuse heaps. Distinctive styles seem to have developed in different regions. Among the vastly more numerous locally made figurines there are a few which are the standard types elsewhere, so that if the little idols were not traded they must have been brought in by pilgrims. When we consider how carefully, even if naïvely, the figures were made and how clay idols were manufactured in later periods to represent specific gods, we must conclude that they had religious significance even at this early date.[5]

The early sculptor did not work in stone or wood, but clay. His figures were small, seldom over six inches high. His method was to model the head and torso first and then add details, like arms and legs, nose, eyes and ears, by pinching on little pieces of clay. Later the figurine was fired, and often after firing the face and body were painted with ornamental designs. The sculptor strove for a naturalistic effect rather than following a rigid convention. Yet standardized ways of doing things produced styles that vary according to site and to changes in fashion. (See Plate 14, top.)

In our modern world we are accustomed to sophisticated and self-conscious art forms. Seen objectively, these Lower Pre-classic figurines are dumpy and gross. Short, fat bodies, blobby noses, protuberant eyes, and stubby arms and legs are not attributes of a graceful form, according to our way of thinking. Yet handling one of these figurines and tracing each step in its formation, one is conscious of an intense seriousness and comprehends a whole world of thought dammed by the want of technical facility in expression. An intuitive person sometimes sees a populous world of shining fantasy behind the meagre scribbling of a child. Behind these figurines must have existed an austere realization of the complex rhythms of birth, growth, and death in nature, epitomized in the miracle of woman and her bearing of children. (See Plate 14, bottom.)

of mankind. The forces were not valued in themselves, as
they are almost always found, hither-and-dissential of the
future stage. Distinctive styles seem to have devel-ped in
different regions. Among the vastly more numerous simple
made a pattern corresponding to the the standard type
elsewhere, so that the figures were not reduced any must
have been broadened by enquiries. What we can in- how
carefully, even if naively, the figured were made, and how the
fields were manufactured to their growth to represent great
gods, we must conclude that they had religious significance
even at this early date.

The only a hero did not work in stone or wood, but they
little figures were small, without over six inches high. The
method was to model the head and torso first, and then add
limbs like arms and legs, most overstall done by piling over a
little pieces of clay. Later the figures were fixed and often over-
firing the face and body were painted well, ornamental design. The arc hope above for a naturalistic effect rather than
following a rigid convention. Yet so attracted ways of doing
things produced styles that vary according to site and to
characteristic sion. (See Plate 3a, top.)

In our culture world the preoccupation of to sophisticated and
self-conscious art forms been objectively the expressive. Features feature: exotic lips and great clusters of bodily lineal.
noses, protuberant eyes, and stubby arms and legs are not
emblem of a grace, they were, they deter was of childlike
Yet handling one of these figures and to make each step well
ornament, one is conscious of a sure sense of manners and com-
portment as. while we feel that disciplined by the want of
technical facility in expression. A primitive people, remember
are a frequent world, a living, sharp, both I the promote
and through a childish-kind rose the tempo, more unconscious;
an acute realization of the complex rhythms of bird,
growth, and death in nature epitomized in the nature of
women, and how is known. Children. (See Plate 3a, bottom.)

The religious significance of the figurines is less intelligible. A common concept in the religion of farming peoples is that of a female principle or generative force, tied in with growth and productivity. A goddess frequently symbolizes that belief, since man often invests the processes of nature with his own attributes and motives. The little clay figures of Zacatenco and El Arbolillo always represent women, some of whom carry children in their arms, but no two wear precisely the same costume. At Tlatilco sexless and a few masculine figures occur, and monstrous types are common.

Such evidence is little to build on, but it is all we have. We do not know what lay behind the sculpture in the way of theology, philosophy, and ritual. The modern Pueblo Indians of our own South-west have few ceremonial objects which could survive destruction and decay, yet such implements by no means reflect the full complexity of religion and ritual which these people possess. We should not, therefore, leap to the assumption that the Lower Pre-classic people were lacking in religious development because of the crudeness of their surviving ceremonial equipment.

The only other index to the religious practices of this period is the treatment of the dead. They were buried, but seldom according to a set plan. Some were contracted, others extended; usually a single person was buried at a time. Yet group burials occurred, and the differences in the age and sex of the occupants of a single grave suggest a family interment. The skeletons exhumed show no marks of death by war or sacrifice. Disease has left no trace, but over a quarter of the dead were children, and few individuals reached old age. Offerings like pots, tools, weapons, and ornaments often accompanied burials, but prosperity in life may have had something to do with the practice. At El Arbolillo one half of the dead, irrespective of age and sex, had offerings, but at Zacatenco, less than five miles away, only one out of eighteen were so honoured.[8] The mourners covered a few of the corpses with red paint made from hematite; they left with one man his ornaments of turquoise mosaic, and endowed a tiny baby with two jade ear ornaments and two pottery bowls, an unprecedented gift, suggesting exceptional parental grief or wealth. Some of the dead they dumped into shallow pits, while they stretched others out in formal tombs, lined and covered with stone slabs and floored with clean beach sand.[9]

The government of the Pre-classic people is not told in this earthy record. The economics are only faintly outlined: hunting, farming, and a little trade to the south. Status in society was apparently recognized, since the burials differed in richness of equipment, and most people grant honour to the dead in the same proportion as prestige to the living. The tenor of life was peaceful in the main, but nature seems to have intervened with occasional violence. At Zacatenco the lake level suddenly rose just at the dawn of the late period. Whether the changes in art styles were brought in by refugees, driven from their homes by the rising waters, or were due to modes and fashions from farther afield is still a moot question. Some communities, inhabited at the end of this period, were abandoned as local floods swept over them, sealing the remains under several feet of silt.[10]

The third or Upper Pre-classic period, from about 600 to 150 B.C., covers the occupation of Ticoman and the beginning of ceremonial centres. To the latter part of this period contemporary writers assign the pyramids of Cuicuilco, Tlapacoya, and El Tepalcate (built apparently after Tlatilco was abandoned), as well as those of the Sun and the Moon at Teotihuacan and the first pyramid at Cholula, in Puebla. The Upper Pre-classic Culture throve in the Valley of Mexico, Morelos, Puebla, Michoacan and in Vera Cruz. It was already in existence during the later phases of the Transitional period in Morelos, south of the Valley of Mexico. Whereas the Copilco-Zacatenco styles ceased abruptly, the Upper Pre-classic techniques persisted into the later Teotihuacan civilization

Trade was much more extensive than in earlier times. Shell was more abundant and more carefully worked, but the varieties were those of the Vera Cruz coast, in contrast to the west-coast origin of the early Pre-classic shells.[13] Ornaments and axes of jade, porphyry, and serpentine also pointed to an eastern origin, but fragments of pottery seemed to disclose a wide radius of commercial activity.

The wave of technical experiment that affected the other artisans also stimulated the sculptors, and they began to elabor-

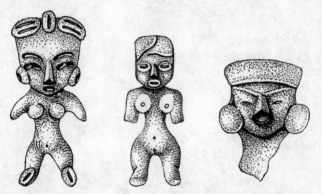

Fig. 10. Upper Pre-classic figurines, types E and H2, Tzacualli E4.

ate these shapes, making grotesques as well as naturalistic human beings, in which they tried to depict different positions and even actions. (See Plates 19, 20, top.) They polished the surfaces to enhance the form by the lustre of its finish. To our modern eye the results are not particularly impressive, but they marked a step in the technical development of the art. Finally, out of this chaos in miniature, two styles developed that must have been satisfactory to the local sculptors, since they were in vogue to the exclusion of all others. In one the figures were coated with a polished white paint, sometimes touched up in red. They were shown seated or standing, arranging their hair, covering their eyes, holding a bowl, and performing various different acts. In the other there was a return to applying pieces of clay in meticulous detail, emphasizing ornaments and hairdress, as well as the limbs and features of the individuals. While most of the figurines were female, a few were obviously male, a suggestion, even though tenuous, that their theology was becoming more complex as outside influences reached them.

Supporting this theory, we find two carefully individualized beings portrayed with more or less skill. One in the Transitional period is a figure with a contorted mouth and the general lineaments of a baby. At Tlatilco in the Valley of Mexico and at Gualupita in Morelos, there are superb and large-sized representations that stand far above the general artistic norm. They seem truly to reflect in clay the strange infantile beings, hewed out of gigantic boulders or graven on stone slabs, that dominated the religious art of the 'Olmecs'.[14] (See Plate 3, top left, bottom left.)

The other being, portrayed in the Upper period both in clay and stone, is an old man who sits with bowed head, supporting on his head and shoulders a bowl for burning incense. This god was also important in the Teotihuacan civilization and in Aztec times, when he was appropriately called Huehueteotl, the old God, and sometimes Xiuhtecuhtli, Lord of Fire. Such a divinity is peculiarly fitting for a volcanic region, and his presentation as an old man suggests the manifest antiquity of mountains. His continuous worship for many centuries would seem to make him the oldest god ritualistically shown in Mesoamerica, even though the mother goddess of corn and growth may represent an earlier concept.[15] (See Plate 17.)

Yet the full impact of Mesoamerican religion on those Central Mexican villagers is symbolized by the great adobe mound of Cuicuilco. On the skirts of the volcanic range of Ajusco, at the south-west of the Valley, they built a massive oval mound, approximately 369 feet in diameter and 60 feet

Mexico and the ballast for its tracks and its motor roads. In exploiting the quarries the early discovery of Copilco was made. Then the artificial mound projecting through the Pedregal challenged the imagination of Dr Gamio, who requested Dr Byron Cummings to undertake the excavation of Cuicuilco. Finding traces of man underneath this impenetrable sheet of rock suggested a culture of immeasurable antiquity. The oldest legendary history of Mexico reached back only to A.D. 900 for the founding of Tula. What happened between that date and the cataclysm of the Pedregal? That was a problem for archaeology to answer, if it could.

First the materials from Copilco and Cuicuilco, the two buried sites, were compared and found to be different. Then these styles were discovered in other parts of the Valley in open sites, unaffected by the local eruptions which formed the Pedregal. Next several seasons of work in these open sites disclosed that not only was Copilco older than Cuicuilco but that Copilco-Zacatenco culture was represented by rubbish heaps twice as deep as those at Cuicuilco-Ticoman. There is no way to measure the rate of accumulation of such heaps. However, on the basis of a deposit at Pecos, New Mexico, the beginning and ending dates of which are more or less known, it did not seem unreasonable to compute six or seven centuries' duration for Copilco-Zacatenco and three hundred years or so for the life span of Cuicuilco-Ticoman.[17] (See Figures 3–10.)

The next step was to fit Cuicuilco-Ticoman to the later phases of Indian history in Mexico. Cuicuilco and Ticoman material is stylistically akin to pottery and figurines found at mound sites in Puebla and Morelos, suggesting that the massive shrine of Cuicuilco in the Valley was an outpost. The baby-face divinity suggests the highly ceremonialized 'Olmec' culture in Vera Cruz, and the Fire God occurs not only at Ticoman and Cuicuilco and the Upper Pre-classic site of Jalapazco, in Puebla, but also very frequently at Teotihuacan.

Actual examples of Teotihuacan culture have appeared in Gualupita and Ticoman. Yet much more significant was the discovery at Teotihuacan that its earliest phase was closely affiliated to pottery and figurines commonly occurring at Cuicuilco, Ticoman, and Gualupita. Thus the beginning of the Teotihuacan civilization was a part of the same cultural manifestation that we have characterized as the Upper Pre-classic. The lava flow of the Pedregal must be dated in terms of the continuous history of the Valley of Mexico. Cuicuilco was abandoned before the flow took place and, to judge from the destruction, an appreciable time before. Geologists guessed the time of this flow anywhere from two to ten thousand years ago, which was not helpful. Fortunately radiocarbon dating can be more precise, placing material from Cuicuilco at somewhere between 828 and 328 B.C. Correlating this with archaeological findings modern writers think the eruption may have occurred about 300 B.C.

Therefore, we must conclude that one or two millennia prior to the dawn of the Christian era sedentary farmers were maintaining themselves in the Valley of Mexico. Their culture was sufficient for their needs, and very little in the way of outside influence affected them for a time. Then influences in art or, more precisely, religious representation began to modify their culture; and new people, perhaps from the regions east and south of the Valley of Mexico, must have come into the Valley, producing a ferment of technical and religious experiment. They showed greater interest than their predecessors in modelling and technique, and exercised something of an artistic independence between villages. Their most impressive contribution was the introduction of religious architecture and the beginnings of defined ritualistic art. Their contacts in trade and in intellectual inspiration were with the peoples of the east coast, but they worked out their styles in their own way. Some groups built clusters of mounds; others seem not to have taken up this type of architecture.

They abandoned Cuicuilco, where they built their largest platform, possibly owing to warnings of the cataclysm that later took place when the Pedregal was formed. Meanwhile other groups, one to the north and one to the east, had built important mounds at El Tepalcate and Tlapacoya.[18] This last continued its importance into the Classic period. Eventually one of these Pre-classic occupations at the north-east side of the lake developed leadership over all the rest, when Teotihuacan evolved into the great ceremonial centre, first and mightiest of the temple cities of Central Mexico.

With the foundation of this new capital the frontier of Mesoamerican civilization shifted from the south and east of the Valley of Mexico to the territory north and west of it. The Valley was no longer merely the home of farmers tilling their fields or of villagers taking their first steps towards ritualized civilization, but the proud domain of the Teotihuacan 'giants', founders of civilization in Central Mexico, whose influence would reach far and wide, and who would lay the foundations for the Toltec and Aztec empires that would follow.

Table 2. SUMMARY OF HISTORY OF PRE-CLASSIC CULTURES

LOWER PERIOD 1500–1000 B.C.: Permanent villages, gradual evolution and changes in pottery and figurine types. Long occupation, stages of which are better defined at some sites than others.

Early El Arbolillo I: Figurines, C_3a, C_3b, $C1–2$, $C2$, pottery incised black with red paint. Pacific shells.

Intermediate El Arbolillo I, Early Zacatenco: Figurines, $C1–2$, C_2, pottery incised black, thick black, white, white-on-red, vague olla necks; laurel-leaf points.

Late El Arbolillo I, Early Zacatenco: Figurines, $C1a$, $C1b$, C_3c, C_3d, $D1$, early F; pottery as in intermediate period.

TRANSITIONAL PERIOD 1000–600 B.C.: Permanent villages, sharp shift in figurine and pottery styles, introduction of new figurine style, type A; evidence of local floods. Atlantic shells.

Transitional El Arbolillo I, Transitional Zacatenco: Figurines, B–C, B–F.

Copilco, Middle Zacatenco, El Arbolillo II: Figurines, A, B, F, C_5; pottery thin black with etched design, red-on-white, red-on-yellow, trade wares; stone points with tangs.

Tlatilco:[19] Figurines A, D_{1-3}, C_5, D–K, 'Olmec' types. White spouted trays and gadrooned black bottles identical to Morelos types. Rich burials.

In Puebla and Morelos pottery and figurines more like Tlatilco than other Valley sites.

Gualupita I, Cholula I: Figurines D_{1-3}, K, O; Pottery, simple silhouette bowls and bottles in brown and red ware.

UPPER PERIOD 600–150 B.C.: Permanent villages, introduction of platforms and altars; evolution from Upper Period in Morelos and Puebla; in the Valley distinctive figurines and pottery which go through gradual evolution; ritualized presentations; some sites better defined than others; first settlement of Teotihuacan and erection of large pyramids; lava flow of Pedregal after abandonment of Cuicuilco.

Early Ticoman-Cuicuilco I: Figurines, E_1, E_2, E_3, I_3; red-on-yellow incised pottery; disk earplugs.

Tlatilco: Continuing into this period?

Intermediate Ticoman, Cuicuilco II: Figurines G_1, G_2, I_1, I_2, E_4, J, M, N; red-on-yellow pottery with white outline; incised earplugs.

Late Ticoman, Cuicuilco III, Late Zacatenco, Gualupita II, Teotihuacan I, El Tepalcate, Tlapacoya: Other sites in Puebla and Morelos; figurines, H_{1-5}; in Gualupita, C_9 and hollow figures; fire gods at Cuicuilco and Ticoman; pottery polished and elaborate tripod supports; carved earplugs hollowed in centre.

Chapter 3

Teotihuacan and the Classic
            Period

A description of a civilization, the monuments
of which are the wonder of Mexico

The dignity and awe in which Aztec tradition holds the
'place of the Gods' affect the modern visitor to Teotihuacan.
Here in the valley which bears its name, a vast area, three and
a half miles long and nearly two miles wide, was given over to
clusters of imposing buildings. The whole zone was paved
with a plaster floor, not once but many times. This was no
ordinary city nor merely a great ceremonial centre given over
to temples and houses for the people engaged in religious
activity. There is little trace of the humble refuse of communal life and there have as yet appeared no mean dwellings
within the zone. But lay people must have lived at the edge of
the sacred precincts, in early times at Oztoyahualco to the
north-west, and later at Tlamilolpa and Xolaplan on the east,
as well. To support this complex society a very much larger
area must have been under intensive cultivation by peasants
subject to the great theocracy. Indeed, Teotihuacan is an impressive monument to the toll which men exact from themselves for their salvation.[1] (See Plate 21.)

The architects built their city in several successive precincts,
extending southwards from the mighty Pyramid of the Moon.
This was not a true pyramid but was truncated at the top to
give space for a temple, and the ascending planes were skilfully
broken to provide terraces. A broad stair led up the south side
from a wide rectangular court. Additional buildings flanked
this plaza, and several hundred yards to the east and west two
smaller precincts added to the symmetry of the plan.

Two rows of buildings of impressive size lead south from
the Moon Plaza. Excavation of one revealed lovely frescoes,

the content of which suggest a temple of Agriculture. Another group of small mounds lies off to the east, and directly south is a second large unexcavated group of temples, which, from the emplacements found in the vicinity, is called the Group of the Columns.

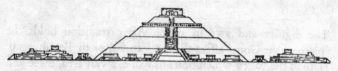

Fig. 11. Reconstruction of Teotihuacan. The Pyramid of the Sun and surrounding precinct.

The Pyramid of the Sun dwarfs all the other buildings in Teotihuacan. This great truncated pyramid, almost seven hundred feet at the base, rises in four terraces to a height of over two hundred feet. The slopes were varied by their builders to create an impression of greater mass. The exterior was faced with stone and covered with plaster, but the pyramid proper was built of adobe bricks, made from the refuse beds of an earlier era. The fragments of pottery, figurines, and tools, imbedded in the interior, belong to the first Teotihuacan period, and were made by the residents of Oztoyahualco in the north-west who are thought to have been the Pre-classic founders of this great civilization and the builders of both great pyramids, though the most recent evidence suggests enlargements in later periods.

The Pyramid of the Sun is surrounded by a wide platform, constructed of square cells, walled by adobe and filled with refuse and rubble, belonging to the beginning of the Classic period. The houses of priests may have lain outside the enclosure. Smaller mounds extend southwards, each group of which seems to consist of several buildings around a plaza, and to have contained a combination of priestly dwellings and a minor temple. Most have been built over, so that the visitor gets the impression of two storeys, whereas actually only one was in use at a time. In one of these there are floors of mica, the ceremonial significance of which is unknown. In another there were found a great many effigy jars representing the Rain God, Tlaloc.

A river makes a natural terminus at the south, but across it lies a magnificent platform, the walls of which are faced with carved stone blocks; but the crowning temple has disappeared. The feathered serpent is the dominant decorative motive, and great heads carved in rugged simplicity project from the balustrade and from the façades. These were originally painted, and glared at the onlookers through eyes of burnished obsidian. Along the façade the serpent heads alternate with those of a strange being, who may be Tlaloc, the Rain God. On the wall behind them the undulating bodies of the snakes are carved in low relief, and sea shells, all Caribbean varieties, are used to fill the spaces left by the curves of the bodies. The effect is massive and awesome. Though lacking the sinuous grace of Maya relief, the decorative scheme, none the less, is that of an achieved art. There was no fumbling in this work of many craftsmen, labouring through the years, cutting stone with stone. This building, called for a long time the Temple of Quetzalcoatl, seems also, as we have seen, to honour the Rain God, Tlaloc.

Once the city was completed in all its mighty scope, a transformation took place. From the Pyramid of the Moon, at the north, to the Temple of Quetzalcoatl, every single building was rebuilt. Rooms were filled in and façades covered up to form platforms for new temples. Not even the gigantic hulks of the Pyramids of the Sun and Moon escaped the addition of new stairs and façades. The Temple of Quetzalcoatl, as was fitting, received the most extreme alteration. (See Plate 22.) The original shrine became the core of a high platform which dominated a huge enclosure, surrounded by a broad rampart. This wall supported four lesser platforms on each of three sides and, on the eastern wall behind the main structure, three such temple foundations.

The later building is less massive than the earlier. There is less use of hewed stone, and rubble is extensively employed. Although the reconstruction extended eventually to rebuilding the whole sacred area, no violent shift in the styles of pottery or figurines suggests conquest. The new architecture has all the earmarks of a religious reformation which destroyed the symbolism of one cult to uplift a new. Moreover, in one sector of the city, the filling between the late and the early pavements produced much burned material such as charcoal, adobe, pottery, and the like, as if the debris from incendiary fires had been utilized for foundation material. There are no written records from Classic times to help us understand what happened, but it may be that the greatness of Teotihuacan did not long survive this third great building period.[2] Certainly the levies of man power, time, and materials sufficient to achieve it would have been enough to bring about serious popular disorders.

People continue to live, though their religion change and their kingdoms perish. Their basic techniques for maintaining life persist likewise. Therefore, tools and pottery give a more continuous guide to unwritten history than the soaring bulk of religious architecture. The material culture of Teotihuacan is an important index to the history of its occupants. The contrast between articles for household use and for ritual became sharper as the Teotihuacan culture reached its full development. The rhythms of change in different types of activity do not always synchronize, but in the Teotihuacan culture we distinguish four periods. (See Table 3.)

The beginnings of Teotihuacan culture are revealed by the contents of the adobes in the Pyramid of the Sun. The pottery fragments and figurines show an amalgamation of four culture strains, one deriving from the Upper Pre-classic, another containing the germs of the later Teotihuacan periods, a third tying in with western Mexico and a fourth of unknown provenance. The little clay figures are hand-made and closely affiliated with Upper Pre-classic types. The early Teotihuacanos developed a new kind of idol made of crudely incised stone. A combination of three-coloured pottery, like that of Ticoman, with a lost-colour process, resulted in a four-colour polychrome which was highly characteristic. Clay earplugs were as common at Teotihuacan as at the other Pre-classic sites. While the early Teotihuacanos did not make, style for style and piece for piece, implements identical to those of their contemporaries at Ticoman or Cuicuilco or Gualupita, their material culture comprised specific elements drawn from each particular site.[3]

There has been no satisfactory radiocarbon dating as yet of Teotihuacan material[4] but most archaeologists today think that the site was occupied for about a thousand years, that the first building period was over by the time of Christ, and that the Classic civilizations then began all over Mesoamerica. After the Teotihuacanos completed their first big building operations their handiwork became more conventionalized and more stylistically unified. Polychrome pottery gave way to simple lustrous wares of black and brown or vases and large jars painted in red on yellow. A flourishing trade sprang up in the importation from somewhere in Puebla[5] of a thin orange ware that attains at times almost an eggshell delicacy. For use in their religious rites the Teotihuacanos constructed cylindrical wares of black or brown which they carved in ritualistic patterns, utilizing such techniques as simple incision, champlevé, and, very rarely, intaglio.

Their stone and bone tools were not capable of much elaboration. However, since abundant deposits of obsidian were close at hand, the Teotihuacanos used this material lavishly, flaking blades to a scalpel-like narrowness and chipping tools of every variety. They made figurines[6] and little animals of this hard and brittle substance and ground it to mirror-like smoothness to make eyes for their great stone idols. In addition they used lava, not only pecking out great blocks for facing their buildings but also carving designs and creating a sculpture. The great step they took was to formalize their religious art. Clay figurines which carried the main trend of artistic development in the Pre-classic cultures, became conventionalized into simple little figures of men and women whose faces were reduced to their bare anatomical essentials. Women were shown dressed in *huipiles* and *enaguas*, men in the *maxtli* or loincoth. The sculptors painted the faces and the costumes of both male and female figures. The growth of ritualistic definition may also be seen in representations of the Old God, of a god in a human skin, later known as Xipe (Our Lord the Flayed One), and in composite figures, having attributes of men and animals among which the jaguar predominated.[7]

Their mastery of stone sculpture was most evident at the Temple of Quetzalcoatl, where able presentation was subordinated to the decorative demands of architectural ornament. To make incense burners the sculptors embodied the idea of the Old God seated under his bowl. Other artists traded for jade and porphyry and wrought these hard substances into beautiful masks and figures which stand out as masterpieces of Mesoamerican sculpture. Much of the work in stone has disappeared, smashed by the Spanish priests or broken into building stones, but two colossal examples still survive. One is the ten-foot statue of the so-called Goddess of the Waters, now in the National Museum. Jade ornamants, *huipil*, *enagua*, sandals, every detail is set forth, not as graceful accents to a suave naturalism but as the ornament to an architectural creation. This goddess is a monument, a sort of monolithic building, that symbolizes the implacable force of nature. The other statue was never finished. It lies still anchored to its matrix of living rock in a ravine near Texcoco. Larger by far than the Goddess of the Waters, battered by the elements,

Fig. 12. Fresco from Temple of Agriculture, Teotihuacan, showing people taking part in an offering ceremony.

the deity of Coatlinchan cannot fail to impress the modern visitor. Its concept is grandiose, but the engineering skill was lacking to cut the sculpture free of its base. Prometheus in his chains may symbolize the tragedy of European thought, but to me this goddess, still an integral part of the land that made her, represents the paralysis of Indian civilization.[8] (See Plate 24.)

Painting and drawing found an outlet in the requirements of ritual. The frescoes of the Temple of Agriculture show an appreciation of decorative design combined with a sense of natural values. One fresco which has now disappeared but which fortunately was copied at the time of discovery depicts a ceremony before two divinities like the Goddess of the Waters. At Tetitla the god Tlaloc can be seen in all his panoply, and at Tepantitla charming little figures represent what is thought to be his paradise. At Atetelco jaguars and coyotes alternate in a sumptuous frieze.[9] (See Plate 23.) Carved vases of the second period present in full ritualistic detail the attributes of tiger gods and other divinities, and little definitive symbols indicate that some sort of writing was in priestly use. Unfortunately no sacred books have survived.[10]

A ceremonial centre like Teotihuacan must have exemplified the best work of which a culture was capable. The civil centres are just beginning to be explored. In the neighbourhood of Teotihuacan, some few miles from the sacred city, great communal dwellings were built, embracing fifty and sixty rooms set about patios connected by passage-ways. The rooms were made of adobe and rubblework covered with plaster, and supported a life of comfort and security. There was also an altar prominently placed, for religious duty was not confined to the ceremonial zone.[11]

Another huge settlement lay across the lake at Azcapotzalco. Here the land is tremendously fertile, so that the old

Fig. 13. Teotihuacan pottery ceremonial vase in champlevé, Miccaotli period; ceremonial vase with fresco decoration representing a butterfly, same period; vase from Azcapotzalco, late period, polished red ware and degenerate design.

buildings have been razed to level the fields for present-day agriculture. Modern excavations to get the clay used in brick and tile have yielded a rich stream of objects, and a few days' digging produces hundreds of specimens.

At Azcapotzalco and at Xolalpan and Tlamilolpa near Teotihuacan, hundreds of skeletons were buried under the floors of the houses. Adults were usually seated, and the quantity of pottery vessels accompanying them suggests the richness of the economy. At Azcapotzalco sometimes the people had great feasts, and after partaking they cast their dishes into pits prepared for the purpose. Since clay idols were thrown in likewise, we may be sure that these festivals were religious in character. Once we found a great red-and-yellow bowl in such a deposit. It contained the remnants of the *pièce de résis-tance*, the upper legs and hips of a human being, the most succulent portions for festive consumption. There is also other evidence of human sacrifice.[12] At the Temple of Quetzalcoatl individuals were buried under the corners as foundation deposits. At both Teotihuacan and Azcapotzalco shallow dishes, cut from the top of skulls, testify to other rituals involving sacrifice and death.

Teotihuacan had a pervasive influence on its neighbours.[13] Remains are found in the Valley of Toluca, in Morelos, and most abundantly in Puebla, where at Cholula the Teotihuacanos constructed a whole temple site of enormous extent. This site has produced no carving, but one temple had a fresco decoration portraying the Butterfly God, a mythological being, important to Teotihuacan religion.[14]

The third phase of Teotihuacan consisted of a tremendous reconstruction of the city and a great florescence of the plastic arts. The figurines of this period represent some of the finest modelling ever achieved in Mexico. The faces were so carefully constructed that some students have considered them portraits. At first hand-made, later they were copied in moulds and retouched to bring them to a detailed perfection. Finally, like the other arts and crafts, the portrait style degenerated, to be replaced by mould-made heads of coarser workmanship. At this time, the fourth period, Teotihuacan ceased to function as a sacred capital. The last architectural change has the appearance of having been made simultaneously, in contrast to the gradual development of the original city. Teotihuacan was built over hastily with the maximum use of original construction. The abrupt change in figurine styles suggests that new gods were being honoured. The drain on human resources, implicit in such large-scale construction, would lead readily to revolt under the strain.

Crop failure could have resulted from deforestation and the consequent drying up of streams.[15] At Teotihuacan lime

Fig. 14. Figurines from Teotihuacan representing the four stylistic stages.

cement covered all the buildings and formed the entire paving. The modern Maya Indians burn ten times as much wood as the quantity of limestone to be reduced, and they have the advantage of steel axes.[16] It is not too fanciful, therefore, to assume that the Teotihuacan masons, lacking metal of any kind, found it easier to use hearths of charcoal, obtained by burning over the forest, than to try to obtain the requisite fuel by chopping out their logs with stone axes. If this inter-pretation is correct, the hills must have been widely denuded of timber, with a consequent drying up of streams and erosion

78

of fields. Furthermore, the barren aspect of the hills of Teotihuacan today must be due to something more than the requirements for fuel and timber of the post-Conquest population. The Teotihuacanos and their successors, the Toltecs, Chichimecs, Acolhuas, and Aztecs, undoubtedly contributed their fair share to this wastage of the forests.

Whatever may have been the basic causes of the abandonment of their ceremonial city, Teotihuacanos still occupied the outlying villages; and the residential cities of Portezuelo and Azcapotzalco across the lake continued to flourish. Teotihuacan however was a city of ghosts. In Toltec times the makers of the Mazapan pottery[17] occasionally crept onto the ruins to bury their dead, but they never disturbed the silence by building houses in the zone. A persistent tradition describes the great Aztec ruler Montezuma as visiting Teotihuacan to make sacrifices, but no evidence exists in the shape of ceremonial equipment left behind.[18]

Azcapotzalco was an enormous city, where dwelt a large population. The decline of Teotihuacan and the gradual abandonment of the eastern towns must have added substantially to its numbers. Its people did not follow the architectural practices of earlier times and have left no great monuments. It originally seems to have been founded at the time of the first great building period at Teotihuacan, because the same hand-made figurines and pottery styles exist at both sites. However, the religious reformation at Teotihuacan suggested by the rebuilding of the city and the making of the 'portrait' type of figurines left no trace at Azcapotzalco. No true 'portrait' heads occur among the thousands of figurines found in the western district.

A fully developed mould-made figurine cult replaced the older hand-made techniques, but this practice was absent from Teotihuacan. Just as Byzantium for centuries carried on the tradition of Rome after the barbarians had sacked the parent city, so, in smaller scale, Azcapotzalco maintained the older tradition of Teotihuacan. Yet the figurine cult was carried to an extreme development. The introduction of the mould led to mass production of images by skilled workmen. Thus the details of dress and ornament, which defined the gods represented, could be rigidly fixed. Each household could be equipped in miniature with the outward elements of a ritual previously confined to special centres. Elaborate incense burners studded with moulded decorations reproduced the main temple altars with their ritualistic ornament. The origin of this practice may well have been in Oaxaca among the Zapotecs, who not only made elaborate incense burners of this type but, since fragments of Oaxaca wares are found in Teotihuacan sites, also shipped pottery to be traded to these northern people.[19]

The Azcapotzalco region was protected by the lakes from invaders on the east. There were perhaps greater water resources there and no such tax on the population as at Teotihuacan, where the people had to carry out a religious reformation in architectural terms. Therefore the pressures from within and without, which caused Teotihuacan to crumble, were not manifested in the west until over a century later. Yet even here, a large cluster of baby burials at El Corral suggests that starvation with a resultant stepping up of infant mortality may have played its part as well. At last here, too, the arts and crafts of Teotihuacan disappeared, and their styles had little continuation in the work of the later people. But the old, old cult of making images persisted, though the idols were now in honour of new gods.

The Classic era, the period of the builders of Teotihuacan, saw the full emergence of Mesoamerican civilization. The culture was unified and seems to have been diffused by an increasing population. In the emphasis on ritual and the direction of technical skill toward the requirements of worship Teotihuacan resembled its great theocratic contemporaries in Mesoamerica and had perhaps the greatest influence of any of them. Evidence of its trade relations help archaeologists to date other sites for they have been traced all over Mesoamerica, from the Huaxteca as far as Guatemala.[20] Its artistic dominance is prevalent in all the Classic sites, either in the architecture or in the pottery styles or in the religious presentations. At Tajin in Vera Cruz and at Xochicalco in Morelos, the traditions were to some extent carried on and modified after the fall of Teotihuacan, and from there in turn came to mould the succeeding civilization of the Toltecs.[21]

Table 3. ARCHAEOLOGICAL PERIODS OF TEOTIHUACAN CULTURE

TEOTIHUACAN I *Tzacualli*,[22] 600 B.C.–200 B.C.

A Pre-classic culture showing influences from Ticoman, Chupicuaro, and Tlapacoya, closely related to sites of El Tepalcate, Chalchicomula in Puebla, and the earliest occupation at Cholula. The figurines are crude and hand-made, the pottery a mixture of four strains, the diagnostic being a negative polychrome.

Occupation of Oztoyahualco, building of large pyramids. The only known god was the Fire God, with the possibility of a pre-Tlaloc at Tlapacoya, and a small Tlaloc jar inside the Pyramid of the Sun, probably Miccaotli.

TEOTIHUACAN II *Miccaotli*, 200 B.C.–A.D. 250.

Transitional pottery, increase of incised black wares, nubbin supports predominating. Figurines more carefully made. Establishment of centre at Azcapotzalco (El Corral I), wide distribution of culture to Cholula, Morelos, etc.

Street of the Dead, Viking group, frescoes of the Superpuestos, the Temple of Agriculture Diosa del Agua. Tlaloc cult definite. Erection of Temple of Quetzalcóatl. Trade with Remojadas, Xochicalco II, Upper Tres Zapotes, Monte Alban II–III, Esperanza, Lower Cerro de las Mesas, Tajin I, Panuco II.

TEOTIHUACAN III *Tlamilolpa-Xolalpan*, A.D. 250–A.D. 650.

Occupation of Tlamilolpa where traded sherds show commerce with Peten Maya corresponding to Uaxactun II. Tomb here with radiocarbon date around A.D. 300. Champlevé incised before firing.

Occupation of Xolalpan, Champlevé incised after firing, plaster cloisonné. The importation of thin orange ware from Puebla reaches its height.

The period of florescence and largest occupation, mould-made figurines showing elaboration of theology. Tlaloc, Xipe, fat god. The frescoes of Tepantitla, Teopancaxco, Atetelco, and Tetitla,[23] showing jaguars, priests, and rain gods. Rich funeral pottery traded to distant parts of Mesoamerica or closely imitated in local wares. Reconstruction of entire city and reoccupation of

81

Aztecs of Mexico

Table 3—continued

Oztoyahualco, abandoned during *Miccaotli* phase. Period ends with abandonment of Teotihuacan.

TEOTIHUACAN IV *Ahuizotla-Amantla*, A.D. 650–A.D. 900.

This late phase of the culture is found at Portezuelo, El Risco,[24] Calpulalpan (Tlaxcala) and many other sites. Shift of centre to Azcapotzalco, great ritualistic development of figurines, complex ceremonial urns (influenced by Monte Alban?). Increase in human sacrifice (influence from Tajin?). New cult of Solar Eagle (Nahua?). At Teotihuacan decadence, and occupation by the makers of Coyotlatelco pottery (Toltec Period) who also lived at Tetitla and Atetelco.

Tajin, Cholula, and Xochicalco meanwhile carry on the great traditions, altering them and filtering them back eventually to Tula.

Chapter 4 The Toltecs of Tula.
First Nahuatl Empire

An attempt to reconstruct its history

The classical era of Teotihuacan was an age of cultural unity. The people of Central Mexico made the same things, lived the same way and worshipped the same gods for centuries. Dissolution set in as famine, revolt, religious disagreements, and the incursions of strange peoples corroded the structure of Teotihuacan civilization. Now a new era begins, called the Postclassic, militaristic as opposed to theocratic: and with this era, history dawns. The Toltecs of Tula or Master Builders were the first people mentioned in the annals of the Valley of Mexico. Their customs and achievements are so wrapped in the mystery which myth draws over the raw facts of history, and so confusing and illogical are the references to them, that a leading Mexicanist once challenged their very existence.[1]

The facts of the matter seem to be that the marauding tribes who poured into the Valley of Mexico during the centuries succeeding Teotihuacan and preceding the establishment of the Tenochca or Aztec empire used the word Tollan to mean a large metropolis whose citizens were Toltecs, or civilized persons. This has led to great confusion among scholars, but since 1941 it has been generally accepted that the Toltecs were a Nahua-speaking people who came to Culhuacan some time during the ninth century, and with the help of other more civilized people already resident in the environs, established their capital in Tula Hidalgo.

The Toltecs have been described as great architects, carpenters, and mechanics, skilled likewise in agriculture, cultivating corn, cotton, beans, chili peppers, and all the other domesticated plants known to Mexico. From cotton they

83

spun thread to be woven into cloth which ranged from the fineness of linen to the thickness of velvet. The men wore robes and loincloths, supplemented in cold weather by sleeveless jackets, and were shod with sandals of henequen, the fibre of a variety of maguey. Women dressed in *huipiles*, sleeveless blouses, and *enaguas*, skirts made by wrapping a long strip of cotton around the waist and legs, a costume which still persists in the Indian villages of modern Mexico. Warriors wore armour made of quilted cotton and used spears and wooden clubs set with blades of obsidian. The club wielders carried shields, and Ixtlilxochitl says that some soldiers had copper helmets, although two copper celts found on the surface represent so far the only example of this metal at Tula. Priests were distinguished by a more elaborate costume composed of a head-dress and a long black tunic which touched the ground.[2]

The 'kings' wore robes like the priests and adorned themselves with necklaces and earrings. They wore socks as well as sandals, a great elegance for sandal-wearing people. They distinguished themselves as much by conduct as by dress, rising early and eating only at daybreak and at nightfall. They spoke little but to the point. A 'king' had one 'queen', and neither could remarry upon the death of the other, although commoners might take a second or even a third wife. A 'queen' could inherit the realm from her husband, and her legitimate sons succeeded her, a statement suggesting that the austerity of the marital ideal did not interfere with the royal pleasure.

The Toltecs built their palaces and houses of stone and mortar and used the *temascal* or steam bath, which still persists among the modern Indians. They held a market every twenty days, or each month in terms of the Mesoamerican year. These markets were located in Tula, Teotihuacan, Tulancingo, Cuernavaca, Cholula, Tultitlan, and several other towns where remains of their occupation still may be seen. There is additional evidence that the Toltecs counted their years and used the sacred almanac of 260 days, according to the pattern followed by their successors.[3]

The religion of this bygone era is difficult to interpret, for both the sixteenth-century Christian mentality and the late Aztec theology distort for us its true structure. Ixtlilxochitl reported a supreme being, Tloque Nahuaque, who surpassed all other gods. Tlaloc, a Rain God (taken over from the Teotihuacanos?) was mentioned as highly important, and a Frog Goddess was also honoured by a sumptuous temple. Quetzalcoatl, Feathered Serpent, was worshipped as the bringer of civilization, but the same name was used as a title for the chief priests. There were persistent myths referring to the conflict between an old worship and a new, symbolized by a struggle between Quetzalcoatl and the war and sky gods of the later Aztec religion[4] and later history tells of the struggles between the votaries of one god as opposed to those of another. The elevation of a god to the role of tribal protector led to the domination of his worshippers in the community and was as important to the ancient Mexican as the domination of an economic or political system is to our modern populations. There was then, as now, the same masking of desire for power with conviction of rectitude. Probably, too, there was the same confusion of motives in the individual.

The history of the Toltecs is as tenuous as their sociology and religion. One history, written by Ixtlilxochitl,[5] began very properly with the creation of the world and the four or five Suns, or eras, through which life has survived. The first era, the Water Sun, was when the supreme god, Tloque Nahuaque, created the world; and after 1716 years floods and lightning destroyed it. The second era, the Sun of the Earth, saw the world populated by giants, the Quinametzin, who almost disappeared when earthquakes obliterated the earth. The Wind Sun came third, and Olmecs and Xicalancas, human tribes, lived on earth. They destroyed the surviving giants, founded Cholula[6] and migrated as far as Tabasco. A marvellous personage, called Quetzalcoatl by some, Huemac by others,[7] appeared in this era and brought civilization and ethics. When the people did not benefit from his teachings, he returned to the east, prophesying the destruction of the world by high winds and the conversion of mankind into monkeys, all of which came to pass. The fourth age, the present, is called the Sun of Fire, and will end in a general conflagration.

These four eras are mythological, with a small amount of historical information incorporated (Table 4). The Aztec versions, which had five Suns, were more purely theological. Yet these mythical floods and fires may recapitulate calamities, such as inundations and volcanic eruptions, which, according to evidence found at Pre-classic sites, beset man in Mexico.

Toltec history, when it breaks through the background of myth, describes a people wandering through Mexico. Under the guidance of an astrologer priest, Huemac, they founded the city of Tollan and elected a king whose reign was fixed at fifty-two years. This was the length of an Aztec year cycle, a major time unit having the same function as our century. The list of the nine rulers is given on Table 5, but historical events were seldom recorded until the end of the period. Huemac died at the age of three hundred in the reign of the second ruler, after compiling a book of history and prophecy. This observation may be a back-handed explanation of the introduction of established ritualistic practices, including a calendar and architecture. The sixth ruler, Mitl, broke the order of length of rule, enlarged his kingdom and built the splendid Temples of the Frog and many other sumptuous structures.

Significant events for the reigns of the last rulers are recorded. The eighth had a dominion extending over Toluca, Cuernavaca, Yolotepec, Cholula, and Jalisco. The old gods were still worshipped, but the cult of two new ones, Tezcatlipoca, the great Sky God, and Huitzilopochtli, the War God, were introduced. During the reign of this king a lady, Xochitl, popularized an intoxicating drink named pulque, made from the fermented juice of the maguey, which is today the standard tipple of Highland Mexico.

Topiltzin, the ninth king, who introduced the ball court, had a reign fraught with disaster. In his time the domain of the Toltecs disintegrated because of local revolts, invasions, and the bitter toll exacted by famine and pestilence. Tollan was abandoned. When they could, the people emigrated south to Tabasco and Guatemala. Those who remained were absorbed into the new tribes, and their lineage was assumed as a mark of honour by the ruling houses of the succeeding Chichimec period. Such is the story of the Toltecs as set forth by Ixtlilxochitl.[8]

The *Annals of Cuauhtitlan*[9] records a list of Toltec rulers that only partially in name and not at all in date corresponds to Ixtlilxochitl's (Table 5). It fits in much better than his with what archaeology has uncovered, however. Modern students of the problem are not entirely agreed as to dates; but the story is roughly the following: Mixcoatl,[10] or Totepeuh, chief of a Nahua-speaking people who worshipped Tezcatlipoca, came from the north-west to Culhuacan, where he established his capital on the Hill of the Star. Legend tells of his encounter there, or in Morelos, with Chimalma, a local maiden, who bore him a posthumous son and died herself soon after. His brother Ihuitimal meanwhile had killed him and seized power, and the son Topiltzin (also called Ce Acatl for the day of his birth) was brought up at Xochicalco in Morelos by the priests of Quetzalcoatl.

Grown to manhood, Topiltzin returned to the Hill of the Star, avenged his father by killing his uncle and from Culhuacan went to Tulancingo in Hidalgo, and from there to Tula, where he founded the Toltec empire. He tried to discourage the practice of human sacrifice (part of the cult of Tezcatlipoca), encouraged the arts, and introduced the ball game. There

87

is a monument to him at Tula with the date of 980. He left Tula after a quarrel about religious practices and went by way of the Mixtec country (where local tradition tells of a chief who carried the symbols of the morning star some time between 940–980) and on to the Maya region where his arrival is recorded at 987. Finally he departed into the east, declaring that he would return.[11]

His descendants continued to rule at Tula (see Table 5) until it was destroyed in the reign of Huemac. The *Historia Tolteca Chichimeca*[12] begins with Huemac, and tells of two groups and their migrations, one of which seems to have reached the Maya area, where tradition speaks of their arrival in 1194.

These, in brief, are the recorded annals of the people whom for many years archaeologists, including this author, identified with the builders of Teotihuacan. Their material culture, of which only part was then known, was assigned by us and by Linné, to a people we called Mazapan, after the suburb of Teotihuacan where we first found their pottery.

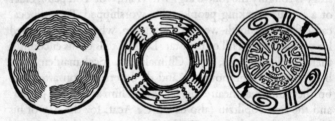

Fig. 15. Toltec pottery. Diagnostic wares of Mazapan, Coyotlatelco, and Culhuacan.

The Mazapan culture was definitely later than Teotihuacan, for its graves penetrated through Teotihuacan floors and its refuse overlay deposits of Teotihuacan discard. These remains were strongly concentrated at the north-west of the Valley of Mexico but extended to the west as well. While in general

Fig. 16. Toltec figurines. Top row: Mould-made figurines, Coyotlatelco style. Bottom row: Mould-made figurines, Mazapan style.

they seem to have been associated with villages, refuse heaps did occur at the ceremonial site of Tula. In the modern town of that name stone sculptures in a distinctive style, neither Teotihuacan nor Aztec, had been, by the process of elimination, assigned to these people. The lavish equipment of their burials suggested that the Mazapan folk were prosperous and well to do. At Chiconauhtla, a frontier town subject to Texcoco, the population, originally Mazapan in cultural affiliation, shifted to Aztec styles with no transition.

The pottery of these people falls into three distinctive main types. One comprises deep hemispherical bowls with decorations made in wavy parallel lines as if by a comb. Allied are other bowls with vaguely outlined maroon designs. A second type is used for heavy bowls with tripod support and floors scored for use in grinding pepper. A third consists of bowls with flat floors and slipped in distinctive colours of white or orange. Such vessels were traded to Puebla, to the slopes of the volcanoes and to other areas bordering on the Valley.

In trade the Toltecs received pottery from distant sources. From Puebla and Vera Cruz they acquired a popular fine

89

orange ware that was also found in Chichen Itza in Yucatan, in Guatemala, and even as far south as Salvador.[13] They had also the distinctive pseudo-vitreous ware called plumbate, which had a wide orbit of commercial distribution, centring in Salvador and Guatemala but reaching south to Panama and east to Vera Cruz, west to Tepic, and north to Tula. This ware is never found in classical Maya centres but appears in the later sites. In the Valley of Mexico it never reached the Teotihuacanos, and its distribution ceased before Aztec times. Wares decorated in plaster cloisonné were also esteemed by

Fig. 17. Bowls from Chichen Itza, Yucatan. These bowls are of Culhuacan-Cholula III type.

the Toltecs, and a few examples appear far from their chief source of manufacture in northern Jalisco.[14] (See Plate 28.)

The Mazapan people made or acquired by trade beautiful spindle whorls with lustrous slips and stamped designs. Their obsidian work was excellent and the scalpels flaked off by pressure were the finest in Mexico. Figurines were mould-made but poorly fashioned, a mother god and a warrior god presaging the Tonantzin and Tezcatlipoca of the Aztec period. They worshipped also the flayed god Xipe, who wears a human skin, and in his honour they broke through the lowly limitations of their clay sculpture to make life-size representations of him, monumental examples of the potter's art. A smaller figure, carrying in his hand a little vase of Zapotec type, was prepared with closer detail. Thus archaeological evidence confirms the traditional origin of Xipe worship in Oaxaca, territory of the Zapotecs and Mixtecs. (See Plate 26.)

90

The Toltec culture was cosmopolitan and was in touch with the products of all of civilized Mesoamerica. Some of the pottery suggests a western origin and, as we have seen, legend tells us Mixcoatl came from the north-west. The Toltecs spoke Nahuatl, but many of their customs and traditions resemble those of the Totonacs who built Tajin. It is possible that they brought their worship of Quetzalcoatl direct from Xochicalco where tradition tells us their great king Topiltzin studied priestly lore, and where archaeologists have uncovered friezes and a ball court like those at Tula. (See Plate 25.)

Excavations at Tula suggest, however, that the Mazapan culture is only one of several strains that went into the make-up of the Toltec civilization. It may be the pottery of the hordes that came into the Valley with Mixcoatl, for it shows both northern and western affiliations. Another strain may well be represented by the pottery that was being made in the Valley at the time of their arrival. It was called Coyotlatelco [15] by Dr Tozzer, who found it mixed with late Teotihuacan material at the type site. (See Figure 15.) At one or two places west of Tenayuca, Coyotlatelco sherds had appeared with Mazapan material; and a collection at the American Museum of Natural History from somewhere near Tula suggested to us a cross-fertilization of a simple early ware (found also at Tenayuca under the fully developed Coyotlatelco) with decadent Teotihuacan elements, resulting in a potential prototype of the style. At Tenayuca, Mr Noguera found the extreme limit in lateness as well, for there Coyotlatelco and Aztec II (or Tenayuca black-on-orange) sherds were at one time mixed. This latter ware is probably diagnostic for the Chichimec occupation of Tenayuca under Xolotl. So it would seem that local populations were making the Coyotlatelco ware at the time the Toltecs came and continued to make it all through the days of the Empire and even after its end. Excavations at Tula have shown that this pottery is earlier than the so-called Mazapan; and the unmixed Coyotlatelco debris at

Azcapotzalco and on the Hill of the Star behind Culhuacan supports the chroniclers who tell of an early occupation of those places before the founding of Tula.

There was undoubtedly also a strong influence on the Toltecs from Tajin, in Vera Cruz, where some of the Teotihuacan complex continued after the collapse of the original capital, as well as from Xochicalco in Morelos.[16] Mixtec codices and certain stones in the famous Monticulo B at Tula attest to the closeness as well of the Mixtec peoples.

No graves have been found at Tula; but at Teotihuacan, we, at a place called Las Palmas, and later the Swedish archaeologist Linné, at Xolalpan, found richly endowed burials which we now know were Toltec. In some of these the entire skeleton was buried; others contained only the skull, covered by a bowl or inside such a bowl with another on top. There is as yet no explanation for the practice nor so far as we know have other burials of this type been uncovered. In Oaxaca the separate burial of heads is supposed to have to do with the cult of Xipe, to whom the Toltecs, in their 'Mazapan' phase at least, seem to have been particularly devoted.[17]

The architecture of Tula is not remarkable but the giant monumental sculptures, the great snake columns of basalt and the seated figures of *Chacmool*, as well as the decorative friezes on the so-called Tlahuizcalli (temple of Quetzalcoatl) (see Plate 25) are a new departure which was to be repeated at Chichen Itza.[18] (See Plate 27.) The constructions at Tula were not built to last, and indeed they did not. Someone, perhaps the Chichimec chief Xolotl,[19] deliberately destroyed the city, and its people dispersed as these new barbarians came to overrun Central Mexico.

The Toltec civilization established the structure of the tribute empire which the Aztec later adopted. Its influence spread from one end of Mesoamerica to the other, but is particularly strong in Yucatan. After the short-lived empire came to an end and its ceremonial centre was destroyed, tradition and archaeology agree, the Toltecs founded dynasties in other places, and continued to occupy Culhuacan, where the later groups of less civilized Chichimecs who invaded the Valley married their women, adopted much of their culture, and eventually spoke their language as well.

Table 4. SEQUENCE OF TRIBES IN THE VALLEY OF MEXICO ACCORDING TO VARIOUS AUTHORITIES

	Phillips[a]	Ixtlilxóchitl I[b]	Ixtlilxóchitl II[c]	Veytia[d]	Duran[e]	Muñoz Camargo[f]	Clavigero[g]	Sahagún[h]	de Jonghe[i]	Mapa Tlotzin[j]	Mapa Quinatzin[k]	Codex Xólotl[l]	Motolinia[m]	Garcia Icazbalceta[n]
Maceguales (created by Gods)	1	–	–	–	–	–	–	–	–	–	–	–	–	–
Quinames (Giants)	2	1	1	1	1	–	–	–	–	–	–	–	–	–
Tarasco	–	–	–	–	–	1	–	–	–	–	–	–	–	–
Olmeca-Xicalanga	–	2	2	3	–	2	–	–	–	–	–	–	–	–
Zacateca	–	–	–	–	–	2	–	–	–	–	–	–	–	–
Toltec	4	3	3	4	–	–	1	1	–	–	–	–	–	–
Nomad Chichimec	3	4	4	2	–	–	2	–	1	1	1	1	1	1
Chichimec	–	–	–	5	2	3	–	2	–	–	–	–	–	–
Teo-Chichimec	–	–	–	–	–	4	–	2	–	–	–	–	–	–
Otomi	–	–	5	6	–	–	2	2	–	–	–	–	–	–
Acolhua I Tlailtoque	–	5	–	–	–	–	–	–	–	–	–	–	–	–
Chimalpanecs	–	5	–	–	–	–	–	–	–	–	2	2	–	–
Chalco-Toltec	–	–	–	–	–	–	–	–	–	–	–	2	–	–
Acolhua II Texcoco	–	6	5	6	–	3	3	–	(4)	3	–	–	2	2
Culhua — 7 Tribes	–	–	–	–	3	–	3	3	–	–	–	–	–	–
Culhua — Tepanec	–	6	5	6	–	–	–	–	–	3	–	–	–	–
Culhua — Culhua	5	–	–	–	–	–	–	–	–	3	–	–	–	–
Culhua — Aztec	–	6	6	7	4	–	–	–	–	3	–	3	3	3
Culhua — Huitznahua	–	6	–	–	–	–	–	–	–	3	–	–	–	–

[a] Phillips, *Codex Ramirez*, 1883, 618–19, 622–4.
[b] Ixtlilxóchitl, *Relaciones*, 1891, 17–21, 75–103.
[c] Ixtlilxóchitl, *Historia Chichimeca*, 1892, 21–45, 61–5, 69–71.
[d] Veytia, *Historia Antigua*, 1836, Vol. 1, 139–56; Vol. 2, 3–10, 39–46, 87–101.
[e] Duran, *Historia de las Indias*, I, 1867, 10–14.
[f] Muñoz Camargo, *Historia*, 1892, 5–116.
[g] Clavigero, *History*, 1787, 93–136.
[h] Sahagún, *Historia General*, 1938, Vol. 4, Book II, 106, 116–17, 138–47.
[i] de Jonghe, ed., *Histoire de Mechique*, 1903, 8–20.
[j] Aubin, *Peinture Didactique*, 1885, 58–74.
[k] Aubin, *Peinture Didactique*, 1885, 75–85.
[l] Radin, *Sources*, 1920, 41–5.
[m] Motolinia, *Historia*, 1914, 3–5.
[n] Origen in Garcia Icazbalceta, 1886–92, Vol. 3, *Origen de los Mexicanos*, 283–92.

Table 5. SUMMARY OF TOLTEC HISTORY

Toltec Kings according to two old sources, compared to Jimenez Moreno, 1956.

According to Ixtlilcxóchitl

Chalchiuhtlanetzin	510–62
Ixtlilcuechahauac	562–614
Huetzin	614–66
Totepeuh	666–718
Nacoxoc	718–70
Mitl-Tlacomihua	770–829
Queen Xihuiquenitzin	829–33
Iztaccaltzin	833–85
Topiltzin	885–959

According to Anales de Cuauhtitlán, *with Jimenez Moreno's dates in italics.*

Huetzin	869–(?)		
Totepeuh (or Mixcóatl)	(?)–887		*900–47*
Ihuitimal	877–923		*947–55*
Topiltzin	923–47	*born*	*947*
Topiltzin	923–47	*at Tula*	*980–99*
Matlacxóchitl	947–83		*1000–34*
Nauhyotzin I	983–97		*1034–49*
Matlaccoatzin	997–1025		*1049–77*
Tlilcoatzin	1025–46		*1077–98*
Huemac	1047–1122		*1098–1168*
Nauhyotl to Culhuacan			*1184*

Chapter 5

The Toltec-Chichimec Period

In which are set forth the complex events, political, social, and cultural, which led up to the formation of Aztec civilization

The succeeding era in Mexican history, 1100–1300, was a chaotic one which eventually resulted in that mixture of cultural unity and political independence which we know as the Aztec civilization. A tempting analogy is to compare the Toltec-Chichimec period to the European colonization of North America, where groups of many conditions and sorts struggled to populate the land and eventually incorporated the sum total of their experience into the North American republic.

Religions and social systems and peoples competed for domination of the Valley. Several of the powerful groups at the time of the Conquest had their origin in this era of confusion, and from their annals we may extract a fairly clear picture of what went on. As each community recorded its own affairs with relatively little attention to those of its neighbours, cross references are rare. History, in our modern sense of utilizing past trends to chart the present and the future, did not exist in the intellectual structure of ancient Mexico, and the traditions of the successive immigrations are in confusing disagreement (Table 4).

The histories of five towns summarize this period: Culhuacan, Texcoco, Azcapotzalco, Cholula, and Tenochtitlan (Table 6). According to the *Annals of Cuauhtitlan*, a long, confused record referring to Culhuacan, Tenochtitlan, and the politically insignificant Cuauhtitlan, the Culhuas conquered the Toltecs and lived for a time at their ancient capital Tula later withdrawing again southward to Culhuacan, where they established a lineage of chiefs, the length of whose reigns they

carefully recorded in their annals.[1] In the middle of the thirteenth century a new dynasty came in which the historians
called 'Chichimec'; it replaced the older line which they
called 'Toltec'. References were made to struggles with other
groups, chiefly at the northern end of the lakes, but there was
trouble with the southern towns as well.

At the end of the fourteenth century civil war broke out and
people deserted Culhuacan, which became weak and a shadow
of its former self. The rise of a new power, the Tepanec, who
had as allies the vigorous but ill-established Tenochcas, contributed to its downfall. Yet before Culhuacan succumbed
completely to vassalage under the new order, members of its
reigning house had twice been sought to found the lineage of
Tenochtitlan.

On the documentary evidences Culhuacan was an extremely important city-state. The consecutive reigns of its
chiefs stretched from the time of the fall of Tula to that of the
rise of the important Aztec state of Tenochtitlan. Culhuacan
was considered a centre of civilization and for three centuries
was a major power in the Valley of Mexico. Yet a visit to the
modern town discloses no lofty remains, for the ancient city is
razed completely. Only the temple on the Hill of the Star,
which rises behind the town and dominates the lakes, is a
memorial to its past splendour. For here, where had been the
first Toltec capital, took place, even after the Culhuas had lost
their power, the New Fire Ceremony which ushered in each
new cycle of fifty-two years and epitomized the spirit of
Aztec religion.

Texcoco, on the eastern shore of the lakes of Mexico, was the
most civilized town in the Valley of Mexico at the time of the
Conquest. Ixtlilxochitl, a descendant of the ruling house, had
access to the annals of his people and left a full history, distorted though it was by his wish to make his lineage rival the
noble lines of Castile; but he had a strong historical sense,
doubtless absorbed from the Spanish priests who educated

him. His ancestors were a nomadic group which lived mainly by hunting and eventually, under a chief named Xolotl, occupied the territory around Teotihuacan. They pushed west to Tenayuca and in the process learned agriculture and assumed a sedentary life. While there they met other peoples of varying degrees of culture and assumed the practice of choosing a chief from a special lineage instead of electing him directly from the clan leaders.[2]

About 1300 two brothers were in line for succession to the chieftainship and one Tlotzin, who was not selected, moved back to Texcoco and headed his own line. When he died and his son Quinatzin took the throne, two groups moved into his territory from the Mixteca area in northern Oaxaca and southern Puebla. They brought with them the worship of the god Tezcatlipoca, the art of writing, and many other useful skills. So completely did these people transform life at Texcoco that the picture manuscripts portrayed the local population clad in skins and the immigrants in woven clothing to emphasize the contrast between their own culture and the superior talents of the newcomers. Quinatzin, who was an extraordinarily competent ruler, extended his dominions greatly by conquering many adjacent communities. The idea of absorbing conquered towns into the victorious state, so obvious to a modern member of western civilization, had not yet occurred to the Mexicans. Instead, defeated towns retained their local autonomy; but they paid a yearly tribute and their chiefs had to make a state visit to acknowledge their fealty to the conqueror. Quinatzin had some seventy towns as fiefs, and his dominion projected down to the shore of Vera Cruz. His successor, Techotlala, succeeded in unifying the Valley dialects into one language, Aztec.

Texcoco and Culhuacan never came into direct conflict, for they were situated at opposite ends of the Lake of Mexico. There is evidence, too, that the Valley was not completely settled, for in the mid-thirteenth century the Tenochca were able to thread their way south to Chapultepec without coming into serious conflict with the settled populations.[3]

However, in the mid-fourteenth century there was serious conflict. A people called the Tepanec, which lived at Azcapotzalco, outgrew its boundaries. Led by an able and vicious chief, Tezozomoc, it began to extend its territories. Culhuacan felt the pressure first, and internal discord developed, as it must when a nation cannot feed itself and has no room to expand. Some of the Culhuas moved up to Texcoco along the eastern shore and added their long-practised skills to those of the Texcocan community. The Tepanec, blocked to the south by dense populations and to the west by high mountain walls, turned north and east to raid and occupy Texcocan lands. Otomi tribes, whose territory lay on the islands and the eastern shore of Lake Xaltocan, were pinched between the opposing forces who would brook no neutrality. They moved north, and the two great powers, Tepanecs and Texcocans, came into direct "contact, and war ensued. Tezozomoc won a signal victory, broke Texcoco, and alienated her vassals. He quickly dominated the rest of the Valley towns, almost obliterating the empty shell of Culhuacan's former dominance. His son Maxtla succeeded this vigorous and ruthless conqueror in 1427. Having the northern Valley at his feet, he oppressed the conquered and interfered in the affairs of former allies like Tenochtitlan. Yet he was to enjoy his conquests only a bare two years.[4]

Indian governmental practice extracted tribute from conquered peoples, but had not developed a technique for forcing payment without declaring a new war and making a fresh campaign. Consequently a bond of sympathy forged from mutually shared ill-fortune grew up between otherwise somewhat hostile communities. Tenochtitlan and Tlacopan, towns at the back door of Tepanec territory, made a pact with Texcoco across the lake; and the allies, rising suddenly, overthrew the new power. Maxtla was slain, his city burned, and,

Fig. 18. Chichimec pottery. Tenayuca black-on-orange, formerly known as Aztec II.

contrary to the practice of the time, his people incorporated into the allied states. Land was apportioned to warriors who had performed notable feats of valour. So completely did the allies break the Tepanecs, that all that remains of their history is the memory of Tezozomoc and Maxtla and some petty local chieftains who succeeded them.

The Texcocans regained their prestige after this war, but the Tenochcas, who had begun as mere vassals, grew so rapidly in strength that at the coming of the Spaniards they had managed to eclipse their former lords, as we shall see in the following chapter.

These events disclose a picture of expanding populations and ensuing conflict. The cultural history shows a diffuse background of various arts and practices gradually welded into a closely similar whole, Aztec civilization. The process was achieved before Tenochtitlan attained eminence, so at the cost of academic tediousness the term Aztec has been reserved for the civilization, Tenochca for the people who so conspicuously made it known.

Culhuacan, so important in the annals as the seat of a famous line of chiefs, shows today little sign of its past greatness. Yet excavations undertaken forty-five years ago proved that its historical importance was not over-estimated, for it seems to have been the base from which Aztec culture spread over the Valley. Pottery, so dismal to read about, so important in reflecting cultural patterns, tells the story of this process.[5]

Aztec pottery is found everywhere in the Valley of Mexico, and, due to the Aztec custom of destroying household goods at the end of each fifty-two-year cycle, it can be identified in terms of relatively exact periods: IV, 1507–19 (the date of the Spanish Conquest, which prevented the cyclical celebration of 1559); IIIb, 1455–1507; IIIa, 1403–55; II early and late, perhaps two centuries prior to 1403, and I. Periods III and IV are represented everywhere. Period II is common on the mainland but less so in Tenochtitlan, which was politically insignificant until after 1400. We have reason to believe that it represents the material culture of the Chichimecs of Xolotl. To date Period I is represented in quantity only in Chalco[6] and at Culhuacan. (See Figure 15.) It seems to be a Toltec ware which continued to be made for a long time, and probably originated in Cholula. The standard ware of Periods II–IV goes through a consecutive evolution, but has a close generic resemblance throughout, while Period I pottery is much closer to the fine orange wares of Puebla which were traded widely throughout south-eastern Mexico in Toltec times.[7] (See Figures 15, 18.)

In the history of the Toltecs we have noted that Topiltzin went to Tula from Culhuacan, and that after the destruction of their new capital some of the Toltecs returned to the old. It may not be stretching the manipulations of the historian too far to suggest that the Coyotlatelco ceramics, which have vague affiliations with Teotihuacan, may represent the material culture of the people who immediately succeeded the Teotihuacanos in the Valley; that it was carried to Tula and outgrown there, but continued to be made in Azcapotzalco and in Culhuacan even after the return of the Toltecs from Tula. The Aztec I pottery, on the other hand, completely alien to the local types, seems to represent the material presence of the returning Toltecs, who in the interval had been influenced by the Cholula culture.

Seeming confirmation of this situation comes from the site of Tenayuca, where great Mexican archaeologists like the late

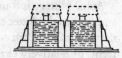

Fig. 19. Chichimec architecture. The first three constructions at Tenayuca. Note the sloping walls of the Aztec-influenced Building III.

José Reygadas Vertiz, Ignacio Marquina, Alfonso Caso, Eduardo Noguera, and others have carried out a superb dissection of one of the temples. It was completely rebuilt five, or possibly six, times. The renovation answered the ceremonial requirement of rebuilding and refurbishing at the beginning of each fifty-two-year cycle in compensation for the destruction at the close of the previously elapsed period. As the site was occupied during the Conquest, the reconstructions probably followed the cyclical ceremonies of 1507, 1455, 1403, 1351, and 1299, with the first building erected some time earlier. The fourth, fifth, and sixth constructions (1403, 1455, 1507) are purely Aztec; the third temple built (1351) is a transition between the Aztec style and the simpler, more archaic methods employed in the two earliest structures (1299 and the original temple). The three completely developed Aztec temples correspond closely to the distribution of Aztec III and IV pottery, between 1403 and 1519. (See Figures 21, 22.) The transitional temple and the second building suggest that cyclical renovations were adopted everywhere along with the Aztec II pottery of the fourteenth century. The original platform of this Tenayuca temple could have been constructed almost any time in the thirteenth century, since the building of a shrine did not entail the celebration of the beginning of a fifty-two-year cycle.[8] (See Plate 29, top.)

The Aztec civilization was brought into the Valley at Culhuacan and Chalco, where it gradually supplanted the defined local cultures. Where, then, was its true source? The most probable answer is Cholula, in the state of Puebla, where still exists the largest structure in the world in terms of cubic content. The devoted group of Mexican archaeologists, whose coordinated efforts have organized the rich background of their Indian past, have been analysing this monument by excavation and archival research for many years. The results are important.

Originally Cholula was occupied by Pre-classic people who later fell under the domination of Teotihuacan civilization. At this time the inhabitants built a large ceremonial precinct, a maze of temples, platforms, and stairs, constructed of rubble covered with plaster. Eventually newcomers,[9] possibly with the aid of the resident population, performed the stupendous task of converting the precinct into a single great platform, traditionally in honour of the god Quetzalcoatl. This mammoth construction entailed filling in every building and courtyard with adobe bricks. On its top they erected altars and quarters for the ceremonial personnel. In one of the altars, Altar de los Craneos, they buried two people and made a mortuary offering of pottery vessels, some of which resemble Aztec I in many respects, while others show affiliation with Mazapan types.[10]

Later on the Cholulans gave up these forms for ornate creations in polychrome, in which pure design and ritualistic decoration were elaborated to an extraordinary degree. The skill of workmanship, the proliferation of ritual, and the quantity of production from Puebla and the south, surpass the work of the Valley peoples even though the content is the same. Therefore, it seems reasonable to assume that in Puebla lay the source and inspiration of Aztec civilization.

The few annals preserved relate chiefly to this period, and their pages are filled with the history of Teo-Chichimec and Toltec-Chichimec lineages. Breaking off from their parent communities, groups wandered away to found homes in new territory. Occasionally they settled in unoccupied lands, but they usually imposed themselves as a ruling class on some already established people.[11] Some of these wandering groups spoke Nahuatl, the native tongue of the Toltecs, the Aztecs, and of many other peoples in western Mexico. Some, like the followers of Xolotl, are believed to have spoken Pame and Otomi, and some, like the conquerers of Oaxaca, spoke the un-related Mixtec tongue. Yet whatever their language, these invaders joined in spreading over southern Mexico, Guatemala, Salvador, even Nicaragua, such kindred cultural elements as chiefly lineage, formal war, distinctive gods, and characteristic ceremonial practices, which we classify as Mixteca-Puebla culture. Other tribes moved north, leaving a strong imprint on the cultures of Sinaloa in the north-west, and elements of this religion affected communities as far distant as the south-eastern United States.[12] (See Plates 30, 31, 32.)

This movement of people, in contrast to that of their civilized predecessors, was not the process of settling unexploited territory. Overpopulation seems the most logical cause, since it forces nations to risk the hazards of war rather than submit to the pangs of slow starvation. The vanquished, whose people had expanded into unpopulated territory during the previous epoch, had had no need to develop military techniques and so fell easily under the domination of invaders. However, in view of the intimate relation between government and religion in ancient Mexican society, such conquest meant the worship of new gods as well as the acceptance of new chiefs. It is likely that some groups adopted the new religion previous to actual physical contact so that they could the better resist invasion. Yet the factor of conquest strongly influenced the spread of Mixteca-Puebla culture by men of Nahuatl and Mixtec speech.

War has its advantages when made on the unwarlike. The thin coating of Western civilization which Europe laid over the globe has its minor counterpart in the late Mexican influence spread over Mesoamerica by these restless people. The winner's gods must be good gods, so cults of Mexican origin spread through the length and breadth of Mesoamerica. Just so the Christian religion had a ready acceptance in Indian America when the missionaries were backed by such redoubtable exponents of our gentle faith as Cortés, Pizarro, and their coadjutors.[13]

Chapter 6   The Aztec Period

In which is recorded the history of the
Tenochcas and the political background of
Aztec civilization

The Toltec-Chichimec period witnessed invasion of the Valley
of Mexico by various tribes and the gradual domination of
these tribes by a culture and manner of life that seems to have
emanated from Puebla and northern Oaxaca. The basic political unit consisted of a group resident in a town supporting
itself from its own land with the supplement, if possible, of
supplies derived from the tribute payments of vassals. At the
head of the state was a chief of lineage who also performed
ecclesiastical functions. Craftsmanship was highly skilled, and
trade flourished to furnish raw materials for the artisans. This
productivity, however, was directed toward religion and
ritual rather than the creation of personal wealth. Religion was
an elaborate polytheism based on nature-worship, with some
god or gods singled out for special adoration, but the working
of the *tonalpohualli*, or sacred almanac, brought the full force of
divine powers to aid man in his life on earth.

The history of the Tenochcas, the Mexico City Aztecs,
shows how a tribal body lived and acquired the position of an
important state. According to their own records, the Tenochcas started their wanderings in A.D. 1168, though this date is
arbitrary and possibly represents the date of the invention of
the calendar system in vogue in Central Mexico.[1] At first they
lived on an island in a lake in western Mexico and crossed in
boats to the shore. In a hillside cave they found an idol of
Huitzilopochtli (Hummingbird Wizard), which had the useful ability to speak and give them good advice. The accounts
differ, and some have the Tenochcas starting off on their
travels with several other tribes from a group of caves in

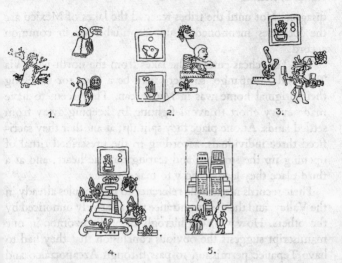

Fig. 20. Historic manuscripts. Excerpts from historical picture manuscripts. 1. Arrival of the nations, in 1300, who brought a knowledge of
writing (*Mapa Quinatzin*); 2. New Fire Ceremony of 1403; 3. New Fire
Ceremony of 1455; 4. New Fire Ceremony of 1507 (2–3 from *Codex
Telleriano-Remensis*); 5. The capture of Tenochtitlan in 1519 (*Codex of
1576*).

which they originated. The names of the tribes are seldom the
same in any two annals, but they always refer to important
tribal entities at the time the particular history was inscribed.
These beginnings may be considered as formalized origin
myths without historical significance.[2] (See Plate 62, middle
left.)

The Tenochcas carried their new god's image with them on
their journey. At each stopping place they set him up to be
worshipped, and in return he advised them. Their method of
procedure was to stay a year or more at a given place, while
pioneers searched the land for another site and planted a crop
there to harvest when the whole tribe arrived. The list of
stopping places is highly dubious, and the different traditions

disagree. Not until the tribes reached the lakes of Mexico are the localities mentioned easily identifiable or in common accord.

The Tenochcas entered the lakes from the north-west, via Tula and Zumpango, so there may be a basis for believing their original home was in Michoacan. They seem to have made every effort to avoid fighting by keeping away from settled lands. At one place they split up; at another they sacrificed three individuals, according to the prescribed ritual of opening up the stomach and tearing out the heart; and at a third place they learned how to make pulque.

Their records make little reference to the peoples already in the Valley, and their own entrance was relatively unnoticed by the others. However, the hieroglyph of Tezozomoc in one manuscript suggests the obvious conclusion that they had to have Tepanec permission to pass through Azcapotzalco and settle at Chapultepec, where the beautiful park now is. Here they remained happily for nearly a generation. Their neighbours seem to have been small but growing communities, so that conflict was inevitable. The Tenochcas began the strife because their young men went up the lake to Tenayuca to raid and steal wives, a common North American Indian method of gaining prestige. Their more powerful neighbours became irritated and made up a punitive expedition in which Tepanecs, Culhuas, and Xochimilcas took part. The result was horrid: the Tenochca chief Huitzilhuitl and most of the tribe had to go to Culhuacan territory to dwell in serfdom, while the rest escaped to the lake where some low-lying islands offered refuge. The main body stayed in Tizapan, near the present San Angel, where they were under the eye of Coxcox, the chief of Culhuacan. The Tenochcas detested the waste which was barren in all except poisonous snakes and insects. Huitzilopochtli they still enshrined, but his worth had sunk so low that the Culhuas came to mock him at his shrine and toss nameless filth into the temples.[3]

Finally, however, the tide turned. Coxcox became involved in a war with Xochimilco and called upon his vassals to aid him. When the Tenochcas reached the field of battle they rushed to the attack and took no less than thirty prisoners, from each of whom they detached an ear with their obsidian knives before sending him to the rear. After the battle Coxcox made a speech praising the valour of his forces in taking so many prisoners but denigrating the Tenochcas who came back empty-handed. The vassals waited until their lord had finished speaking and then inquired of him why each captive was short an ear. The attention of the Culhuas being riveted to this

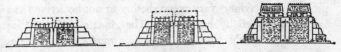

Fig. 21. Aztec architecture. Last three constructions at Tenayuca, corresponding perhaps to the cyclical renovations of 1403, 1455, and 1507.

extraordinary circumstance, the Tenochcas opened their pouches and displayed the missing ears, proving beyond cavil the measure of their prowess. Clearly the war-sacrifice cult had reached the Valley by this time, for the emphasis set on the taking of prisoners indicates that this was one of the chief purposes of war. Furthermore, a drawing shows the later sacrifice of the prisoners, a cult practice the accomplishment of which was to make the Aztecs dreaded by other peoples throughout the length and breadth of Mexico.

So great had the prestige of the Tenochcas become that they went to their lord, Coxcox, and asked for his daughter as a wife for their chief so that they might found a dynasty. Coxcox granted their request, and the Tenochcas were so overcome with gratitude that they sacrificed the luckless girl and draped her skin on a priest to impersonate a nature goddess, Toci. Then with somewhat less than tact they invited the father to the ceremony. He, expecting a marriage celebration,

109

was utterly horrified and summoned his warriors to exterminate the Tenochcas, who forthwith fled to the lake, rejoining their brethren already there.

There were two communities on the islands at the middle of the fourteenth century: Tenochtitlan, which seems to have become an entity in 1325, and Tlaltelolco, which recent excavations indicate had been occupied before 1200. They both were havens for malcontents from the mainland, and about the middle of the century each was large enough to petition the mainland peoples for a chief to found a dynasty. Tlaltelolco received a leader from the Tepanecs, and the Tenochcas again induced Culhuacan to provide them with a chief, Acamapichtli. The accounts vary as to whether or not he arrived as a lad accompanied by his mother. The *Annals of Cuauhtitlan* mention that at this time the Tenochcas were erecting houses of stone, an indication that a community had to reach a definite stage of development before enjoying the prestige of an important lineage.⁴

In the time of Acamapichtli the Tenochcas were tributaries and allies of the Tepanec and fought successfully against Tenayuca and Culhuacan. Yet their field of operations was minute, and a morning's automobile ride will enable the curious to see the whole scene of Tenochcan history. Huitzilhuitl II succeeded Acamapichtli at his death and prudently ensured the future of the nascent state by marrying the daughter of Tezozomoc. He was chief during the final struggle between the two great lake powers, the Tepanecs and the Texcocans, a war which ended in the death of the Texcocan chief, Ixtlilxochitl, and the dispersal of his fiefs.

Chimalpopoca succeeded his half-brother Huitzilhuitl, and his reign was fraught with disaster. Tezozomoc died, and his son Maxtla succeeded him at the cost of murdering a brother. Maxtla was frankly out for power and kept the city-states of the Valley in a ferment of intrigue and oppression. Finally he murdered Chimalpopoca and also the chief of the neighbouring town of Tlaltelolco, adding insult to injury, according to Indian thinking, by stepping up the tribute payments as well.

The people of Tenochtitlan were seething with indignation, and the small mainland town of Tlacopan (Tacuba) was sympathetic to the oppressed. Nezahualcoyotl, the legitimate successor to the chieftainship of Texcoco, had taken to the hills after the defeat of his nation and was stirring up opposition to the enemy. He induced the Tenochcas under their new chief Itzcoatl to attack Azcapotzalco through the back door of Tlacopan, while he rallied the Texcocans and their tributaries to assault the enemy with columns coming both by canoe and overland round the lakes. After a long war of several weeks the allies were successful.

Nezahualcoyotl doubtless intended that his state should regain its position as the dominant power in the northern lake country. But he did not realize that when he formed the triple alliance for mutual defence and offensive profit he laid the foundation for a rival state which would surpass Texcoco. The Tenochcas and the Texcocans were each to receive two shares of all loot, the Tlacopans one, but the division was probably liberally interpreted by whichever chanced to be the strongest of the three allies. The Tenochcas gained land on the lake shore, which gave them a strong foothold for further conquest. Since this new territory was granted to the leading warriors, a caste of power and wealth was established. Thus outwardly the conquest brought the Tenochcas from the condition of a feudal tributary to that of an independent state. Inwardly there was a change of feeling, a shift from an inferiority to a superiority complex. Itzcoatl, the fourth Tenochcan chief, expressed this attitude by ordering all the historical picture manuscripts to be burned, 'as they were not appreciated by the ordinary people'.[5]

From the time of Itzcoatl the state histories are in very close accord. Those written prior to his accession in 1428 exhibit considerable conflict, often resulting in discrepancies of a fifty-two-year cycle or more. I think this lack of agreement arose from the split in continuity at the time of the Chapultepec defeat in 1300. Part of the tribe refugeed to the islands in the lake and founded a town in 1325 or thereabouts, ruling it under a tribal council and a main chief. The other group was taken to Tizapan and became civilized according to Culhuacan standards. The founding of Tenochtitlan, from their point of view, did not take place until they joined the original colony on the lake where, as soon as possible, they erected stone temples and tried to found a dynasty.

Itzcoatl enabled the Tenochcas to assume Aztec civilization. His historical reforms doubtless coincided with ritualistic regulations as well, for he undertook the construction of temples and the ordering of a religious hierarchy. He ordained the ranks of the civil government and superintended the building of the city, constructing causeways to the mainland to ensure easy access. Systematically Itzcoatl began to mop up those independent Valley groups not subject to Texcoco; he also won victories and acknowledgements of supremacy from the powerful Chalcas and Xochimilcas, people culturally allied more closely to the Puebla groups than to those of the northern Valley. To show his independence Itzcoatl had a brush with Nezahualcoyotl's Texcocans, and thereafter the peace between the former allies was somewhat precarious.

Montezuma I, surnamed Ilhuicamina, the Wrathful, succeeded Itzcoatl after his death in 1440. This chief, already marked as a leader in the wars of Itzcoatl, extended the domination of Tenochtitlan even further. He successfully fought the Chalcas, who detested the people of the northern Valley, and crossed the mountains to raid eastwards into Puebla and Vera Cruz and southwards to conquer towns in Morelos and Guerrero. A fairly close military cooperation must have existed between Texcoco and Tenochtitlan, for conquests claimed for Tenochtitlan by Tenochcan historians appear as gains for Texcoco in the Texcocan annals. Poor Tlacopan disappears from the scene, possibly independent still but certainly unconsidered in the division of pelf, a situation recalling that of Italy in 1918.

Under Montezuma I the cultural aspects of Tenochtitlan progressed mightily. He took measures to ensure the health of his people, building an aqueduct from the springs of Chapultepec to bring an abundance of sweet water to the city. Around the eastern rim of his capital he caused a great dyke to be erected to dam off the spread of the lakes during the rainy season.

The conquests into Puebla brought the Tenochcas in touch with the highly developed religion of that area, so that many additional temples were built in honour of gods and goddesses which were revered by the conquered tribes. In times of relative peace he revived the War of Flowers, a ceremonial contest between warriors of two groups in order that prisoners might be taken for sacrifice without the economic dislocation of formal war. This practice was known long before in the Valley, the Tenochcas participating in such struggles with the Chalcas in 1376–84, but the Tenochcas had been so continuously at war that they were accustomed to take their prisoners the hard way.[6]

The crops failed from 1451–6, owing to severe storms and frost. Many people died, and others, unable to support themselves, adopted voluntary slavery in order to share the bounty of the more fortunate. Usually a famine led to increased military activity to replenish the empty larders with supplies exacted as tribute. But in this case the situation was so severe and the Tenochcas so weak that they had to be content with a War of Flowers.

Axayacatl succeeded his father Montezuma I in 1469. He extended Tenochcan domination over a still wider area, spreading west into the Matlatzinca country and south to Oaxaca and Tehuantepec. He conducted a campaign into the Tarascan territory and met with a dreadful defeat which ensured the independence of these people of Michoacan up to their conquest by the Spaniards. This was the only serious Tenochcan military disaster until the grim days of 1519.[7]

Neither Axayacatl nor his successors was able to transform domination of a region into dominion. He did succeed, nevertheless, in reducing the neighbouring town of Tlaltelolco, killing its chief and denying its council the right to meet with the Tenochcas in matters of governmental importance. Tlaltelolco up to that time had maintained its independence and had grown at the same rate as Tenochtitlan, aiding in many of the campaigns. It was famous for its merchants; and its market, even after its subjugation, was the greatest in Mexico. Local jealousy, however, did not lead to war until both towns competed in building temples to Huitzilopochtli, the War God. Apparently this competition for divine favour led to war, whereas economic conflict did not. Ridiculously enough the open break was induced by the insulting behaviour of the Tlaltelolcan women, who flaunted their backsides at the enraged Tenochcan visitors.[8]

The religious arts reached their full development under Axayacatl. In his time was made the great Calendar Stone which weighs over twenty tons and is thirteen feet in diameter. The block was quarried on the mainland, and the allied rulers sent help to drag this gigantic mass across the causeways. Designed to symbolize the Aztec universe, it is a masterly example of a pattern, the detail of which adds, rather than detracts from, the spaciousness of the concept.[9] (See Plate 50, top.)

In 1472, early in the reign of Axayacatl, the life of a great figure in American Indian history, Nezahualcoyotl, came to an end. This Texcocan chief had begun his manhood in political exile fleeing from Tepanec vengeance, but had fought and intrigued his way back into power. He even restored the fortunes of his people who, in the previous century, had rivalled the Culhuacanos in the formative years of Aztec civilization.

Nezahualcoyotl had a broad judicial sense which enabled him successfully to elaborate the administrative structure of a far-flung realm. Since the Texcocans, before the Tepanec domination, 1419–28, already had a chain of tribute-paying vassals, this resumption of control in after years was not so much a conquest as the forceful exercise of due rights.[10]

He took a lively interest in the construction of temples and public buildings so that, for all its tattered decay today, Texcoco was one of the most imposing cities on the Central Plateau. His palace near by and his bath, hewn from the solid rock of Texcotcingo, are visible proof of the rich luxury of his life.

Nezahualcoyotl took a profound interest in religion and the arts. He transformed theological speculation into a philosophy of religion and worshipped a single god, the force through which nature manifests itself and from which the lesser gods derived their power and being. He encouraged the arts and in his own right attained great renown as a poet and orator. The lore of the stars fascinated him, and he had a deep knowledge of the astrological astronomy of his day and age. In contrast to the bleakly austere records of the Tenochca overlords, his career was a model of wise administration. Not the least of Nezahualcoyotl's achievements was his keeping the peace with his arrogant island ally, Tenochtitlan, which was every ready by intrigue, murder, or open warfare to add to its wealth and power.

Nezahualcoyotl was succeeded by his son Nezahualpilli, who ruled until 1516. The length of his reign indicates the possession of an administrative skill equal to his father's. He successfully undertook a number of conquests, but they are not so dramatized as those of the Tenochcan chiefs.

Nezahualpilli had an interest in astrology, religion, and necromancy, as would be natural in a chief whose religious obligations were as onerous as his civil and military duties. His later years were weighted with trouble with Tenochtitlan. He had married a sister of Montezuma II and, as she was unduly free in granting favours to the young men of the court, in 1498 he took advantage of his legal right to kill her. The Tenochcas took this act as a gross personal affront and directed every effort, short of war, to overcoming their ancient ally.[11]

Axayacatl of Tenochtitlan died in 1479, while Nezahualpilli was young in his rule, and his brother Tizoc, who had previously been the war chief, took his place. Tizoc's most important act of office was to begin the reconstruction of the great temple to Huitzilopochtli, the War God, and Tlaloc, the Rain God. In commemoration of his conquests he also had carved the so-called Sacrificial Stone. This monstrous-sized vessel for burning human hearts has a relief on the edge, depicting Tizoc dressed as Huitzilopochtli seizing captives representing tributary tribes. Most of the towns, unfortunately, must have been merely reconquered, since their names appear in the previous conquest lists of earlier rulers. It is not a complete surprise to read in some accounts that Tizoc died of poison administered by chiefs disgusted by his lack of military success.[12]

Ahuitzotl succeeded his brother Tizoc in 1486. His first task was to complete the great temple the others had begun, in the dedication of which the gathering of sacrificial victims played an important part. He invoked the aid of Nezahualpilli, and the allies made a two-year campaign into northern Oaxaca, amassing no less than twenty thousand victims, the high point of the sacrificial cult in Mexico. At the start of the dedication the captives stood in two rows, and Nezahualpilli and Ahuitzotl began the grisly work of tearing out the victims' hearts. Lesser dignitaries succeeded each other according to rank, until the awful immolation was completed.[13]

Ahuitzotl's military campaigns extended south into Guatemala and as far north as the Huaxteca in Vera Cruz. He was constantly engaged in putting down revolts, especially in Puebla, where the Tlaxcalans and Cholulans had resisted

Tenochcan domination. His capital, meanwhile, had grown so enormously that he had to construct another aqueduct, a fact which indicates that sheer pressure of population was an important cause for the military exploits of Tenochtitlan. An unusually disastrous flood beset the city in 1503, so that Ahuitzotl had to send to Texcoco for aid in restoring the dykes. While superintending these public works he received a head injury which proved fatal. Ahuitzotl's personality was strong and vicious. He was passionately fond of war, being a vindictive and relentless foe. Likewise he had those traits which so often accompany military character, lust for women and fondness for display.

The luckless Montezuma II, surnamed Xocoyotzin (the Younger), son of Axayacatl, succeeded his uncle. Not only had he to keep the conquered tribes in order, but also he had constantly to provide captives for sacrifice. This bloody cult, which to the Tenochcan mind had brought such eminence, had to be maintained lest disaster ensue. He approached his uncle's piety on one occasion when twelve thousand captives from a rebel province in Oaxaca were delivered up to the War God.[14]

The last New Fire Ceremony took place in 1507. The years immediately preceding, with their threat of an ending world, were especially ominous, since in addition to earthquakes and other supernatural portents word came in of white strangers, propelled in odd craft, who were ranging along the coast. But the ceremony took place, and the world continued. (See Figure 20.)

Montezuma fought an unsuccessful war against the Tlaxcalans, but at the same time he succeeded in avenging himself on his Texcocan allies for the death of his sister, by allowing their force to be ambushed and wiped out. In 1516, at the death of Nezahualpilli, he appointed his successor without recognizing the choice of the Texcocan council. The ousted candidate revolted and the already strained alliance was broken.[15]

A year later Grijalva reached Vera Cruz, and in 1519 Cortés started his march to Mexico. Montezuma died that winter, stoned by his own people, according to Spanish accounts, strangled by the Spaniards, in the Indian versions. Cuitlahuac succeeded him but died of smallpox in four months, and the last of the free chiefs, Cuauhtemoc, conducted the heroic defence of Tenochtitlan, only to be hanged four years later on Cortés's march to Honduras.[16]

Thus ends the bare record of Tenochcan history, without a description of the people, their government, their laws, their gods or their arts. Lacking, also, is an account of the clash between the two civilizations: Aztec and Spanish. The records are abundant, and we can form a lifelike picture of the time. Before we examine the nature of Aztec civilization and the causes of its downfall, let us recapitulate briefly the history of the Valley peoples before the Conquest.

This chapter has covered the rise of the Tenochcas and how they came to be the greatest example of Aztec civilization. Yet the events set forth show quite clearly that they did not originate this civilization or, beyond the sacrifice cult, contribute much to it. During their migration period, from 1168 to 1248, they were simple primitive folk. In their sedentary period, from the settlement at Chapultepec in 1248 to the election of Acamapichtli in 1376, they were busily absorbing the culture of their neighbours and overlords, especially that of the Culhuas who, remember, were originally Toltec. The tributary period, from 1376 to 1428, saw the Tenochcas under the control of the Tepanec, cautiously trying out the formal Aztec city-state organization. Not until Itzcoatl assumed the chieftaincy in 1429 did Tenochtitlan really advance, at which time the city took part in the general great rise of Aztec civilization.

On the other hand, Culhuacan was associated with the earliest phase of Aztec culture in the Valley and was the heir of the great Toltec civilization. The evolving Aztec culture in its ceramic aspect had surpassed its predecessors and was well established throughout the Valley at a date when the Tenochcas were nonentities. The historical position of Culhuacan closely paralleled the archaeological record, yet this early Culhuacan phase did not seem to be a spontaneous development so much as a derivative from Puebla and the Mixteca.

The availability of annals and the existence of competent excavations in sites like Tenochtitlan, Texcoco, and Culhuacan have caused us to weight heavily the testimony of the people on the northern half of the lakes. Chalco and Xochimilco, to the south, whose annals have disappeared and whose sites are largely unexcavated,[17] may have had a far more important part in the history of the Valley than appears here. Pueblan influence is far stronger in these southern city-states.

Aztec civilization, therefore, was a dynamic composite of many elements, some developed as an answer to growing needs, others incorporated by contact with foreign peoples. Constant change took place, as in all other human societies, resulting from the continual adjustments man must make to fresh situations. Since individual men and women make up a community, let us in the following chapters begin with a single person and work our way through his social obligations and economics to his governmental organization and religion, finally reaching the Conquest and its aftermath.

Table 6.[18] SUMMARY OF AZTEC HISTORY AFTER THE RISE OF
TENOCHTITLAN

1403–55, EARLY AZTEC III PERIOD

Eastern Phase: Political elimination of Texcoco in first half of period with later
recovery; prosperity and cultural advance under Nezahualcóyotl; expansion
of palace at Chiconauhtla; Aztec IIIa pottery; Cholula V pottery; cyclical
dumps at Chiconauhtla and Los Melones, Texcoco.

Western Phase: Political extinction of Culhuacan; rise and fall of Tepanecs;
rise of Tenochtitlan with organization of Triple Alliance; growth of conquest and war-captive pattern; cyclical reconstruction at Tenayuca, Building
IV; cyclical dump in *Zocalo*, Mexico City; broad diffusion of Aztec IIIa
pottery; sixth Aztec cycle counted, 1403–55.

Culhuacan	*Cuauhtitlan*	*Cuitlahuac*	*Texcoco*	*Tenochtitlan*
Nauhyotl	Xaltemoc	Tepolozmáyotl	Ixtlilxóchitl	Chimalpopoca
1400–13	1390–98	1393–1415	1409–18	1414–28
	(1408)			
			Tepanec Tyrants	
			Tezozomoc	Itzcóatl
			1343–1427	1428–40
			Maxtla	
			1427–29	
			Texcocan Lineage	Montezuma I
			Resumed	1440–69
			Nezahualcóyotl	
			1418–72	

1455–1507, LATE AZTEC III PERIOD

Eastern Phase: Continued development of culture at Texcoco; growth of
Chiconauhtla palace; elaboration of ceramics; Aztec IIIb pottery; cyclical
dump at Chiconauhtla.

Western Phase: Political power of Tenochtitlan; extension of conquest over
Mexico and Guatemala; reconstruction of great temple; increase in captive
sacrifice; elaboration of ritual; diffusion of Aztec IIIb pottery; cyclical reconstruction at Tenayuca, Building V; cyclical dump at Nonoalco, Mexico
City, seventh Aztec cycle counted, 1455–1507.

Culhuacan	*Cuauhtitlan*	*Cuitlahuac*	*Texcoco*	*Tenochtitlan*
unimportant	unimportant	unimportant	Nezahualpilli	Axayácatl
			1472–1516	1469–81
				Tizoc
				1481–6
				Ahuitzotl
				1486–1503

1507–1519 (CONQUEST) AZTEC IV

Eastern Phase: Growing friction between Texcoco and Tenochtitlan; last expansion of Chiconauhtla palace; Aztec IV pottery styles with good life forms. Conquest.

Western Phase: Tenochtitlan domination with coercion of Texcoco; maintenance of old conquests rather than success of new ones; cyclical reconstruction of Tenayuca, Building VI; Aztec IV pottery with many life forms; eighth Aztec cycle counted, 1507–59, incomplete with Conquest.

Texcoco	*Tenochtitlan*
Cacama	Montezuma II
1516–19	1503–20
	Cuitlahuac
	1520 (4 months)
	Cuauhtemoc
	1520–4
	(murdered on way
	to Honduras)

In which are set forth the basic ideas of Aztec
Education, Government, Law, and Social
Customs

The social organization of the Aztec tribes when they came
into the Valley was in theory completely democratic. An individual was a member of a family which, in turn, belonged to
a cluster of families or a clan.* Theoretically twenty of these
clans made up a tribe, each of them regulating its own affairs,
but in matters of tribal importance joining with the others in
a council composed of all the leaders. The council appointed
one chief to control civil and religious affairs and usually a
second for war. Originally designed for simple farming
communities and presumably of an antiquity dating back to
Pre-classic times, this organization later ramified into the
governmental complexity of a populous and highly complicated city-state.[1]

The working of a community is best illustrated by the position of the individual in it, a process which is described in the
third part of the *Codex Mendoza*. Immediately a child was born
it was washed and swaddled by a midwife. Since the gods
governed the fate of man on earth, the parents consulted a
priest who looked in the *tonalamatl*, or book of fate, to see if
the day of birth was lucky or unlucky. Four days later the
child's family held a feast both to celebrate the birth and to
name the child. If the day of birth proved to be unlucky,
custom sanctioned a religious fiction whereby the naming
ceremony was postponed to a more favourable period. At the
feast the guests sprinkled food and pulque over the sacred fire,
which had been kindled at the accouchement as an offering to

* The term clan is used to mean a tribal division without connotation
of male or female descent.

the Fire God, the Old God, whose cult originated in the time of the Pre-classic Cultures. The child, if a boy, was shown toy weapons and tools which the parents placed in his hands, guiding them in the motions of use. If the child were a girl the parents made her pretend to weave and spin with toy instruments. A name, that badge of identity so important to man, was given to the child at this time. A boy was often named for the date of his birth, One Reed, Two Flower, Seven Deer, or for an animal, like 'Nezahualcoyotl' (Hungry Coyote), or for an ancestor, like 'Montezuma the Younger', or for some event at the time of birth. Often the day name was given with an alternative animal title. Girls' names frequently were compounded with the word for flower, *xochitl*.

Education began after weaning in the third year. Its purpose was to induct the child into the techniques and obligations of adult life as promptly as possible. A world in which handwork is universal offers a child a chance to participate in adult activities far earlier than in our heavily mechanized culture. Fathers supervised the training of sons, and mothers instructed their daughters. Up to six years of age the children listened to frequently repeated homilies and advice, learned the uses of the household implements and performed minor household chores.[2]

The principal food was the tortilla, a flat cake of unleavened corn meal, which measured a good foot in diameter to judge from the size of the clay griddles used in cooking them, in contrast to the modern tortilla which varies between four and six inches. At three the child received half a tortilla a day; at four and five his ration was doubled; from six to twelve a tortilla and a half were prescribed, and at thirteen the allotment was two. Supplemented by beans and game, this diet was filling and nutritious.

The *Mendoza* manuscript reflects the current Aztec ideas on child psychology. Admonition was the chief method of discipline up to the eighth year. From then on a rigorous corporal punishment awaited the recalcitrant child. This disciplin ranged from pricking the hand with the maguey spine to ex posing the child to the chill rigours of a mountain night, lying bound and naked in a mud-puddle. In view of the almost uni versal kindness which Indian parents show to their children they probably seldom applied these extremely imaginativ corrections for wrongdoing by the young.

This type of training, not unlike that of a modern farn child, initiated him directly into the economic life of the home The satisfactions in playing a man's part by contributing to th family welfare compensated the child for the heaviness of hi social obligation. At fifteen or sixteen most boys went throug a special training before assuming the full rights of manhood under certain conditions they were younger when they re ceived this special instruction. There were two types o schools: the *telpuchcalli*, or house of youth, for standard train ing, and the *calmecac* of uncertain etymology, for instruction i priestly duties. The *telpuchcalli*, maintained by the clan for th children of its members, offered instruction in citizenship, th bearing of arms, arts and crafts, history and tradition, an ordinary religious observance. The *calmecac* was in the natur of a seminary for special training in priestly and chiefly duties and several of them were maintained near the temples of im portant gods. The *calmecac* seems to have been an addition t ordinary training, required by the development of ritual whereas the *telpuchcalli* carried on in special quarters instruc tion given in a simpler day by the old men of the clan. Othe schools trained young women to be priestesses; they als learned to weave skilfully and to make featherwork for pre paration of priestly vestments. (See Plate 38, top left.)

A youth was ready for marriage at twenty, and a girl wa deemed mature at about sixteen. The parents arranged th marriage with the consent of the boy and girl. A priest wa consulted to decide whether or not the fates of the coupl were harmonious. Incest laws like our own prevailed, with th further restriction that marriage must be outside the clan. Having satisfied these conventions, the father of the boy sent two elderly clanswomen with gifts to the girl's father, who, following custom, rejected the suit. The old ladies returned again to consult in earnest with the parents of the prospective bride. Such a discussion was necessarily intricate, since it involved the amount of the bride's dowry, which was to be balanced by the gifts of her suitor.

On the evening of the wedding one of the matchmakers carried the bride on her back over the threshold of the husband's house. Elaborate speeches were made by everyone, following which the mantles of the bride and groom were tied together, symbolizing the union. The old men and women gave tongue again in the form of long-winded homilies, and at last a feast, liberally lubricated with pulque, took place. The bride and the groom, after this merciless treatment, retired for four days of penance and fasting, and not until that period elapsed did they consummate their marriage.

As is often the case in a warrior nation which suffers from reduced manpower, polygamy was prevalent. Yet the first wife took precedence over the others, and her children alone had the right to inherit. Concubines were permitted and there was, likewise, prostitution. Desertion was frowned upon, but a court would grant a decree of divorce under certain conditions. A man could obtain the right to cast out his wife if she were sterile, were subject to prolonged ill temper, or neglected her household duties. The wife could be freed from a husband who failed to support her or educate the children or who illtreated her in the physical sense, for the Aztecs had not invented mental cruelty. A divorced woman could remarry as she chose, but a widow had to marry a brother of her deceased husband or one of his clansmen.[3]

Women had definite rights, but they were inferior to those of men. They could hold property, enter into contracts and go to courts to obtain justice. In matters of sexual morality girls

had to be chaste and wives faithful to their husbands. A ma
transgressed the rules of propriety only when his illicit relations involved a married woman. Otherwise his wife could no
formally demand his fidelity. While the legal position of women was relatively low, judged by modern standards in th
United States, personal influence was great, and there wer
several instances where a woman acted as regent when her so
was too young to assume the office of chief. In matters of triba
alliance we have seen how the marriage of a chief's daughter o
sister to another ruler cemented an alliance. Moreover, mar-
riages were carefully arranged between families, so that for
husband grossly to neglect his wife's rights was a breach, if no
of etiquette, certainly of social contract. The priesthood ma
have offered a modest field of influence and attainment to
women. However, history records no mention of any advantage deriving from temple service.

Men had the chief opportunities, and these lay in variou
directions. The early chroniclers, conditioned by their medieval Spanish background, spoke of hereditary classes. In al
probability, judging from Indian communities as a whole
there was *rank* but not *class* in the hereditary sense until th
Empire was well established. As in our own society, a ma
could attain high *rank* through his own efforts, and throug
his eminence his children would consequently profit in thei
own social adjustment. Yet they could not reach their father'
position unless they earned it through equivalent service
Wealth did exist, and property in the form of rights to use land
tools, and other possessions created a social and economic stratification. In theory if not always in practice Aztec society wa
democratic, and the communal ownership of productive property was its economic base.[4]

A man attained rank through the measure of his service to
society. The wise farmer, the wily hunter, the brave warrior
or the dexterous artisan gained admiration from his fellows because of superior skill. If his wisdom and judgement were con-

picuous he might be elected as the clan representative to the tribal council, or even as chief. Similarly an individual who dedicated himself to learning the magic rituals to placate the gods could become a medicine man or priest. However, in the populous and advanced city-states activities tended to become specialized, and greater opportunity led to a more finely graded scale of social eminence. (See Plates 33–35.)

A married man received a plot of land directly from the clan or else took over his father's fields if the latter were too old to work. Diligent husbandry, eked out by making stone tools, pottery, or practising some such craft for barter, could produce a good living. Unmarried men helped their fathers and were able to add to their prestige by taking part in the numerous military campaigns.

Since the capture of victims for sacrifice was the chief glory of war, an able soldier who could subdue his enemies and drag them to the rear received much honour. According to the number of captives taken, a warrior had the right to wear an increasingly elaborate costume. Consistently successful warriors could enter an order, like the Knights of the Eagle or the Ocelot (often referred to as Tiger), which performed special dances and rituals. Sometimes a warrior of unusual prowess received additional grants of land or more often obtained an increased portion of the clan's share of tribute. Having reached an established position by this means, he had a more important voice in clan councils and might attain a seat in the council itself. A special honorific, *tecuhtli* (grandfather), which corresponds to chief among the North American Indians, distinguished these men. The title signified high social rank, and from these men who had distinguished themselves by probity, bravery, and religious observance, high elective and appointive posts were filled.[5]

In this stratum there were many positions of honour and influence, which, like petty political offices in small North American towns, were held in connexion with some other means of livelihood. There were officials who kept order in the markets and tribunals which settled disputes in clan affairs. Men of proven wisdom and experience taught the young in the *telpuchcalli*, or houses of youth. Others kept the records of tribute and wealth in the clan storehouses, superintended the distribution of this communal property, and even went abroad to supervise its collection.

Each clan had its elected officers whose positions dominated its administration. One official, the *calpullec*, performed the duties of secretary-treasurer and kept economic order within the kinship, drawing upon the members of the body for a much administrative assistance as his task required. Ranking with him, the *teochcautin* acted as sheriff, preserving social order and enforcing it. In war-time he commanded the military forces of the clan. Linking the clans to the tribe were the *tlatoani*, or 'speakers', the supreme council, composed of a member from each clan and exercising judicial and directive functions. The wisest men and the most distinguished attained this post, for on them depended the well-being of the whole society. (See Plate 38, top right.)

Just as the clan had its executive officers, so each tribal body elected four officials who controlled the military forces of the four quarters, or phratries, into which the twenty clans were evenly divided. They maintained order among the clans and exercised authority in disputes and crimes that could not be settled by the clan itself. Two were especially concerned with judicial matters; the third was an executioner, and the fourth acted as an intermediary between civil and military affairs.[6]

These four offices were the proving ground to test the abilities of the supreme chief and the religious leader. In Tlaxcala it appears that they jointly exercised the executive leadership. In Tenochtitlan the supreme chief, *tlacatecuhtli*, 'chief of men', was always chosen from the four and often occupied first the position of 'Snake Woman', a name also given to an important fertility goddess, Cihuacoatl. The func-

Plate I. EXCAVA-
TIONS IN CENTRAL
MEXICO

TOP, *Left:* Dissecting a
palace at Chiconauhtla,
State of Mexico; for plan
see Plate 42a. MIDDLE,
Left: Stratigraphy of
Burials at Tlatilco. BOT-
TOM, *Left:* Excavation at
Nonoalco. *Right:* Deep
pit at El Arbolillo, Federal District, Mexico. The
earliest discovered figurine types (Plate 14) were
found at the bottom of
this trench

Plate 2. CLAY FIGURES FROM GRAVES
IN WESTERN MEXICO

TOP: The dog is a hairless edible breed,
the large ancestor of the modern dwarf
Chihuahua. The accompanying figure shows
a fresh vitality unobscured by ceremonial
details. BOTTOM: Seated woman from western Mexico, a fine example of direct realism. The lack of sophistication is compensated
for by the lively understanding of the subject matter

Plate 3. SCULPTURES IN THE 'OLMEC' STYLE

TOP, *Left:* Clay figure from Pre-classic site at Gualupita, Morelos. *Centre:* Jade bead from Chiapas in similar style; note face marking. *Right:* Outline of jade tiger (below) with facial marking like that of the head. BOTTOM, *Left:* Clay figure from Pre-classic site at Tlatilco. *Right:* Jade tiger, Necaxa, Puebla, a superb example, in miniature, of the jade cutter's art

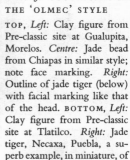

Plate 4. SCULPTURES IN 'OLMEC' A
EARLY MAYA STYLES

TOP: Model of Temple E VII–sub Uaxac
Peten, Guatemala. Later structures seal in
earlier monument of rubble covered
plaster. The second tier of masks clo
resembles the sculpture on the left. MIDI
Left: Porphyry mask from Tabasco. BOTT
Left: This stone figure of a man from
Quiche province of Guatemala sh
evidence of strong 'Olmec' influence in
Maya area. *Right:* Stone mask represen
tiger-like god

Plate 5. 'OLMEC' STONE SCULPTURE

Top: Altar 4 from La Venta, showing seated figure in the jaws of a jaguar. BOTTOM, *Left:* Colossal head from La Venta, known as Monument I. *Right:* Stone figure of a Wrestler, 'Olmec', from Southern Vera Cruz

Plate 7. MAYA ARCHITECTURE AND SCULPTURE,
LATE PERIOD

TOP, *Left:* Stela, twenty-five feet high, from Quirigua,
Guatemala. These stone time markers bore calendric calculations. *Right:* Figure in low relief, Jonuta, Tabasco. This is a
superb example of Maya art. Contrast the dignity of the
kneeling man with the vivid realism of the parrot. BOTTOM:
House of the Dwarf, Uxmal, Yucatan. Late Maya temple
architecture increased the size of the rooms and lavished
decorative detail on the façades

Plate 8. MAYA PAINTI[NG]

TOP: Detail from a To[ltec] period wall painting [at] Chichen Itza. Warriors [are] raiding a town and [tak]ing prisoners, suggesting [the] troubled days of the To[ltec] expansion. BOTTOM: De[tail] from classic wall pain[ting] at Bonampak

Plate 9. ZAPOTEC SCULP-
TURE AND ARCHITEC-
TURE, OAXACA, MEXICO
TOP: The ruins of Monte
Alban, near Oaxaca. This was
the great Zapotec ceremonial centre, where a whole hill
was terraced to make space for
temples and tombs. BOTTOM:
Relief from the earliest period at Monte Alban. This earliest art has certain resemblances
to the 'Olmec' style. Glyphs
accompanying some of the
figures show that a form of
writing was known

Plate 10. ZAPOTEC SCULPTURE IN CLAY

TOP: Mortuary urn depicting a rain god. Ritual demanded a formal and conventional treatment in defining this god. MIDDLE: This tiger god recalls the 'Olmec' divinity of Plates 3 and 4. It is a splendid example of Period 2, combining the freedom and the conventionalization of the two other sculptures. BOTTOM: This figure in the Oaxaca Museum shows how Zapotec sculpture could break through the bonds of convention to produce fine realistic art

Plate 11. 'TOTONAC' SCULPTURE, VERA CRUZ

Impressive art forms have been found in this state and have been inaccurately grouped under this single term. TOP, *Left:* Palmate stone, of undetermined use, representing a dead wild turkey. *Right:* Back of a slate mirror which probably had a reflecting surface of iron pyrites. BOTTOM: Clay head from Vera Cruz. Classic period. Note resemblance to Teotihuacan, Fig. 4

Plate 12. 'TOTONAC' SCULPTURE AND ARCHITECTURE

TOP: Rear view of Temple of Tajin, Papamtla. The niches may have held sma[ll] idols, or may represent the days of the year, but more probably are simply a[n] impressive example of the versatility of Mesoamerican architecture. The buildin[g] was covered with burnished and painted stucco, and there was a sanctuary on to[p] BOTTOM: Mural sculpture in stone from one of the six ball courts at Tajin, depictin[g] a sacrifice

Plate 13. PRE-CLASSIC IMPLEMENTS

TOP: Obsidian tools; *top row,* Upper Preclassic; *middle and bottom rows,* Lower Preclassic. *Right:* Equipment of Upper Pre-classic leatherworker, awls, grainer, scrapers, and rodent teeth for cutting and scraping. BOTTOM: Lower Pre-classic ornaments, earplugs, beads, and whistle. Note the jade ornaments, second in both rows

Plate 14. LOWER PRE-CLASSIC
FIGURINES

TOP: Figurines (Type C 3) from
the earliest level. The features are
made of applied bits of clay. Although the general appearance is
crude, the technique shows long
experimentation. BOTTOM: These
Figurines (Types C 1 and C 1–2)
develop from those above. They
seem to show a more slovenly procedure, but there is more variety in
form than in the earlier style of
female figures above

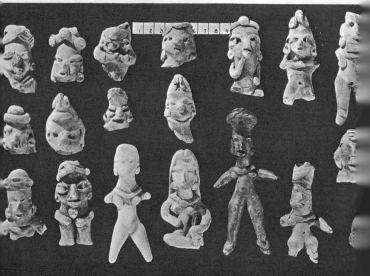

PLATE 15. TRANSITIONAL PRE-CLASSIC FIGURINES

TOP, *Left:* The head (D 1) in this much enlarged reproduction represents a style in which the craftsmen exercised more care and skill. The source of the type seems to have been outside the Valley of Mexico, in Morelos. *Right:* This complete figure is from Vera Cruz. BOTTOM: A group of similar heads from Central Mexico, showing the variations within a single style. The scale is in centimetres

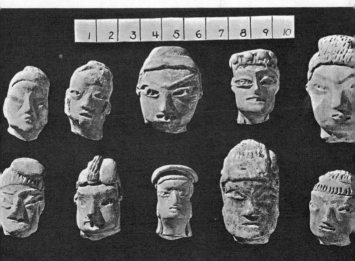

Plate 16. A TRANSITIONAL FIGURINE TYPE

Drawings of a Transitional Type (D-K) showing connexions between Morelos and the valley. The figure on the right is from our excavations at Gualupita, the one on the left is from Tlatilco

PLATE 17. TRANSITIONAL PRE-CLASSIC FIGURINES AND ART OBJECTS

Top: Figurines (Type A). Close scrutiny will disclose that this style is in a different tradition. The source may perhaps be Tres Zapotes, Vera Cruz. BOTTOM, *Left:* Figurines (Type B) which are the survival of the local tradition, contemporary with Type A (*top*). Degeneration has set in, since the craftsmen's interest has shifted to the new style. *Right:* Incense burner of lava, the oldest stone carving found yet in the Valley of Mexico. The bowl rests on the back of a hunched human figure. *Below:* Earplug of carved baked clay. A collar at the rear was inserted in a perforation in the ear lobe

Plate 18. UPPER PRE-
CLASSIC ARCHITECTU.
TOP: Pyramid at Tlapaco
D.F. This building is proba
ly contemporary with t
earliest constructions at Teo
huacan. BOTTOM: View
platform at Cuicuilco. T
oval structure of adobe fac
with stone had fallen in
decay before the lava (visi
at upper left) flowed over t
debris. On the left, circli
the base of the platform, m
be seen a parallel row
stones of unknown signi
cance

P: Three figurines (E) represent the plastic art of this era. The bowl is polychrome
d is ornamented with embossed birds. BOTTOM: The Type H figurines of the
t phase of the Upper Pre-classic are covered with a white slip and painted. Their
sitions are lively and animated. The jar in the background is painted red on a
own background with a subsidiary pattern in black applied by the batik process.
e small pot is of quartzite

Plate 20. POTTERY AND FIGURINES, UPPER PRE-CLASSIC

TOP, *Left:* This large seated figure of clay from Gualupita, Morelos, shows individuality not found in the run of the sculpture. It belongs to the same per as the other figure (*right*), which is similar to some found at Tlatilco. BOTTO These bowls from Ticoman show the standard shapes of this era. Note the elabor tripod supports that distinguish these shapes from the preceding Lower Pre-cla Era

PLATE 21. TEOTIHUACAN ARCHITECTURE

TOP: Reconstruction of Teotihuacan by Gamio and Marquina. The long axis runs north and south and includes, beginning with the Temple of the Moon, the Plaza of the Moon, the Agriculture Group, the Group of the Columns, the Pyramid of the Sun, the Superimposed Buildings, and the Citadel Group. Note the arrangement in terms of precincts and axes. BOTTOM: Air view of Teotihuacan today, looking south-east. In the foreground is the Pyramid of the Moon, and in the centre the monstrous Temple of the Sun

Plate 22. TEOTIHUACAN ARCHITECTURE

Detail from the Temple of Quetzalcoatl, which was later covered up to mak
Citadel Group. The massive serpents' heads had eyes of obsidian

PLATE 23. TEOTIHUACAN PAINTING

TOP: Fresco of jaguars and coyotes, Atetelco. See Plate 25 for comparison with later representations of the same concept. BOTTOM: The paradise of Tlaloc at Tepantitla

Plate 24. TEOTIHUACAN SCULPTU[RE]
TOP: This massive figure, ten feet tall, se[ems]
to be a water goddess. It is noteworthy [for]
its monumental quality. BOTTOM, *L[eft:]*
Mask of porphyry, showing a marvel[lous]
skill in reproducing their physical t[ype.]
Right: Stone mask from Guerroro, T[eoti]-
huacan type, but note 'Olmec' mouth

Plate 25. TOLTEC SCULPTURE

TOP: Stone relief of coyote from the Great Temple at Xochicalco. Compare with Teotihuacan painting, Plate 23, and with the frieze from Tula below. BOTTOM: frieze in stone representing coyotes and jaguars. Compare with painting in Plate 23 and frieze of jaguars alone in Plate 27, as well as with coyote from Xochicalco above

Plate 26 TOLTEC POTTERY, SCULPTURE AND ARCHITECTUR[E]

TOP, *Left:* Life-size figure from C[o]linchan, Valley of Mexico. It represe[nts] the god Xipe dressed in a human s[kin] *Right:* Effigy vase, one of a pair, Maza[pan] Culture, from a grave at the type site. [It] seems to represent a dead man. These [two] figures indicate that the Toltecs had [de]veloped clay sculpture into a major [art] BOTTOM: Tula, Hidalgo. Temple show[ing] columns

te 27. TOLTEC INFLUENCE IN YUCATAN

the turn of the twelfth century the Toltecs conquered Yucatan and built a
emonial centre at the former Maya city of Chichen Itza. TOP, *Left:* Head of the
xican Rain God Tlaloc. *Right:* Temple of the Jaguars at Ball Court (ⓒ *National
graphic Society*). BOTTOM: Detail of the Jaguar frieze and serpent columns so
iniscent of Tula. (See Plate 25)

Plate 28. TOLTEC TRA[DE] WARES

TOP and MIDDLE: Des[igns] from a vase, and another [vase] decorated in plaster cloisor[né] from Jalisco. Vases orname[nt]ed in this technique w[ere] extensively traded in [the] tenth and eleventh centu[ries.] BOTTOM: Jar in plumb[ate] ware, a quasi-vitreous wa[re] made in Salvador and Gua[te]mala, which was tra[ded] widely through Mesoame[rica] in this period

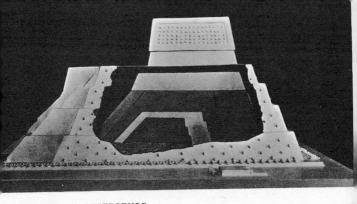

CHICHIMEC ARCHITECTURE

...del of the Temple of Tenayuca, showing the original building and the ...nstructions, possibly corresponding to the cyclical ceremonies of 1299, ...3, 1455 and 1507. BOTTOM: Temple at Teopanzalco, Cuernavaca. The ...f the later stairs and walls may be seen in the foreground, with the original ...d stair behind, and are larger than the first two Tenayuca buildings in the ...e. The later temple, to judge from the stair and lower walls, had an ...ral style as typically Aztec as the last three Tenayuca temples above

Plate 30.

MIXTECA-PUEBLA A[...]

This culture became dom[...]
ant after the eleventh c[...]
tury and had a wide [...]
fluence on the establis[...]
regional styles. TOP: P[...]
from the *Codex Nuttall* [...]
picting warriors attack[...]
a town in a lake. The ba[...]
at top left represents [...]
heavens, and the ot[...]
symbols the name and nu[...]
ber of the character's bir[...]
days. MIDDLE: Gold [...]
ornament representing [...]
parrot head. BOTTOM: [...]
temple or palace at Mi[...]
the largest roofed room [...]
Mesoamerica. Observe h[...]
each block of stone [...]
carved to combine int[...]
mosaic pattern

ate 31. CEREMONIAL VASE

is vase from Mihuatlan, Oaxaca, is a masterpiece of Mixteca–Puebla ceramics.
represents the god Macuilxochitl (Five Flower), God of Games and Feasting.
s dress, necklace, and face painting are faithfully represented in polychrome, and
ove the left collar-bone a turquoise bead has been inserted to indicate the god's
art. Jade and turquoise were precious, so also was the heart of a god. Therefore,
re was no symbolic conflict in showing as green an organ which is red

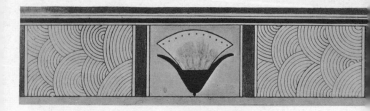

Plate 32. TRADE POTTERY, AZTEC PERIOD

Vessels like these from Puebla and Tlaxcala were much prized in Central Mexico, and obtained by trade or tribute. At the top, a design composed of a feather fan and concentric circles, taken from a hemispherical bowl. The middle cup utilizes a simple grecque pattern, while at the bottom is the hieroglyph for the day. Reed set against a black background decorates the neck of a vase, the body of which is painted a lustrous red

Plate 33a. PROCESSION OF NOTABLES, DOING HONOUR TO
MONTEZUMA

This drawing by Keith Henderson, in the Henry Holt edition of Prescott's *Conquest
of Mexico*, was adapted from native picture records. The artist reconciles the
dubbed fidelity of the Indian drawing with our own representational standards

Plate 33b. AZTEC WOMEN

Rich embroidery enlivened the dress of Aztec women, as shown in this drawing by
Keith Henderson. The measure of this artist's accuracy may be taken by comparing
this and the above with the *Codex Florentino* paintings on Plates 34 and 35

Rich Man

Poor Man

Beggar Man

Thief

Goldsmith

Feather Worker

Warriors

Doctor

hief

Lawyer

erchant

Women

lor, beware

Ant Bite

tes 34–35. AZTEC SOCIETY AND COSTUME FROM THE
DEX FLORENTINO

ring the mid sixteenth century, the Spanish friar Bernadino de Sahagún made a
ous study of the Aztecs, *Historia General de Nueva España*, which was not
lished until 1829. He had the Indians prepare copious illustrations to clarify his
s, but they did not reach public circulation until 1905. The selections here show,
des the social divisions expressed in our nursery rhyme, 'Rich man, poor
a . . .', various other activities, caught with a fresh and humorous eye. Although
e of the background details show that Spanish influence was already strongly
a generation after the Conquest, the general details disclose a strong persistence
e Aztec way of life

Plate 36. THE AZTECS' MEXICO

TOP: Ignacio Marquina's reconstruction of Tenochtitlan as it was in 1519. The reader looks slightly south–east. At the left looms the great temple; at the right stands the skull-rack; in the foreground is the northern canoe basin. Left and right of the great temple may be seen the palaces of Axayacatl and Montezuma. The sacrificial stone, and behind it a round temple to the Wind God, Ehecatl-Quetzalcoatl, occupy the middle distance. BOTTOM: The 'floating gardens' of Mexico are fast disappearing, Xochimilco, where this picture was made, is occupied by the same Aztec-speaking people who lived there before the Tenochas ever entered the valley

Plate 37. AZTEC ECONOMICS AS SEEN IN THE CODEX FLORENTINO

TOP ROW: A farmer plants his corn, using a digging stick, and later he and his wife store the harvest for the winter. Basic farming methods still persist among the modern Indians. MIDDLE, *Left:* A produce market which recalls the neatly arranged wares of a modern Indian vendor. *Right:* King Ahuitzotl receives produce of the coast: shells, jaguar skins, plumage, jade, and cacao. BOTTOM, *Left:* Members of a slave family wearing bars across their necks as a sign of bondage. *Right:* A merchant from the coast chaffers for such Highland produce as cloth, gold ornaments, copper, obsidian tools, and maguey-fibre rope

Plate 38. SOCIAL OBLIGATIONS, REWARDS, AND PUNISHMENTS

TOP, *Left:* Boys are taken by their fathers the school or *Calmecac*. These people are the poorer classes. *Right:* Four chiefs senten criminals to death by noose and clubs for ou rageous crimes. MIDDLE, *Left:* Warriors proven worth engage in ceremonial comba They wear the costume of warriors' orde or of chiefs. *Right:* A tribal ruler invests tw leading men with badges and trappings rank. BOTTOM, *Left:* Montezuma had pr fessional entertainers, hunchbacks, juggler and musicians

Plate 39. EAGLE KNIGHT, NATIONAL MUSEUM

This head represents the ideal warrior, steadfast, hardy, and devout. The 'very
perfit gentle knight' of the Middle Ages would meet his peer in this noble Aztec.
Photograph by Sunami

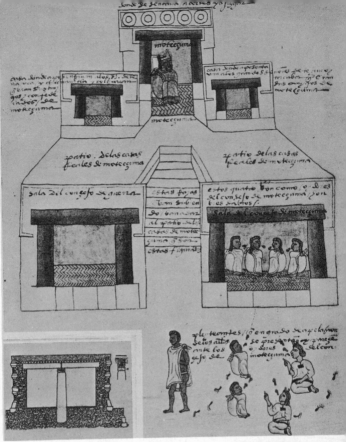

Plate 40. AZTEC ARCHITECTURE

TOP: Montezuma's palace, from the *Codex Mendoza*.
His apartments are on a platform reached by a stair.
At right and left are rooms for allied chiefs, such as
the rulers of Texcoco, Culhuacan, Chiconauhtla,
Tlacopan, and Tenayuca. The left-hand room on
the first floor is reserved for the war council, and the
quarters on the right are for the judges, who may be
seen settling a case between several litigants.
MIDDLE, *Left*: Section through a temple at Mitla
showing details of construction. BOTTOM: A two-
storey house of probable post-Conquest date. The
palace above with ascending platforms shows the
customary Aztec method of elevating rooms

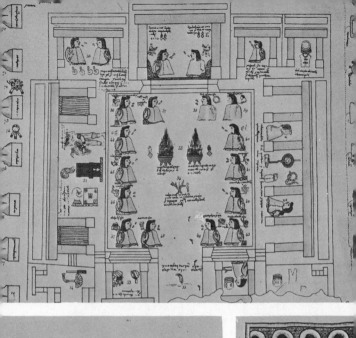

Plate 41. AZTEC ARCHITECTURE

TOP: An Aztec palace of Texcoco from the Mapa Quinatzin, drawn in elevation without perspective. Nezahualcoyotl and Nezahualpilli, father and son, face each other in the throne room. In the courtyard sit vassal chieftains, including the chief of Chiconauhtla (No. 46). The right side of the court is walled by storehouses for tribute; on the left is a temple, designated by the scribe as a hall of science and music. The top rooms are for the judges (*left*) and the arsenal (*right*). The bottom rooms house the war council and visiting ambassadors. BOTTOM, *Left:* House of wattle and daub, still used in Mexico. *Right:* A chief's house with adobe walls on stone foundations, wooden pillars for the anteroom, and fresco painting on the facade

Plate 42a. AZTEC ARCHITECTURE

Palace at Chiconauhtla. Note how closely the plan resembles that of the Texcocan palace on Plate 41

Plate 42b. AZTEC ARCHITECTURE

The Lienzo Chalchihuitzin Vasquez shows the chief and founder of his line in the central house. The topmost row of figures discloses his descent, and the smaller houses joined to his palace by roads are those of his subjects. The people in the two large houses at lower right and left are allies. Post-Conquest painting on cloth

Plate 43. AZTEC FEATHERWORK

Plate 44. AZTEC POTTERY

TOP: Design from bowl of the Aztec IV period, representing a marine worm, water plants, and a fish. SECOND ROW: Polychrome bowls, with, *left*, 'grecque type' decoration, and *right*, figures of a snail in section, symbol of Quetzalcoatl. THIRD ROW, *Left:* Cup, black and red; *centre:* Polychrome bowl with stellar symbols; *right:* Cup with 'grecque type' decoration and symbols of fire, white and coffee colour. BOTTOM, *Left:* Double bowl with fine black designs. *Right:* Aztec mortar with symbol of summer

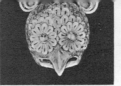

Plate 45. MEXICAN GOLDWORK

Almost all Aztec goldwork went into the Spanish melting-pot. Most surviving examples come from Oaxaca, where the supply was doubled by Caso's discovery of Tomb 7 at Monte Alban. (See Caso, 1932.) TOP ROW: Small gold ornaments from Oaxaca reveal exquisite workmanship. MIDDLE: This lip ornament has a movable tongue that makes a very lively serpent indeed. BOTTOM, *Left:* A gold worker from the *Codex Florentino* makes a mosaic ornament like that at right, in which turquoise mosaic enhances a gold reproduction of the shield and arrows, constituting the sign of war

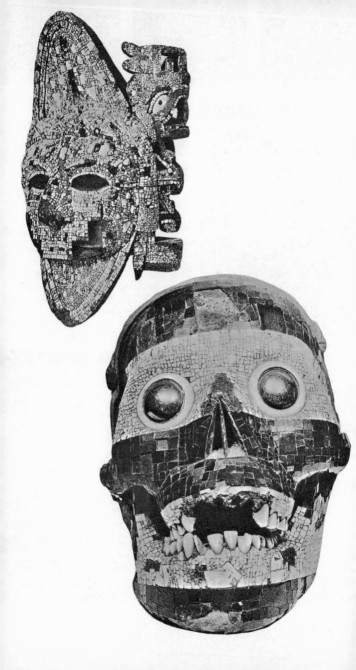

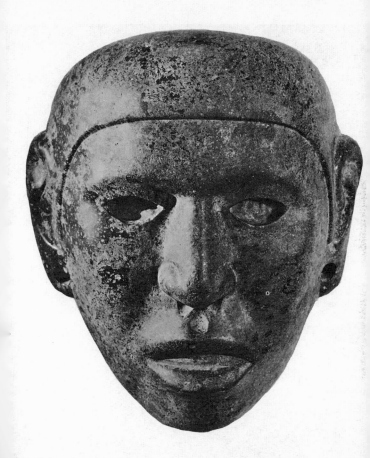

Plate 46. MOSAIC WORK

(Left): Mosaic work was one of the most elegant crafts, and demands colour reproduction to give a just impression. The mask in jade and turquoise, now in Rome, was part of the original loot of the Conquest. The skull (*below*), a British Museum treasure, is composed of light bands of turquoise and dark ones of lignite, set on a human skull, cut away behind to form a mask, possibly representing Tezcatlipoca. The technique was a Mixtec one

Plate 47. AZTEC ART

(Above): Porphyry mask, Teayo, Vera Cruz. This mask is an outstanding example of Aztec art, even though it was made outside the borders of their domain. This carving, and the Eagle Knight (Plate 39) are perhaps the finest secular sculptures from the Aztec period

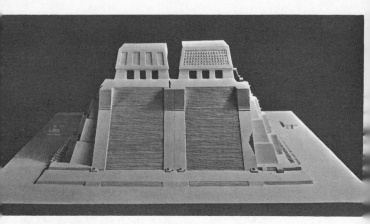

Plate 48. AZTEC ARCHITECTURE

The temples were the most imposing aspect of Aztec architecture. TOP: Model of the Temple of Tenayuca as it looked at the time of the Conquest. BOTTOM: The temple as it looked after excavation. The staircase focused the attention of the worshippers on the culmination of each ceremony, a human sacrifice. (Cf. Plates 60 and 61.)

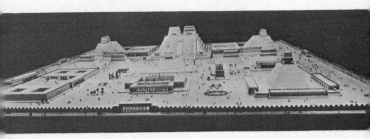

Plate 49. AZTEC ARCHITECTURE

TOP: Model of the great Plaza of Tenochtitlan, showing the great temple and surrounding buildings as they looked at the time of the Conquest. Reconstruction by Ignacio Marquina. BOTTOM: The Zocalo, Mexico City, looking north-east. This was the site of the great plaza of Tenochtitlan. The President's palace (*upper right*) rests on the foundations of Montezuma's palace. The great temple to the Gods of War and Rain stood just east of the cathedral. At the tram crossing in the foreground a large disk like the Calendar Stone (Plate 50) still lies buried. The present square is built on the remains of Tenochcan city, twenty feet above the ancient level

Plate 50. AZTEC ART

TOP: The Calendar Stone, thirteen feet in diameter, represents the history of the world. It is arranged in concentric circles, at the centre of which is the sign Four Motion, the date of the present era. The dates of the preceding eras are given in the four arms of the Motion sign. The twenty day names encircle the central symbols, and they are enclosed by glyphs for turquoise and jade, signifying 'precious', and the colour of the heavens. Beyond this band radiate sun's rays and star symbols, while the outer border consists of two great fire snakes, symbolizing Time. BOTTOM: The National Stone, a monolithic block in the Mexican National Museum, suggests how the Calendar Stone was probably set on a platform. Its symbolism represents the Sacred War, the eternal conflict between the contrasting and opposing forces of nature

PLATE 51. AZTEC ART

TOP: This feathered snake in the Mexican National Museum may well symbolize Quetzalcoatl, God of Learning and the Priesthood. This representation differs from the fire snake in that it lacks a raised crest over the head. BOTTOM: The enormous snake at the foot of the balustrade to the great temple in Mexico is a dramatic architectural ornament, frequently employed in Aztec temple building. Snakes were a major ornament at Tenayuca (Plate 48, above) and many other Aztec buildings, appearing also far to the east in Mexican Chichen Itza

Plate 52. AZTEC ART

TOP: Coatlicue, the Mother of
Gods, a highly important member
the pantheon. This representati
over eight feet high, displays
power in terms of such fearsome
tributes as two snake-heads, a ne
lace of a skull, hands, and hearts
skirt of writhing snakes, and claws
her feet. The bottom of the stat
feet is carved to represent the ea
monster. BOTTOM: Wooden dr
with two tongues (*teponaztli*) in
form of an ocelot. The smooth si
ple outlines contrast with the maca
congestion of the presentation abo

p: Another presentation of Coatlicue, the
•ther of the Gods. An earth goddess, she is
• associated with death, so that in this case her
d is a human skull. BOTTOM, *Left:* Small
k-crystal skull representing Death God. This
m the Mixtecs. *Right:* A box, symbolically
ved, to hold human hearts. Note the glyph
jade, i.e. 'precious', banding the sides of the
tainer

Plate 54. AZTEC ART

TOP: This Corn Goddess is envisaged
young girl. Her soft Indian beauty is bro
out with the same sure simplicity w
characterizes the warriors on Plates 39 an
BOTTOM: A colossal head, nearly four feet
of Coyolxauhqui, sister of the War God.
is shown dead. Simple handling of d
enhances this monumental conception

55.
EC
GION

e figure of
olteotl,
c goddess
aildbirth

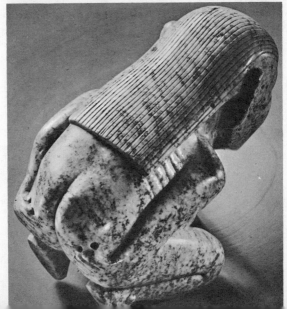

Plate 56a. AZTEC RELIGION
Jadeite figure of a rabbit, a pulque
giving birth to an Eagle Knight

Plate 56b. AZTEC RELIGION
Head of Tezcatlipoca, considere
many to be the finest Aztec scu
known

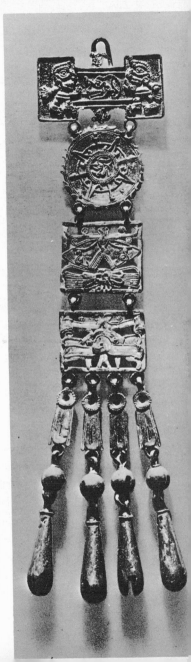

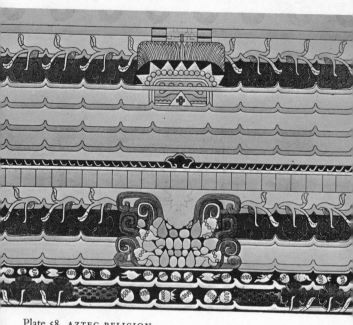

Plate 58. AZTEC RELIGION

TOP: Altar at Teotihuacan with symbols of agricultural worship. Note glyph at centre. BOTTOM, *Left: Codex Florentino*, (Aztec) special ceremony involving g[...] descent to earth, with birdmen, snake dancers, rain gods, and priests dressed as chief gods of the pantheon. *Right: Vienna Codex*, (Mixtec) scene partly ceremo[...] partly historical. Gods, dates, temples, chiefs, and fire-making are shown

Plate 59. AZTEC RELIGION

TOP, Left: Tlaloc, God of Rain. Right: Quetzalcoatl, God of Learning, in guise of Ehecatl, God of Wind. BOTTOM: Page from *Tonalamatl* of *Codex Borbonicus*. The Goddess Itzpapalotl, presiding over the fifteenth week, One House, is shown in the large division. The broken tree signifies Tamoanchan, a legendary homeland; the house below, with a man on top and the night sign in the door and the spider above, signifies the realm of darkness. The other symbols are offerings. The rectangular divisions refer to the days and their Gods. The day signs and numbers begin at the lower left with One House and end at top left with Thirteen Eagle. A Night God is drawn in each day square, beginning with Piltzintecuhtli and ending with Chalchiuhtlicue (Table XII, 194). The squares above the bottom row and to the right of the vertical row reveal the Gods of the Day Hours and their birds, beginning at the left with Xiuhtecuhtli and ending at the top with Ilamatecuhtli (Table XV)

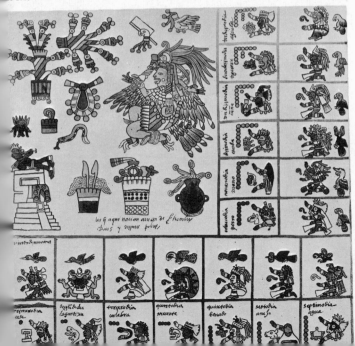

Plate 60. AZTEC RELIGION

TOP, *Left:* Priests and laymen sacrifice two
victims in honour of the War God. *Right:*
War captive on sacrificial stone defends
himself against members of the warrior
orders. MIDDLE: Sacrificial knife with
mosaic handle representing an Eagle
Knight, in the British Museum. The
pictures from the *Codex Florentino* reveal
the technique of using a stone knife to
make a deep enough incision to reach the
heart and tear it out. BOTTOM: Sacrifice to the sun

PLATE 61. AZTEC RITUAL

TOP, *Left:* Dressing a victim and equipping him with a proper headdress, shield, and magical mirror to play the part of Tezcatlipoca. *Right:* Sacrifice of the victim after a year. Note the flutes discarded by him as he ascended the stair. MIDDLE, *Left:* Dressing a priest in the costume of Xipe, the Flayed God, who wears a human skin. *Right:* Musicians with rattle and skin-covered drum, *huehuetl*. BOTTOM: Ceremonial cannibalism. The *Codex Florentino* artist had obviously never taken part in such a feast, fairly common before the Conquest

Plate 62. AZTEC RECORDS

TOP, *Left:* Conquests of Montezuma II; see [page] 59 for method of reading (*Telleriano-Remen*[sis]). MIDDLE, *Left:* Migration of the Aztec tribes. T[hey] leave an island by boat and reach a hill with a [cave] where Huitzilopochtli lives. They divide into [sev]eral migrant groups. List here includes, from [top] to bottom, Matlatzincas, Tepanecas, Chichim[ecs,] Malinalcas, Cuitlahuacas, Xochimilcas, Chalcas, [and] Huexotzincas (*Codex Boturini*). *Right:* Meetin[g of] Montezuma, Cortés, and Marina (Lienzo de T[las]cala). BOTTOM, *Left:* Monthly Ceremony (C[odex] *Borbonicus*). *Right:* Tribute Roll (*Codex Mend*[oza]).

Tenochtitlan.

ano de 30 zeco negos y se 1426 segunla nrā murio chimalpopoca y
fueelexido poes snor vts cohuatl krey nando este vtzcohua ll sehal
garon los mexicanos queno qui sieron servir mos alos de azcapa
çalco vasi quedaron ya aqui hecentos ses tab vos sobre gerao
el cayitā b gano azcapuçal co sedezia maxtla
y tierra eclisada

63. AZTEC WRITING

…age from the *Codex Telleriano-Remensis* describes the period from 1424–39.
… cartouches give the year names, indicating the succession of the four days with
…thirteen numbers. The sequence may be readily followed: Ten House, Eleven
…use, Twelve Rabbit, Thirteen Reed, One Knife, Two House, etc. The death of
…malpopoca (Smoking Shield) is recorded for the year Twelve Rabbit (1426), as
…e accession of Itzcoatl (Snake of Knives). Each ruler is designated by his hiero-
…ph. The defeat of Maxtli (Loincloth) is depicted as well as an eclipse of the sun
…wn by the disk obscured by the stone. The figures and descriptions were
…rted after the Conquest by two priests (to judge from the handwriting), who
…e use of native informants. (Cf. Plate 62, *top left*.)

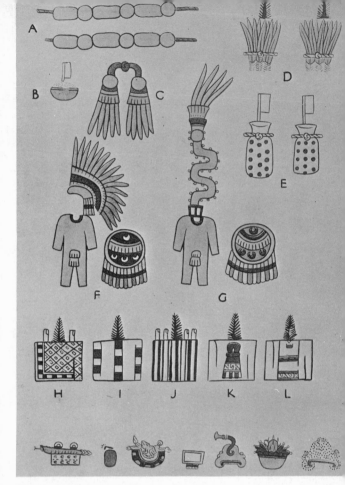

Plate 64. AZTEC WRITING

A page from the Tribute Roll of Montezuma (after Spinden, 1928). The tribute towns are in the columns at bottom and right, designated by numbers. The goods comprised: (a) two strings of jade beads; (b) 20 gourd dishes of gold dust; (c) royal headdress; (d) 800 bunches of feathers; (e) 40 bags of cochineal dye; (f–g) warriors' costumes; (h) 402 cotton blankets of this pattern; (i) 400 blankets; (j) 400 blankets; (k) 400 blankets; (l) 400 blankets. Note the use of fingers for units, flags for twenties, and three-like signs for four hundreds. The sign for eight thousand may be found on Plate 62 (*bottom right*) in the top left-hand corner, designating the number of containers of honey

tions of these high chiefs are difficult to interpret in terms of Western civilization. Roughly the 'chief of men' may be said to have represented the group in its external affairs, like war and alliances. As such the office had highest significance to the Spanish observers who saw its holder as the leader of the community. The 'Snake Woman' was the executive peak of the internal affairs of the group, where civil custom and religious demand governed almost every act. It is important to realize, however, that these chiefs could be deposed by the council at any time, if their services were unsatisfactory.

The continual election of such high officers from the same family or lineage, when democratic procedure obtained theoretically, is harder to explain. Tradition is strong in primitive communities, and a family that produced one effective man might in the next generation produce another. The council in Tenochtitlan chose successive chiefs from a fairly wide range – brothers, sons, nephews, and half-brothers were scrutinized in the rigid proving ground of public service. Furthermore, a wise council, exercising its tremendous powers, could make a puppet 'chief of men' seem effective as its representative. Even then, to be considered for election a person of privileged birth had to meet the long series of tests on which eminence was based.

Two other specialized fields were open to Aztec youth: trade and craftsmanship. Trade was a new development in an economy which was based on living off the land. The opening up of contact with other groups through settlement and warfare and the growth of material and ritualistic wants, led to the establishment of a class, the *pochteca*, whose members travelled all over Mexico, exchanging local for foreign produce. They had their own god and apparently lived in a special quarter. From the valley they carried obsidian, cloth, and rope, which in the hot country they exchanged for shells, tropical feathers, jade, cacao, and other regional riches. In time they performed an important political function, spying out towns to conquer and reporting on the tribute which could be exacted. There is a very modern touch about the economic and political functions of these merchants who so often brought military conquest in their train.[7] (See Plate 37.)

Craftsmanship, with the growth of technique, must have attracted many men to whom straight agriculture seemed drab and unrewarding. Potters, jewellers, weavers, and feather-workers came to pursue these crafts to the exclusion of other labour. The enormous elaboration of the religion called into almost continual activity sculptors, masons, and painters. The market, still important in Middle American Indian communities, had a profound social significance, for there, in addition to bartering his products for those of others, an Indian could hear the news and widen his social and intellectual horizons. (See Plates 34, 35.)

The priesthood offered a relentless sort of career. Religion penetrated into every part of daily life, and the individual participated in great and complicated rituals. Civic eminence depended greatly on religious observance, and chiefs led in the direction of ceremonies. Therefore, it is hard to recognize a priesthood completely separate from civil officialdom; both were mutually dependent. There was a priestly hierarchy, it is true, but it probably operated in conjunction with civil position. Permanent positions may have existed, but in the chapters on religion we shall describe more fully how completely the realms of Church and State coalesced among the people of ancient Mexico, in contrast to the cleavage between them in our own society.

Mexican society existed for the benefit of the group, and each member was supposed to do his part in preserving the community. However, the bane of working social orders as well as hypothetical social schemes are those unfortunates who, by mischance, maladjustment, or just plain devilry, do not do their part. The Aztecs, too, had this problem to cope with, and there developed a social class of people who had lost their civil rights and become slaves. This they might do voluntarily or because they were prisoners of war or were punished for crimes or were sold by their parents. Their treatment differed according to the circumstances of their enslavement.[8] (See Plate 37, bottom left.)

Military captives usually were sacrificed, but those who demonstrated some unusual skill were sometimes bought for domestic service or put to work on some communal enterprise. Criminal slaves lost their free status for such offences as failure to denounce treachery, membership in a traitor's family, kidnapping for sale a free man, selling another's property without his consent, theft without restitution when over ten years old, or hindering a slave from gaining the sanctuary of a chief's house. Penal slaves were privately owned, usually to make restitution to those whom they had injured.

Voluntary slavery was assumed by the poor and landless who needed food, by the indolent who were too lazy to provide for their own support, by gamblers, and by prostitutes who wanted finery. Parents often sold a child, to be replaced by a younger one when the first was old enough materially to contribute to the family welfare. Sometimes destitute people offered a bondsman in return for a loan from a more fortunate neighbour. If the bondsman died in service or the master took any property unlawfully the debt was discharged. To avoid this contingency the owner made the slave live at home and perform only personal services. Slavery, except in the case of war prisoners, was not too exacting. A slave could control his family, own property, or even have slaves of his own. His children were always born free. What the slave lost was his eligibility for civic office, which depended, as we have seen, on public service and was negated by his reliance on the bounty of others or his commission of anti-social acts.

An important aspect of the legal code of the Aztecs involved the loss of civil rights as a result of flagrant anti-social acts. In general, custom dictated and regulated human behaviour. Membership in the community brought safety and subsistence. To break away or to be cast off meant death at the hands of foes or isolation as a solitary wanderer, a prey to marauding beasts. Competition for rank and renown existed in the field of public service rather than in the acquisition of wealth. Hence the anti-social behaviour implicit in attaining many of our own higher grades or ranks was held to a minimum.[9]

Growth of the community to a size where none but the great were known to society at large probably tended to break down the sense of membership and participation, so that thefts and like petty crimes increased as mutual responsibility diminished. The growing complication of tasks and manners of livelihood led to disputes and injustices. In a nation of warriors skilled in arms, personal animosity flared up into bloodshed. Thus the tribunals mentioned had to be set up to exercise their jurisdiction in community affairs and to reinforce the powerful influences of public approval and disapproval. (See Plates 35, 40.)

Religious crimes, like blasphemy or robbing temples, were rare, for the disfavour of the gods brought disaster on the community and on the individual as well. Religion, however, did not enter into the field of ethics, and no post-mortem punishment awaited the sinner. Special heavens existed for warriors and for women who died in childbirth and for people who died in certain specified ways, but this belief had to do with the favour of particular gods. It was not a carefully defined system of rewards and punishment.

Restitution for the sinned-against was the chief basis for dealing with anti-social acts, in contrast to our pattern of punishing the sinner. Exile or death was the lot of the evil-doer who endangered the community. A random sampling of crimes and punishment will show the tenor of Aztec law and why it was never necessary to resort to imprisonment as a means of enforcing expiation of a crime. Cages or detention pens, however, were used to confine prisoners before trial or sacrifice. (See Plate 34.)

Theft was punished either by slavery until restitution was made or by a fine of double the amount stolen, one part to the robbed, the other to the community treasury. Highway robbery received the death penalty, and pilfering in the market-place meant instant death by stoning, since that petty crime militated against the social advantages of the gathering. To steal corn, the staple of life, when growing in the field, was a serious offence, demanding the death penalty or slavery, but a wayfarer might with impunity satisfy his hunger by plucking ears from rows adjacent to the road. To filch gold, silver, and jade, precious substances usually reserved for religious ornaments, was also a mortal crime.

Murder, even of a slave, brought the death penalty. Rebels and traitors received the same fate, but kidnappers were sold into slavery. Drunkenness was a serious crime except at prescribed ceremonial occasions. Social disapproval, public disgrace, even death by stoning or beating, were penalties suffered by the intemperate. However, the old of both sexes, who had fulfilled their social obligations, were allowed great latitude in their potations.

The witch or practiser of black magic was sacrificed, and death was likewise the lot of him who impersonated a high official. A slanderer had his lips cut off and sometimes his ears as well. Brawling and fighting in the market-place were dealt with severely, but in an ordinary case of assault the assailant paid for the cure of the assailed and for any damage done. Adultery was punished with great severity, even death, when committed outside the pale of the divorce laws. Hanging was the usual penalty for violation of the incest laws, and sodomy was punished with revolting brutality.

Thus reduced to cited instances, Aztec law was harsh. Actually, from childhood on, the individual grew up into correct social behaviour; the violator of the code met with serious consequences. All people had some kind of personal property, but most land belonged to the community and only its produce to the individual.[10] Therefore, the elaborate legislation surrounding our own property concepts was unnecessary.

There was little to harass the individual intellectually or economically. Existence was subject to divine favour, and a man fared much as did his fellows. Large as some towns were – Mexico City had three hundred thousand people – the sense of community was strong. Freedom of thought, individual liberty, personal fortunes, were non-existent, but people lived according to a code that had worked well and continuously for centuries. An Aztec would have been horrified at the naked isolation of an individual's life in our Western world.

Chapter 8　　　Economy

The domestic and tribal economy of the Aztec people

The Aztec social system provided a means by which people could exist harmoniously together in considerable numbers. The domestic and tribal economy of the Aztecs offered the food, shelter, tools, and clothing to which man largely owes his dominant position on earth. The measure of a human society may be gauged by the relationship between the organization of the people themselves and their use of materials to build houses and equip them. The Aztecs' economy had the same basic simplicity as had their social organization; likewise it had the same flexibility in expanding to meet the needs of a growing population.[1]

Agriculture was the basis of Aztec life, and corn, *Zea mays*, was the chief food plant. The cultivation of plants ensured a food supply near at hand, which was not subject to the fluctuations of game and thereby enabled man to take thought for the morrow. The clan system, as we have seen, recognized that the fruits of the land supported the community. Therefore, it was only natural that the community should own and control the land which supported its members.[2] (See Plate 37.)

The central council divided the land among the clans, and the leaders of each, in turn, apportioned its share among the heads of families justly and equitably. Sections were also reserved for the maintenance of the chief and the temple staff, for war supplies and the payment of tribute; these were worked communally, with some amount, no doubt, of slave labour. At the death of a tenant the land passed to his sons. If he died without issue the holding reverted to the clan for redivision, as was also the case if a tenant failed to cultivate his plot for a period of two years. Such a system could work equitably and profitably for all concerned so long as a society was relatively static and plenty of arable land was at hand. However, in the Valley of Mexico inequalities developed in the system.

The growing population of the Valley peoples used up all the available land, and families or clans had no way of adding to their farm holdings. A plot which produced ample supplies for a small family might yield a bare subsistence or less for a larger one. Normal variation in the richness of soil would result in similar injustices. Under such conditions the chiefs and priests who lived off the public lands would be far better off than the ordinary citizen whose holding, generation by generation, tended to diminish. Thus friction leading to foreign war and internal revolt was bound to result whenever a group could not expand its territorial limits to meet the needs of its population. The considerable migrations, like those of the Culhuas to Texcoco and Tenochtitlan or the Mixtec people to Texcoco years earlier, had their basis in a pressing economic necessity.[3]

The Tenochcas, who came late to the Valley, at a time when land was at a premium, had, we have seen, a difficult time in withstanding their hungry neighbours. Forced to retreat to islands in the lake, they met the land problem in the same ingenious way as did the Chalcas, Xochimilcas, and the tribes to the north-west, in Lake Zumpango.

This method was to create *chinampas*, the so-called 'floating gardens'. The *chinampa* was, in reality, a small artificial island, made by scooping up mud from the marshy borders of the lakes and at first holding it in place by a revetment of reeds and later by trees whose roots bound the earth solidly together. Water flowed into the narrow pits, making them into canals. Fresh mud was always added before planting, so that the fertility of the earth was constantly renewed. The Tenochcas and their neighbours thus converted great sections of otherwise unproductive marsh, flooded in the rainy season, into a grid of canals and fields, the fertility of which is equalled only by the river-flooded lands of the Nile Delta. *Chinampa* agriculture continues today in the districts of Xochimilco and Chalco, where most of the vegetables are grown for the modern metropolis of Mexico City. The inhabitants still use the Aztec language and occupy the same land as did their ancestors, renewing them each year by the same methods used in Aztec times. The outlines of former beds may be seen for a considerable distance round about, since the modern draining of Lake Texcoco has dried up much of the lake area of the Valley of Mexico.[4] (See Plate 36, bottom.)

When the Tenochcas moved into the lake they achieved living room. As the city grew it could incorporate the adjacent garden beds for house foundations, while the increase in population could be fed by building new *chinampas* on the outskirts of the farming area. Thus much of their success may be attributed to the freedom from internal strife achieved by the relatively unlimited possibilities of *chinampa* agriculture.

The Tenochcas supplemented their land hunger by another means. In conquered territories successful warriors received grants of land which were worked by members of the defeated people. Small colonies sometimes lived off this land to guard against revolt in the subjugated area. Such property passed from father to son, but if there were no heir it reverted to the tribal authority, not the clan in which the tenant had membership. Other such land must have been held for the benefit of the religious organization. Thus the central authority of Tenochtitlan, and presumably Texcoco as well, held considerable property to support the elaborate pomp of Church and State without straining the resources of the people. The relative fluidity of such real estate gave the central authority a wherewithal to adjust inequalities and dissatisfactions among the more ambitious members. Naturally, as the Aztec peoples were less highly developed socially than ourselves, they did not attain our own elaborate system of rewards and adjustments by means of federal, state, and municipal appointments.[5]

The Aztec state had another source of support: tribute. The levies often consisted of foodstuffs and raw materials, both native and foreign to the Valley, and also included warriors' and priests' costumes, mantles, pottery, and other articles of craftsmanship. Distributed throughout the community these goods enriched both communal enterprise and private convenience.[6] (See Plates 62, bottom right; 64.)

Manufacture and trade were beginning to play an important part in Aztec economy, although not to the extent of societies which have developed media of exchange, like money, and therefore emphasize personal wealth in the possession of such a commodity. Manufacture was in the handcraft stage, carried on as a supplement to the main business of raising food. Most households were self-sufficient, making whatever they required in the way of tools, utensils, or clothing. However, certain towns had access to natural resources which others had not and developed special skill in exploiting them. A town might have a good clay bed, for example, and its pottery would be far superior to that of surrounding communities. Another village would be especially successful in growing peppers, while a third might have in its territory a good quality of obsidian or flint for making stone tools. Thus such products would be exchanged by one town for the produce of another and even redistributed by the same process. Shells from the Caribbean have been traded from hand to hand as far as the central United States; pottery vases from Salvador were carried to distant Tepic in Mexico; gold ornaments from Panama appeared as votive offerings in the Sacred Well of Chichen Itza in Yucatan.[7] (See Plate 37.)

Such regional specialization was accompanied by the perfectly natural tendency of individuals to exploit what they made and produced with greatest aptitude. As technical knowledge grew specialization increased, and the market became an important institution. Each town held one at specified intervals to which people came from great distances. At Tlaltelolco the daily market was a wonder of the Western world, exciting by its lavish variety the admiring envy of the Spaniards. The importance of the market still persists in Indian communities, so much so that in Guatemala the people travel miles to exchange their produce; and so important is the market as a social function that a merchant will not dispose of his produce except at that place, even though offered payment far in excess of its market value.[8]

Barter was the only means of exchange, and value was established by desirability and rarity. Money, an exchange medium of fixed value, did not exist. However, something had to be found which would balance an inequality of exchange by being not too valuable to use in adjusting small transactions and at the same time universally wanted. The cacao bean answered this requirement and was easily portable as well. The Aztecs were extremely fond of chocolate (the word itself is of Aztec derivation), so that beans were gladly converted into the national luxury drink. Quills of gold dust sometimes were used as an exchange medium, as were crescent-shaped knives of thin-beaten copper. These last had not the common acceptance or the utility of cacao beans, although they represented easily portable value.[9]

The most precious substance among the Aztecs was jade, or stones resembling it in texture and colour. Both jadeite and nephrite occur in the New World, and the American variety is distinguishable from the Asiatic stone. Uncut stones are seldom seen today, for there is no lapidaries' market in modern Mesoamerica or the United States,[10] whereas jade is still extensively worked in China, so that men find it worth their while to search rivers in Burma for boulders of this rare substance. (See Plate 3.)

The testimony of the Conquistador Bernal Díaz is conclusive on this point of value. During the night when Cortés retreated from Mexico, the leader, after taking off his share of treasure, turned the surplus over to his troops. Many, burdened down with gold, drowned ignominiously in the canals. Díaz, however, noted Indian usage and confined himself to four jades which he was able to exchange later and which, in his words, 'served me well in healing my wounds and gathering me food'.[11]

The Aztecs did not have our modern esteem for gold, so the Spaniards had great difficulty in getting it at first. The Mexican Indians responded to the invaders' demands for objects of value by offering jade and turquoise, those substances most precious to themselves. Such misguided compliance was highly irritating to Cortés and his men, who had no ethnological training; nor, it is only fair to say, would they have wanted such education, were it available. Gold was valuable to the Aztecs only for the ornaments which could be made from it, and silver may have had an even greater value, since nodules were rare and the Indians had no technique for smelting the ore.[12] (See Plate 45.)

Thus the Aztecs did not hold our ideas of value and wealth. Yet they contributed much to our prosperity and well-being, partly through being forced as slaves to work the gold and silver mines, whose modern economic significance they so little understood, and even more through the enrichment of the world's supply of foods. In addition to corn of several varieties, the Aztecs developed many sorts of beans, a very nutritive addition to human diet because of the high protein content. Squash, gourds, *chia*, *damotes*, green and red peppers, avocados, and tomatoes were products of the versatile Mesoamerican farmer, enriching the Aztec diet and that of the modern world. Trade with southern Vera Cruz brought chocolate, vanilla, and pineapples to the Aztec larder.[13]

The maguey plant, or agave, was important to household economy for its sap, which was fermented to make a kind of beer. Not only was this pulque used both as a tipple and a ceremonial intoxicant, but it had an important nutritive effect as well in counterbalancing the lack of greens in the Mexican diet. The plant itself had many other uses. Its fibres could be twisted into twine or rope and woven into containers or even clothing. The thorns were excellent needles and had a more lugubrious use as instruments for mortifying the flesh in religious penances. The leaves as a whole sometimes were employed in constructing shelters or roofing huts. Small wonder that the maguey and the corn plants were symbolized as goddesses and worshipped accordingly.

The Aztecs cultivated cotton in many varieties. Tobacco they smoked for the most part in hollow reeds as a sort of cigarette. Late in their history they also used elbow-shaped pipes, probably for some ceremonial purpose, much as our modern Pueblos restrict pipe smoking to rain-inducing rituals. They consumed quantities of copal gum as incense during religious ceremonies and obtained rubber from Vera Cruz and the south, as well as from the dwarf guayule plant found in northern Mexico. The Aztecs, like us, found this material indispensable to their culture, for balls in their ceremonial game, *tlachtli*, and as a gum to fix feathers and other adornments to costumes. Bitumen, which came from the oil seepages in Vera Cruz, had its function as an adhesive and as a body paint. In western Mexico the Indians prepared a serviceable lacquer which they used to coat gourds and wooden trays. This incomplete list of plants and substances cultivated and exploited by the Aztecs and their neighbours gives an idea of our deep indebtedness to these past civilizations. The original inventors and innovators are lost in the black obscurity of American history, but the fruit of their ingenuity plays an important part in our modern economy.

As opposed to this wealth of plants, the Aztecs were poor in domesticated animals. They had several varieties of dog, one of which was bred for food, but they never used this animal for transport as did Indians of our Northern plains. The turkey was their chief domesticated fowl, although there is some evidence that they bred geese, ducks, and quail also. In plantations of the nopal cactus they carefully tended the cochineal bug for the rich crimson dye it yielded when crushed. A second insect, the maguey slug, still retains its place as a delicacy of the Mexican table, served with another typically Aztec dish, *guacamole*, a thick mixture of tomato, avocado, and chile.

Hunting, when possible, produced food, but as early as Upper Pre-classic times the deer were nearly all killed off. The seasonal migrations of the birds, which still visit the lakes of Mexico, offered a profusion of geese, ducks, and other wild fowl. Small fish, netted or speared with a trident, were sometimes consumed, and the eggs which a certain fly lays on the lakes were made into a paste still eaten in Mexican communities. The high functionaries, since they were supported by the community, kept a much better table than the poor, who lived meagrely off the produce of their own fields; the daily repast of Montezuma was described by the Spanish conquerors as the height of Lucullan luxury.[14]

Tools showed relatively little variation from Pre-classic to Aztec times. The *coa*, or digging stick, was the chief farming instrument, and the *metate* and *mano* even now reduce the kernels of corn to flour. Stone tools still persisted for cutting and grinding, and cold, beaten copper was beginning to find favour as a material for needles, axes, and ornaments. The volcanic glass, obsidian, because of its sharp edges and its abundance, was as satisfactory as most of their edged metal tools. The simple loom and the weighted spindle were sufficient equipment for the weavers, and pottery had a variety of uses in the storage and service of food. The bow, throwing stick, lance, and club were the chief weapons. By and large, mechanical inventiveness was not conspicuous in Aztec culture, although craftsmanship, through the superior use of simple tools, was developed to a high degree, as we shall show in the next chapter. (See Plates 34 and 37.)

The great cities of the Aztecs had their origin in the simple villages of sedentary farmers. Just as in their social organization and economy, there was a simple base, comparable to the settlements of some of our sedentary North American tribes. The houses on the outlying *chinampas* represented the primitive state of Aztec housing. These were huts with thatched roofs resting on walls of wattles smeared with mud, a type of shelter probably in use in Pre-classic times and persisting two thousand years later in the Indian villages of present-day Mexico. (See Plate 41.)

More imposing establishments graced the older portions of the city, where generations of successive residents had brought care, renovation, and innovation to domestic architecture. Each house rested on a raised platform faced with stone, which gave some protection against floods. Rooms for social purposes, sleeping, cooking, storage, and quartering slaves were arranged in a rectangular plan about a central court. The house walls had stone bases and, according to the wealth or taste of the owner, were finished in stone or adobe. The roof was constructed by covering crossbeams with small poles tightly fitted together and spreading a layer of lime plaster over the whole. As there were no windows, the houses had to be shallow. To admit light and air the buildings were usually two rooms deep and prolonged according to taste and wealth. The back room, which contained a hearth for cooking, was completely enclosed save for the door to the outer chamber which was left largely open on the patio side, columns or short wing walls supporting the rafters. Two-storey houses probably did not exist before the Conquest, but there are cases where, to have light and circulation of air, a rear court with its surrounding rooms was elevated on a platform to the height of the roofs of the rooms around the patio in front.[15] (See Plate 40.)

Our excavations in the palace of the chief of Chiconauhtla, a fief of Texcoco, revealed interesting data on the growth of a chiefly establishment. This palace was continually being rebuilt and expanded to meet the demands of a growing population and richer economy. Patios were arranged at different levels, according to the plan described above. The earliest rooms had the congested quality of a Teotihuacan plan, but the later chambers were more spacious and open to sun and air. Each renovation called for more space so that, allowing a family of five to each hearth, the entourage of the chief more than trebled in a century and a quarter.[16] (See Plate 42a.)

The plan of an Aztec town tended to have a rectangular form, since the division of the land among the clans usually followed a more or less orderly rectilinear pattern. A central plaza was essential for communal gatherings; the market and the principal structures, like the main temple and the chief's quarters, were situated at this point. In Tenochtitlan, which was reported to have sixty thousand fires or hearths or, figuring on the same basis as above, three hundred thousand people, additional centres existed for each clan and for the four larger districts into which the city was divided for administrative purposes.[17] (See Plate 36, top.)

We have been left a description of an Aztec city in 1524 from a Spanish monk, Fray Toribio de Benavente, called by the Indians 'Motolinia', or 'poor', in reference to his Franciscan simplicity of life. His first-hand observations have a fresh reality:

They called these temples *teocallis*, and we found all over the land that in the best part of the settlement they made a great quadrangular court, which, in the largest pueblo, was one crossbow shot from one corner to another, while in the smaller places it was not as large. This court they enclosed by a wall, many of which enclosures were with battlements; the entrances looking towards the chief highways and streets, which all terminated at the court, and even, in order to still more honour their temples, they led their roads up to these in a straight line from two and three leagues' distance. It was a wonderful aspect, to witness from the top of the chief temple, how from all the quarters and the minor places, the roadways all led up in a straight line to the courts of the *teocallis*, . . . the devil did not content himself with the aforesaid *teocallis*, but in each pueblo and in each quarter, as far as a quarter of one league off, there were other small courts containing, sometimes only one, sometimes three or four *teocallis*. . . .[18]

The streets of Tenochtitlan were the canals bordered by footpaths, and frequent bridges allowed easy access to all parts of the town. Three great causeways led north, west, and south to the mainland, touching it respectively at Tepeyac, now Guadalupe, Tlacopan, now Tacuba, and Coyoacan. Canals paralleled these main roadways where they entered the city proper, following them as far as their terminus at the main plaza. Two aqueducts also joined the city to the mainland. The one to Chapultepec seems to have been constructed exclusively to carry water and had two channels, so that when one was being cleaned or repaired the other could remain in use. The Coyoacan aqueduct, built later by Ahuitzotl, may well have followed the great southern causeway. The problem of sanitation must have been serious, but boats were tied up at strategic points for public use, and when filled their contents were sold to fertilize the fields. Pottery vessels were kept in the houses to preserve urine, which the Aztecs used as a mordant in dyeing cloth. Hence sunlight and these simple methods for getting fresh water and disposing of offal kept down the pestilence that beset the city in Spanish times when the ancient methods of sanitation were abandoned.[19]

A city so advantageously situated had no need of fortifications, and formal military architecture was rare. The temples, which dominated the city, were natural strong points; indeed, the hieroglyph for the capture of a town was the burning of a temple, an indignity to which no people would submit unless driven from this last rallying point.

The temples had stone or rubble walls surmounted by a high roof, the construction of which consisted of a cribwork of logs, either thatched with straw or covered with plaster. Each temple usually had a chamber and an antechamber, and in some cases two or even three shrines rested on the same plat-form. This platform or substructure gave height and mass to the temple. The usual practice was to lay up rough stone, set in adobe or lime, into a truncated pyramid, the sides of which were broken up by three narrow setbacks and by a steep ramp leading to the top. The surface was of veneered cut-stone slabs, and additional blocks were laid along the ramp to make the stair. Wide balustrades bordered the staircase and often ended in gigantic serpent heads. Aztec construction was the simplest type of engineering, but imposing architectural effects were gained by the consummate artistic sense and superb craftsman-ship of the builders.[20] (See Plates 48, 49.)

The adequate, even imposing, housing of the Aztecs and their gods by no means eclipsed their dress. Clothing, besides protecting man from the weather, has an important social function. It is a guide to the sex, age, group, occupation, rank, and even character of its wearer. The simple and standardized clothing of our modern society performs the same service, and with a moment's observation one can tell much about a stranger from his clothes. The Aztecs, like many peoples of the world, strove by their dress to accentuate the social differences between people, and pomp and panoply dominated their costume. On the barbaric splendour of high civilian dress was superimposed the fantastic garb of the priests and priestesses in their impersonation of the complex and ornately represented divinities in their pantheon.[21]

The *macehual*, or ordinary tribesman, left his head un-covered, his hair long, and customarily wore a *maxtli*, or loin-cloth, a mantle knotted over one shoulder, and sandals of leather or woven maguey fibre in cold weather. Women wrapped about their loins a finely woven cloth, which they sustained with a narrow belt. A sleeveless slip-over, or *huipil*, completed their costume. They plaited their hair into braids, sometimes interlacing them with ribbons, and these they wrapped around their heads. This woman's costume may still be seen in many parts of Indian Mexico. (See Plates 33a and b.)

The poor made their garments of maguey fibre or coarse cotton. The rich wore the same clothing fashioned from finer textures and decorated with elaborate embroidery. The many names given to the different kinds of mantles show their interest and importance to the wearers. Wool was almost never made into cloth, since dog hair was all they had, but feather cloaks were highly esteemed. Chiefs wore a fillet of leather from which hung two tassels, and administrative chiefs had a sort of diadem of gold or jade and turquoise as a badge of office.

The warriors frankly gloried in their costumes. Rich mantles and ornate feather head-dresses were not enough for some, who carried on their shoulders a harness of wicker supporting an elaborate structure in feather mosaic. Others wore costumes modelled on the appearance of an ocelot or an eagle. On specified occasions the priests assumed the dress of the gods and goddesses, whose costumes were sumptuous and ornate and defined by exacting ritualistic marks of identification. (See Plate 61.)

Jewellery consisted of ornaments of copper, gold and silver, shell, various-coloured stones, like jade, turquoise, emeralds, opals or moonstone, and mosaics laid on a backing of clay, wood or reed. Large plugs were inserted in the ear-lobes of men and women alike. Men often wore ornaments passed through the septum of the nose or suspended from a slit in the lower lip. Elaborate necklaces and pendants, armlets and leg bracelets, gave brilliance to a costume for state occasions. Cosmetics were not used to touch up nature, as with us, but instead a lavish application of face and body paints in red, blue, yellow, green, and black enhanced with prismatic richness the softer tones of their brown flesh. (See Plate 45.)

It is obvious that the Aztecs were no pitiable craven savages. They lived upon variegated and delicious foods and dwelt in houses that were comfortable and airy. Their dress stimulated the exercise of merited self-satisfaction, not to be confused with the compensations of vanity. Their manner of life enabled them to take advantage of their personal aptitudes and exchange the products of their own creation for whatever they lacked. Articles for daily and ceremonial use were made with the loving care of master artisans, and rare indeed was the object that did not have the impress of some little decorative touch that makes a pleasant possession of a drab utensil. Their crafts deserve to themselves a complete chapter.

Chapter 9   Craftsmanship

A consideration of how the Aztecs attained a high degree of skilful craftsmanship with relatively few mechanical aids

Craftsmanship allows an exercise of the creative impulse, satisfying the individual through his domination of the raw material. In our modern mechanized age most of us suffer from the lack of opportunity to create, since almost everything we use comes machine-made, and not even the skilled mechanic feels that his ingenuity and craftsmanship alone have produced a useful and attractive object. The ordinary modern floats like Mohammed's coffin, without contact with the earth on which he lives or the universe of which he is an infinitesimal part. The Aztec, however, lived in the most intimate contact with nature in its finite and infinite manifestations. Because his conscious being was set in terms of the group mind, he seldom felt that sensation, common to the Western intellect, of having cut himself from the tree of natural existence with the saw of his own reason.

The home production of articles for daily use gave an impetus to craftsmanship, since wealth and prosperity lay in a man's possessions, not in the abstract ownership of rights to the work of others. Thus a successful man had a well-made house, finely fashioned and decorative clothing, carefully worked utensils and tools and well-tended and productive fields, while an unsuccessful man had a small and miserable equipment. Yet except for the intervention of natural disaster the differential was largely due to the ability of a man and his household to produce with their own hands the symbols of his wealth or to exchange his specialized product for equivalent superior equipment made by others. The entrepreneur and broker had small place in the undertaking of production and its distribution.[1]

The gods also stimulated good craftsmanship. Every home had an altar, and every act was accomplished through the favour of some deity. Ceremonies to appease these custodians of natural force were of frequent occurrence. Thus the use of symbols, referring to the god whose favour was sought, came to exercise an important influence on design. Since a man does reverence with his most esteemed social attitudes and his best material possessions, each household must try to surpass its previous efforts to honour the gods. The temple equipment, therefore, tended to represent the cream of local craftsmanship.

Work in stone, the most durable natural substance available, is a common gauge of human ability. Since the tools last forever, it is possible to compare the technical abilities of peoples over an enormous span of human history. However, for basic equipment like projectile points, axes, grinding stones, and the like, satisfactory forms are reached fairly early and do not change in proportion to cultural advances in other directions. Thus the arrow or the dart points of Aztec times were not technically better than those used by the Pre-classic peoples. However, the technical demands of the sacrificial cult called for a heavy broad-bladed flint that could tear through human flesh at a single stroke, and this type of knife, not found in earlier horizons, was produced commonly with the extra care in chipping which is to be expected in a ceremonial object. (See Plate 60.)

The three-legged *metate*, or grinding stone, was not better made in Aztec times than before. In Pre-classic, Classic and Toltec times it had an edge, so that the *metlapil* (son of the *metate*, i.e., *mano*, or grinding stone) was bevelled and fitted within the confined space. The Aztec *metate* was flat, and the *mano* had swollen handles, projecting on either side of the grinding surface of the *metate*. I have never had the misfortune to break my back grinding corn in a *metate*, so that I have no way of knowing whether this represents a technical advance or a mere change in style.

The demands of ritual necessitated stone boxes for burning and storing human hearts. These boxes were pecked out of lava and lavishly decorated inside and out with reliefs, referring symbolically to the gods for whom the sacrifice was made. Some of these eagle vases (*cuauhxicalli*) fall into that area of superior craftsmanship we designate in our own culture by the term 'fine art'. The great circular cup, ordered by Tizoc and mis-called the Sacrificial Stone, eight feet in diameter and two and one half feet thick, attained the stature of a monument. Stone incense burners, often in the form of the Old God, were common in Teotihuacan and rare in Pre-classic times. The quantity of religious sculpture, produced chiefly in late Aztec times, to judge from the style, did not detract from the quality of the workmanship, so strong was the control of religious and social factors.[2] (See Plate 53, bottom right.)

Obsidian must have had important economic value for the Valley peoples, and since volcanic glass is portable and very useful for its sharp cutting edge, it was widely traded to the inhabitants of non-volcanic regions. Techniques were established early in the Pre-classic, and the art of polishing this stone was known to the Teotihuacanos, who utilized it as eyes for the idols of the Temple of Quetzalcoatl. Ceremonial bloodletting called for a constant supply of thin blades (made by pressure flaking), some of which are exquisitely long and narrow. Yet scalpels of comparable fineness were made in Teotihuacan and Toltec times as well. Indeed the principal innovation of the Aztecs was in fashioning vases from obsidian, a formidable task, owing to its hardness.[3]

The making of mirrors called much ingenuity into play. They are so rare that they must have been used solely for ritualistic magic. Blocks of obsidian were sometimes polished to produce an eerie and mysterious reflection. However, iron pyrites, burnished and shaped, were more common; and rarer examples had thin pyrite flakes laid in a mosaic and glued to a background of wood or shell. In another technique used on the coast the artisan detached a surface of pyrites in its matrix of slate, burnishing one side and carving the other to fashion a mirror with a carved back. One example, at least, is known of a mirror or marcasite with its surface so ground as to produce a magnified reflection.[4]

Stone sculpture we shall consider more conveniently under art, but the mass production of dressed stone for building must have required patience and skill to accomplish. Stoneworking throughout Mesoamerica was achieved without metal tools. Flaking and chipping for the hard stones, pecking and hammering for the softer ones, were the preliminary steps in every case. A final polishing with some simple abrasive like water and sand often completed the process. Some hard stones seem to have been detached from their matrix by applying the abrasive and sawing with a cord of rawhide or a tool of harder stone. The Mesoamerican people also developed tubular drills of bone and reed, which, rotated by a bow and aided by an abrasive, could hollow out vases or bore out places that were otherwise inaccessible to the clumsy tools of the time.[5]

Save for descriptions and drawings, the destruction of time and man has left us only a few examples of the weaver's art. Weaving of some kind is very old, and no people, however primitive, exist in the world today who do not make at least some kind of basketry. Textiles are made as a rule by higher groups, but they are found in the American continent as part of the material equipment of peoples who had not yet learned how to make pottery. An early example of cloth, combining threads of cotton with some fibre like yucca, was found in the Lower Pre-classic horizon of Zacatenco.

The long practice of weaving must and did have a significant effect on decoration, for the rectangular patterns, to which the weaver is confined, influence all of Indian art in Continental America. Design and the arrangement of elements are more important than form in Indian art. While many geometrical patterns appear in pictures of Aztec clothing, fine embroidery could produce the effect of curvilinear designs or even naturalistic patterns drawn from the regional flora. Batik and tie dyeing also enriched the decoration of Aztec clothing. Other processes produced the effect of velvet and brocade, and some garments even imitated in texture and pattern the skins of animals. Judged on a visual basis, the designs on Aztec clothing were by no means inferior to those of the celebrated textile art of Indian Peru. However, we have no positive evidence that technical development of Aztec weaving was equal to Peruvian, for those ancient South American weavers knew and practised every method known to man and even a few unique to themselves.[6] (See Plates 33–5; 62, bottom right; 64.)

Feather mosaic is probably an old craft, since evidence seems to show that it was known to the Upper Pre-classic Cultures. Feather- and the technically allied fur-cloth appear in primitive horizons in North America. The process consisted in tying the stems of feathers into a fabric during the weaving process. Featherworkers adorned shields in this way, dispersing the feathers to represent animals or else purely decorative designs. They made cloaks, too, and created sumptuous insignia worn on the head or harnessed to the body. In these objects the blending of colours was so delicate and perfect as to rival paintings. As late as the nineteenth century, although the art had declined, the Mexicans still depicted landscapes and scenes from daily life in this medium, and today they make charming pictures for the tourists with cardboard, feathers, and glue.[7] (See Plate 43.)

Feather mosaic had an early counterpart in stone and shell; we found a turquoise mosaic in a Lower Pre-classic grave. The wooden handles of sacrificial knives were sometimes ornamented in this way, as were masks, shields, and even small gold ornaments. A *tour de force* of the mosaic worker is a wooden shield from the Mixteca, on which little pieces of turquoise were fitted together in a relief sculpture depicting a religious scene.[8] (See Plates 46; 60, bottom left.)

Mosaic workers utilized stones of different colours and shells of various kinds. Pure designs were common, but elements representing the costume or the body paint were shown when the mosaic covered a figure in wood or stone. An application of mosaic on a larger scale was frequent in architecture, a veneer of cut stone being applied to the rubble of a platform or building. The temples of Mitla, Oaxaca, influenced by the same Mixteca-Puebla culture to which Aztec civilization owed its origin, are masterpieces of this technique, for individual blocks have their surfaces carved to fit together in an intricate geometric design.[9] (See Plate 30, bottom.)

The woodworkers, owing to the impermanence of their medium, have left little to exhibit their prowess, but the few surviving masks, idols, drums, and *atl-atls*, or throwing boards, bear ample witness to their superb craftsmanship. The very fact that they had to work wood with stone tools makes their achievement noteworthy. Their copper tools were dull and unserviceable in cutting even the softer woods, and these implements came into use relatively late in Aztec times.[10] (See Plate 52, bottom.)

Wood was used extensively in buildings for roof beams and door-jambs. A beam in the palace at Texcoco was ninety feet long and five feet thick, so that its preparation and transport must have been an arduous task. There was probably little use of planks in Aztec building, since it would be difficult to prepare them with the rudimentary equipment at Aztec disposal, and adobes and plaster were easier to make and just as serviceable. Wooden canoes, however, were essential for life in the lakes. Some were dugouts hollowed out by fire, but others, to judge from the type used by the Xochimilcan Indians today, were flat-bottomed punts, constructed of planks which were probably tied together in Aztec times rather than pegged, as they are today. The portable bridges used to cross the canals were also simple combinations of planks, or planks resting on beams. (See Plate 35, bottom left.)

Furniture, which in European culture has done much honour to the woodworker, was little used in Mexico. Mats sufficed for beds and seats. High dignitaries sat on a sort of wooden throne which had legs and often a back and was called *icpalli*, from which the Mexican word *equipale* for a modern wickerwork and leather chair is derived. Mention is made of screens and chests and ornamental sheathing for room interiors, but no examples are left for us to judge their craftsmanship. (See Plate 38, top right.)

The wooden drums, on which musicians beat out ceremonial rhythms, were handsomely carved, as befitted their religious use. There were two types, a vertically cylindrical drum (*huehuetl*), which had a skin head, and a horizontally cylindrical drum (*teponaztli*), the top of which was slotted to form two tongues. While the notes differed, there was usually the same interval between the resonant sounds emitted when the tongues were struck. The task of reaching the pitch must have been excessively difficult, for the wood had to be hollowed by fire and then chiselled to a nicety. At times the artist fashioned these drums to represent a crouching man or animal. Masks were often used in temple ceremonies when a god was impersonated, and ceremonial staffs were part of this equipment. So, also, were the throwing boards, or *atl-atls*, with which a warrior flung a javelin, the lengthening of the arm thereby giving the missile an increased propulsive force. Some of these *atl-atls* were most delicately carved and represent the best of Aztec design. (See Plate 52, bottom.)

Metallurgy was in its infancy: though it appeared in Toltec times it introduced no real metal age. Copper was cold-hammered; the art of adding alloys to make bronze had not

155

reached Mexico from the south, but the gilding of copper and mixing of gold and copper were adopted by Mexican gold smiths. Copper was cast into bells and ornaments, and the process, used also for gold, was the cire-perdue, or lost-wax method. The desired shape was modelled in clay, over which was dusted finely-ground charcoal, followed by an even layer of wax. This coating was also dusted with charcoal and the whole enclosed in clay, which was perforated at the top and bottom. The molten metal was poured in at the upper hole after the wax was melted and the lower orifice plugged. When the metal cooled the cast was broken and the finished object removed.[11] (See Plate 45.)

Although most of the native goldwork found its way to the Spanish melting-pot, a few lovely ornaments survived; in 1932 the quantity was more than doubled by Dr Alfonso Caso's discovery of the undisturbed tomb of a high Mixtec official. The design and shape of these necklaces, ear-plugs, and rings, by their sheer intricacy and bulk, make one realize that the Spanish descriptions of Cortés's loot understated the rich ability of the Mexican goldsmiths.[12]

Metal-working, without much question, had its origin in Ecuador or Peru, and various techniques were transmitted up the Pacific coast to Panama and Costa Rica, where important gold-working industries were founded. Although the inter vening area produced little metal, another centre was estab lished in Oaxaca in Mixtec times. The Oaxacan ornaments although deficient in some of the southern technical develop ments, surpass in design and workmanship the best of the older goldwork of Peru and Ecuador.[13]

Mining methods were rudimentary. Gold was collected in nugget form or panned as dust; copper also was mined as nodules or nuggets; silver, which seldom occurs pure in nature, was for this reason rarely converted into ornaments. The melting furnaces were heated with charcoal and their draught forced by a man blowing on the embers through tube. The casting we have already described. This work in gold, one of the great wonders of the Conquest, was achieved by the same simple methods of all Aztec handiwork and was another triumph of sheer skill, unassisted by technical aids.

Pottery making was the greatest New World craft, and probably no other continent has such a complex range of form and design. The pliability of clay made it easy to work, and firing was simple, so that pottery products were an important part of Indian craftsmanship. In the Valley of Mexico we have seen how every group, almost every village, had its own particular style, which changed gradually through slow shifts in the popular taste as time wore on. In the absence of written records the archaeologists fortunately have been able to rely on pottery styles to peg out in time and space the relationships of these ancient and forgotten peoples and thus lay a basis for New World history.[14]

The Aztecs, like all the other New World peoples, did not use the potter's wheel but built up their vessels with strips of clay, relying on their keen eye and sensitive fingers to achieve the desired shape. They did not use moulds to form their vessels, as was occasionally done in late Teotihuacan times; nor, apparently, did they make use of the *kabal*,[15] a block on which Yucatecan potters rested their vessels and which they turned with their feet in shaping the raw clay.

The Aztecs had an abundance of finely textured clay, orange after firing, from which they fashioned vessels for the storage and serving of food. The Toltec potters of Culhuacan used this ware first, making plates with flat bottoms resting on cylindrical legs.[16] On the floors they painted curvilinear designs which were sometimes faintly naturalistic. In the second period, when the Chichimecs began the manufacture of this ware all over the northern Valley, the vessels were made more coarsely, and the hollow legs degenerated to thick, elongated ones.[17] The decoration was converted into an abstract combination of curvilinear *motifs* that had the quality of European script writing.

The third phase of this style, which probably developed in Texcoco during the fifteenth century, saw a gradual conversion of the linework into crude, continuous patterns, but the construction of the vessels proper was much finer.[18] A few potters rejected this slovenly manner and drew elaborate geometric designs. The closely parallel lines in some of these patterns were done freehand on the curved interior surfaces of the bowls, revealing extraordinary control in draughtsmanship. Perhaps in trade, perhaps in tribute, many foreign vases were introduced at this time and stimulated the local potters to develop new styles of their own.

In the fourth period, during the chieftaincy of Montezuma, the potters broke away from these extremes of concentrated meticulousness and slovenly linework. Naturalism found favour, with birds, fish, and plants used as designs and executed with that careless finesse of brushwork which characterizes Japanese sepia drawing. After the Conquest draughtsmen accustomed to working in this style were able to copy accurately such elements of Spanish design as the double eagle of Charles V and the coats of arms of nobles.[19] (See Plate 44, top.)

Polychrome pottery was made locally, usually consisting of a red slip, or wash, adorned with a geometric design in black and white. Coarse construction with painfully careful, if crude, draughtsmanship characterized the fourteenth-century ware. In the fifteenth century the hands of the potters loosened so that they were able to paint more sophisticated designs on vessels as thin and delicate as any pottery ever made in the Americas. Trade wares were rare at first and emanated chiefly from Puebla, but in the fifteenth century the quality and quantity increased, indicating the effects of trade and tribute. The historical reports that Texcoco was culturally superior to Tenochtitlan are borne out by archaeology; the Texcocan wares, although following the same styles as the Tenochcan, were better made and had a greater variety of design. Also there is evidence of more trade with foreign groups.[20] (See Plates 31, 32.)

Goblets were made for pulque; graters were made for grinding chilis, and clay vessels were made for every con-

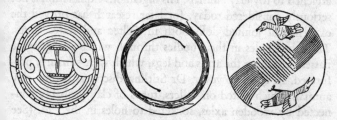

Fig. 22. Aztec pottery, types IIIa, IIIb Texcoco black-on-orange found respectively in the cyclical dumps for 1455 and 1507, and a third type IV, Tenochtitlan black-on-orange, made from 1507 through the Spanish Conquest of 1520–1.

ceivable use; one form was a small oval platter with a special compartment for sauce, resembling the 'blue-plate special' dishes of our modern restaurants. The circular roaster or griddle for cooking tortillas came in with Mazapan culture and continued to be popular through Aztec times. The bottoms of griddles were roughened so that heat would penetrate rapidly and evenly to the dough on the smoothed upper surface.

Clay utensils had their use in weaving. The Aztec spinner rested the end of her distaff in exquisite little cups, often charmingly ornamented. Her spindle weights were also made of clay. In the fourteenth century these were heavy and had holes large enough for a heavy spindle. Often their burnished black or red surfaces were cunningly adorned with stamped or incised designs representing conventional patterns or human and animal figures. In the fifteenth century the spindle weights became much smaller, so that at times it is hard to distinguish them from beads. This reduction in size perhaps indicates the spinning of more delicate cotton threads.

The spindle weight, or whorl, has an important bearing on discussions as to whether or not the Aztecs knew the wheel. The weight had the function of a flywheel in accelerating the rotation of the distaff. The explorer Charnay may have mistaken spindle whorls for wheels which might have been attached to toy clay animals. His ingenuous explanation is not seriously considered today, for later research has proved the existence of jointed dolls both in Toltec and Aztec times. These had holes in their bodies through which strings were passed, attaching the arms and legs, which were similarly perforated. In 1940, however, Dr Stirling discovered some clay animals which rested on rollers, tubes of clay probably connected by wooden axles, socketed to holes in the legs. (See Plate 13.) This knowledge does not seem to have been put to any efficient use. In the history of invention there are several similar cases, notably the Chinese discovery of gunpowder. They used it to make a noise in ceremonies, but not until the Europeans took over the substance did its application have any practical purpose.

In Aztec times stone sculpture was the usual medium for reproducing the human form. The figurine cult, which in Preclassic and Toltec times manifested the chief development of the plastic arts, became insignificant. The use of the mould did not induce superior craftsmen to fashion even the originals. Yet in these dull reproductions of gods and goddesses there still lurks that ability to capture the spark of essential vitality so characteristic of this field of art in earlier times. Curiously enough, the goddesses, more kindly and less ridden with abstract virtues than the gods, usually awoke a response in these ancient idol makers that resulted in perfectly charming little figures.[21]

Pottery was not confined to household chattels; great roof ornaments of baked clay were made to adorn the temples. Sun-dried adobes were commonly used for general house construction. However, they were sometimes fired into bricks which formed the back walls of fireplaces or were substituted for dressed stone in the corners of buildings. A temple at Tizatlan carries brick construction in the pillars before the altar, but rubble faced with cut stone was preferred as a general building material for temples. Before the great temples, braziers the height of a man combined ritualistic usefulness

Fig. 23. Aztec figurines. *First two,* Aztec figurines made prior to 1403. *Last four,* made between 1403 and the Conquest, representing Xochiquetzal, Xipe, Xochipilli, and Tonantzin, respectively.

with architectural ornament. Cones of baked clay were used as studding to keep the plaster from slipping off the temple walls and to serve as a decorative element as well.[22]

The Mexican craftsman had at hand an abundance of good pottery clay, which from the earliest times provided a medium for plastic experiment and experience. Work in clay created the background for that sureness and security in creation that stands out in the later Mexican sculpture in stone and wood. According to our Western standards, clay is a substance inferior to wood or stone for plastic expression. However, the ancient Mexicans, like the old Chinese, considered it fit for the finest examples of their arts and crafts.

Mexican craftsmanship, whoever the craftsmen and whatever the era, was superb in that it answered the necessities and ideals of both the time and the people. There is little evidence of a wide gap between superior and inferior workmanship, as in our Western civilization, where there is less need or opportunity for high-grade handwork. In unindividualized societies the general skills of the people, so far as can be judged by their work, follow a more even course than in elaborated and specialized groups. To turn such craftsmanship into art required a mere flick of the switch of social demand. The arts, as considered in the next chapters, were just projections of the craft background.

The measure of Aztec civilization cannot be gauged solely by its technical achievements. The arts and crafts transcend the products of Old World peoples at the same mechanical level. The spirit of the Aztec people, as exemplified in their religious art, soared to the lofty heights attained by the creators of all those ancient civilizations, like Egypt and Mesopotamia, whose monuments reflect the glory of their builders' religious devotion.

Chapter 10   The Fine Arts

A consideration of those aspects of Aztec craftsmanship which we segregate as fine art

The Aztecs did not have a term for 'fine arts', nor did they
speculate about aesthetics nor make objects to be contemplated
for their beauty alone. They had none of the socially sterile
attitudes towards art which we adopt in our own culture.
Instead, they recognized the value of superior workmanship
and used its products to honour the gods who were intermedi-
aries between man and the infinite power of the universe.
Aztec art, in this respect, is no different from the great traditions ancestral to our modern aesthetic. Religion has always
evoked man's best in thought and deed so long as human
society believed that religion was essential to its survival.

Aztec art was powerful in architecture and sculpture, weak
in painting and drawing. The dance was more advanced than
music, and literature, in the absence of an effective method of
writing, was confined to the evanescent output of oratory.
The years and the elements have left us only such examples as
could survive the ravages of time, and we have no way, except
by analogy with living groups, to ascertain the Aztec attitude
towards their creations in those fields of endeavour which we
moderns dignify as art.

The most impressive expression of architecture was in religious building. Houses might have a fortuitous beauty of
proportion, but the main consideration was adequate shelter.
Public buildings of a secular character, like the clan house or
the chief's quarters, were large-scale projections of the
domestic architecture. The addition of many apartments for
attendants and concubines, a swimming pool and a menagerie,
such as composed the palace of Montezuma, did not alter

structurally or in basic plan the scheme of rectangular rooms set about a patio.

The temple architecture, on the other hand, achieved real majesty. The great gods lived in the sky, so that their shrines and images were very naturally elevated above the level of wordly affairs. The climate contributed indirectly to the conversion of religious requirement into an impressive art form. It was not necessary to house the congregation or protect it from the weather. The altar or shrine alone needed to be elevated, and the worshippers stood in the plaza below. Thus the temple capped the substructure and was the culmination of a harmonious series of ascending planes, calculated to increase the illusion of height by emphasizing the effects of mechanical perspective.[1]

Such aesthetic canons were probably not laid down as laws but were reached after centuries of experimentation had produced a standard procedure. An early temple found in the Valley is Cuicuilco, of Upper Pre-classic date, where the altar was exposed upon a massive oval mound.[2] There is no trace of temple walls, and the use of fire precluded a canopy. However, at Teotihuacan, in the Classic period, the temple had replaced the open altar, and in all probability it housed a representation of a god in wood or stone. In the whole of Mexico there is no more harmonious treatment of gigantic mass and planes than the substructure of the Temple of the Sun.[3] (See Plates 18, bottom; 21, bottom.)

The floors of the temple survive, though the roof and walls were destroyed long ago,[4] but the illusion of infinite height and space still remains. The planes between its terraces are so cunningly calculated that the observer standing at the foot of the great staircase cannot see people at the top. He is conscious only of the massive ascent disappearing into space. When the stair was used by a religious procession, in all its pomp and colour, the effect must have been stupendous. The elaborate hierarchy of a great civilization moved upwards to meet, at a point unseen by the beholders, the infinity of the heavens, concentrated aloft in the god's image.

The plan of the sacred city of Teotihuacan was calculated to maintain the illusion of mass and height. The buildings were laid out in groups along a north-south axis, broken laterally by several precincts oriented to the east and west. From whatever angle one approached Teotihuacan the eye was led towards a point of interest, guided by the arrangement of the planes and masses. Thus the diminishing effect of distance was avoided. Within each precinct the surrounding walls insulated the observer from the rest of the city and emphasized the mass and height of the principal precinct temples. Not even the Pyramids of Egypt present so carefully calculated a plan to dominate the individual with the sheer weight of supernatural power. The modern visitor to Teotihuacan, now in ruins, cannot escape the ancient association of ideas that the greater his temple, the more powerful a god must be. (See Plate 21, top.)

Teotihuacan was probably the result of the cooperation of communities scattered over a large part of the Valley. Its scale and vastness could not have been achieved by a single resident community and, as we have seen, it probably served and was served by a great area. In Toltec times again, Tula was the capital of an empire of sorts, which dominated a group of peoples. In Chichimec times, when there was no central authority, each community built its temple or temples as best it could and few survived. Tenayuca still has a temple of this period, the platform walls of which ascend almost vertically. Apparently shrines to two gods rested on the summit. At this same time, across the mountains in Puebla, the Cholulans were piling sun-dried brick on sun-dried brick to make a man-made mountain. So huge is this structure that the priests' quarters as well as the temple were located on top of one of the platforms. A large colonial church founded on the pyramid has obliterated evidence of the ancient temple proper, which tradition dedicated to Quetzalcoatl. It would seem logical to assume that the priests' houses were on a lower level than the shrine, since the tenets of Aztec religious architecture required a dominating position for the earthly residence of the god.[5]

However, in the Valley of Mexico the communities prospered and their peoples multiplied. As resources and manpower increased, the temples became larger and more numerous. Yet so complete was the destruction by the Spaniards and their Indian converts who transformed many a temple on its platform into a large parochial church, that the modern visitor finds little to suggest the architecture of the past. Archaeology has abundantly confirmed, in fragmentary form, the amazed descriptions of the conquerors.

The last two reconstructions at Tenayuca bear witness to the excellent proportions and dramatic principles of Aztec architecture. Excavations in the hill above the railway station at Cuernavaca revealed a temple intact in all except its roof. The temple of the Tepozteco, perched high in the hills over Tepoztlan, is another nearly perfect example of Aztec architecture on a small scale. A pit sunk in a vacant lot across the street from the cathedral in Mexico City reached the corner between the stair and the western wall of the great temple of Huitzilopochtli, War God of the Aztecs, and the massive size and ornate decoration prove that the startled descriptions of the Spaniards did less than justice to this tremendous monument.[6] A recent excavation in a cliff overhanging Malinalco, near Tenancingo, State of Mexico, brought to light a temple complex, largely hewed from living rock, which thrusts the famous Egyptian rock tombs of Abu Simbel into the limbo of provincial opera-house scenery.[7] (See Plates 29, bottom; 36, top; 48, 49.)

The Aztec temple had a platform, the sloping sides of which were generally broken by three terraces. A steep, broad stair flanked by balustrades, occasionally with a third dividing it into two, gave access to the top. Carved stone blocks, projecting in rows from the sides of the platform, represented snakeheads, skulls, or some other symbolic form of the cult. At the foot of the balustrades huge serpent heads with gaping jaws added to the architectural design and created awe in the beholder. The stair rose broad and steep, focusing the attention on the sacrificial block at the top, over which victims were stretched to await the searching knives of priests.

Behind the block stood the temple or temples, which generally had a back room for the idol and an antechamber for the priests. The walls were usually of dressed stone and sometimes ornamented with carving or relief. The roof, which was thatched in poor or primitive temples, in important shrines was made of beams laid like a corncrib, growing smaller towards the top. Plaster laid on twigs or poles sealed the roof against the rain and was carved with designs symbolic of the god inside. The interiors were noisome places, coated with blood and smoke, for incense was burned in profusion, as were the hearts of sacrificed victims. The proportions of terrace to terrace, temple to platform, stair to façade, were maintained irrespective of size, producing an effect of height and mass which yet in no way detracted from either the platform or the temple. This sense of proportion extends into every aspect of Aztec art and craftsmanship.

Some temples were cylindrical and rested on square or circular platforms.[8] These were dedicated to Quetzalcoatl, often represented as Ehecatl, God of the Wind, to whose passage a rounded surface offered no obstacle. Sometimes the door of such a temple was fashioned in the form of a serpent head, while the circular building suggested its body. A superb temple of this type is part of the Malinalco group mentioned above, which is hollowed out of the living rock. The door is carved at either side in low relief to suggest a serpent head in profile, while the whole also can be visualized as a snakehead in full face, of which the open mouth constitutes the door. A

167

bench circles around the walls within, and the *skins* of eagles and ocelot, emblematic of the rising and setting sun, are carved in relief as if they hunt from the wall to drape over the bench. An altar in the centre of the room represents another eagle. This elaborate concept is carved from the solid rock cliff and is a marvellous blend of architectural design and sculptural skill.[9]

The Aztec sculptors worked in relief and in the round, in heroic and in miniature size, and were equally able in symbolic and naturalistic conceptions, which they could execute in whatever medium was available. Our modern appreciation of their work is hampered by the prominence of religious *motifs*, which often detract by crowded detail or grotesque fantasy from the clean lines of their basic proportions. (See Plates 57, 60.) Aztec art, we have insisted, was never completely secular. Yet, in compensation, the Aztecs allowed a lively appreciation of natural elements to enter purely religious conceptions wherever possible.

From the time of the Pre-classic Cultures the Mexicans used baked clay extensively for sculpture and worked out in it their artistic standards. The few surviving examples of wooden sculpture suggest that this medium was carved in accordance with stone techniques and did not, as in Egypt and Greece, serve as a training ground for standards later transferred to stone. If anything, the plastic methods of Mexico had their origin in a long and continuous handling of clay. Both media entail an emphasis on surface and contour; and the technical process of reducing stone by pecking and polishing, if more laborious, is not, in the last analysis, very different from the final smoothing and finishing of a work in clay. Thus the sculptors achieved a delicate appreciation of the contours and lines of the human form.

Partly owing to the past tradition and partly because the images of the gods were set in the temples, the Aztec artists showed their figures in passive attitudes, more often seated than erect. The austerity of their life led the Aztecs to attribute similar attitudes to their gods, and, as a result, the soft emotionalism so characteristic of European art is almost totally absent. Thus Aztec sculpture is even more forbidding and gloomy than other Mesoamerican arts, which have at first a depressing effect on observers accustomed to Old World aesthetics.[10] (See Plates 50–6a, but also 39, 47, 56b.)

The same sense of proportion so evident in Aztec architecture produced a monumental quality in their sculpture. The smallest piece has the same dignity that attends the most massive temple carvings. A photograph reveals no impression of the original scale, and in one case the head of a goddess was carved identically in a small piece of jade and a four-foot block of basalt, with no loss of plastic or monumental values to either.[11]

In relief sculpture the forming of the object and the disposition and subordination of details show the mastery of design inherited by eyes trained in centuries of weaving. The vast block of the thirteen-foot Calendar Stone is carved with as delicate an appreciation of the relative values of space as similar designs painted on pottery vessels or graven on jade. (See Plate 50.)

The finest Aztec sculpture, to the Western eye, reproduces the young gods and goddesses that presided over the crops. Thus the Aztec body, long of trunk, short of limb, softly rounded in its well-fleshed strength, is simply and accurately portrayed with passive grace. The patient and resigned features were perfect subjects for the sculptor and his medium. Some gods could assume the guise of animals, and the sculptors took full advantage of their close observation of nature to carve a coyote with ear atilt or to dignify a red basalt grasshopper with the armoured malevolence of an insect in heroic scale. The serpent, emblem of Quetzalcoatl, symbol of time and the year, representative of mystery and power, was frequently carved. The sinuous curves ending in the savage symmetry of the head offered a challenge which the sculptors accepted with a success that evokes the mysterious horror of the Aztec universe. (See Plates 51, 54, 60.)

The grotesque gods are abstract and horrible to our modern eye. Coatlicue, the 'Lady of the Serpent Skirt', and mother of Huitzilopochtli, was thought of as powerful and awesome, so the task of the sculptors was to transmute those qualities into stone. The great statue in Mexico, whose head is twin serpents, whose necklace human hands and hearts, whose feet and hands are viciously armed with claws and whose skirt is a mat of writhing snakes, brings into a dynamic concentrate the manifold horrors of the universe. A smaller carving, simpler and less detailed, produces this same effect, implying that the very essence of fear was honoured and worshipped. An altar of red lava, dug up in the street behind the cathedral, is grimly adorned with ranked skulls, but the design is so harmonious that death becomes an abstraction, part of a distant universe of fear, and not the imminent individual disaster which besets us moderns. (See Plates 52, 53.)

The Calendar Stone embodies a finite statement of the infinity of the Aztec universe. In the centre is the face of the Sun God, Tonatiuh, flanked by four cartouches which singly give the dates of the four previous ages of the world and together represent the date of our present era. The twenty names of the days circle this central element, and they, in turn, are ringed with a band of glyphs denoting jade or turquoise, which give the idea of being precious and symbolize the heavens and their colour. This strip is girdled by the signs for stars, through which penetrate designs emblematic of the rays of the sun. Two immense Fire Serpents, symbolic of the Year and Time, circle the exterior to meet face to face at the base. Boring back through these forms to the significance behind them, we have a grandiose conception of the majesty of the universe.[12] (See Plate 50, top.)

In 1926, under the Presidential Palace in Mexico City, a

monolith over a metre high was found, which represented a platform and a stair crowned at the top by a similar solar disc. Reliefs on the sides show Huitzilopochtli, God of War, and Tezcatlipoca, God of the Smoking Mirror, symbolizing the sacred war between night and day. Probably the Calendar Stone was set up in much the same manner, and it is tantalizing to think of the lost reliefs which explained and ornamented the great disc when it was in position.[13] (See Plate 50, bottom.)

The historical accounts record that the Calendar Stone was made in 1479 and the great eagle vase of Tizoc during his rule from 1481 to 1486. A trough, extending from the basin to the edge of the vase, has been explained as a drain for blood to run out. However, the design is not keyed to this drain, and the purpose of the basin is to burn hearts, not to receive blood. Therefore, the furrow was probably made by the Spaniards, who sought either to use the vase as a nether millstone or tried unsuccessfully to smash it as an example of idolatry.[14]

The dates of these two monuments indicate that this was the time when Aztec civilization burst into flower. It is a tribute to Aztec artists that, originally fettered by the more lowly tasks of handicraft, they could accept the tremendous economic, social, and religious stimulation of their sudden rise to power as a licence to convert craftsmanship into great religious art.

The Aztecs did not create their art forms or their religion, which seems to have seeped in from the Mixteca–Puebla country. There the religious manuscripts and the ritualistic concepts hewn in stone and painted on vases were more complex and better drawn than their Aztec equivalents. Unfortunately, as yet, archaeological investigation has not extended to more than a sampling of this potentially rich area of Mexican civilization. However, the Valley people, given the opportunity, eagerly accepted these forms and created their own versions of the parent art.[15] (See Plates 57, top; 58, 59.)

The same elements portrayed in stone monuments appeared in smaller objects. Wooden drums and *atl-atls* had relief carvings the equal of the temple ornaments in all except scale. The same divinities were graven in bone against a background of turquoise mosaic. The goldworkers reproduced in miniature the images of the gods and goddesses and the symbols of their cult, carrying out in costume ornament the elements of the ritual in which they were used. Lapidaries succeeded in reducing jade, obsidian, rock crystal, opal, moonstone, and amethyst into tiny sculptures which carry the same emotional authority as the grand-scale art. The bulk of first-rate material is enormous. It would seem that the products of Mexican craftsmanship had been raised *en masse* into arts. Virtually overnight a cluster of primitive villages had transformed themselves into great creative centres.[16] (See Plates 43–6; 53, bottom left.)

The great mural paintings of Teotihuacan and the Maya area[17] are not equalled in Toltec or Aztec times. True, we have recovered a few examples, but they come from sources which produced fine sculpture. The surviving frescoes at Tizatlan and Malinalco are in no way superior to the drawings in the codices or manuscripts. The use of colour is lavish, but the drawing is crabbed and conventional, confining itself to correct delineation of ceremonial elements rather than to the combination of composition, perspective, and colour values into a significant emotional experience. Apparently the finer workers devoted themselves to sculpture, while drawing and painting subordinated in the outward expression of ritual, fell to less skilled hands. Yet design was a requisite in a work in two dimensions, and, considered on this basis, the symmetrical disposition of the figures renders less serious the anatomical flaws and rigidity of presentation.[18] (See Plate 57, top.)

The pictographic annals often exhibit an engaging charm in the little historical scenes recorded. The humour cannot be entirely fortuitous. There is something inherently fascinating about drawing little men that impels a draughtsman to humanize his figures with a resultant and welcome loss to their dignity. Even the supremely competent draughtsmen who decorated the Egyptian tombs in the Fourth Dynasty could not resist a casual impishness. Aztec drawing was hardier than the sculpture and was able to survive until the close of the sixteenth century. The Indians copied old records, and some annals were carried on in the same style until 1560. The friars used Indian artists to illustrate reports on indigenous affairs, and there are several manuscripts in which Indian and European drawing methods are inextricably and delightfully mingled. Pictured history has always had its appeal, to which emphasis of the essential and the suppression of the irrelevant, implicit in drawing, largely contribute. In our present day, with all the superb methods of photographic recordings and reproductions, the comic strip has a vogue unparalleled in our history.[19] (See Plates 62, 63.)

Aboriginal music has largely disappeared. The friars quickly adapted the chants and dances of Europe to Indian needs and substituted Christian for Indian ritual practices, using song and dance as formulas easily understood by primitives. To judge from the instruments, Aztec music was strong in rhythm but lacking in tone. The two-tone and one-tone drums could emit sonorous rhythms, but the bone and clay flutes pipe pitifully and are not gauged to a fixed scale. The conch shell could be blown with varying notes, according to the intensity of the blast, although it was more suitable for summoning people than for making music. Whistles, rattles of clay and gourds, bells, and shell tinklers enhanced the effect of carefully regulated rhythms. Notched bones, often human, were rasped with a stick and produced quite pleasant sounds. A strange type of drum, which seems to have been indigenous, had an amazing resonance attained by beating an inverted gourd floating in a large container of water.[20] (See Plates 38, bottom left; 61, middle right.)

The dance was highly important, but native steps seldom persist except in the most primitive outlying districts, for they were transformed by the friars into Christian patterns. The chroniclers describe dances of many types in which masses of people participated. It is impossible that the Aztecs, with their profound sense of design and form, should not have had elaborate rituals in which great bodies of people moved in complex patterns to complicated rhythms. Song was used to reinforce the ceremony, and the words of some chants survive without, alas, the musical notation. These dancers, acting out mythical events pertaining to the lives of the gods, must usually have been highly theatrical. Thus, as with other peoples of the past, religious service fulfilled the function of the drama.[21] (See Plate 62, bottom left.)

The pictographic writing of the Aztecs was too simple to record a literature. However, the many references to oratory and the wealth of allusions and synonyms referring to the gods and goddesses give a picture of rich fantasy and poetic imagination. The emphasis on the spoken word, the complex background of the religion, the closeness of the supernatural world, would not have produced lean, accurate prose. Rather a semi-poetic, highly symbolic verbiage came from the practice of oratory and the chanting of prayers. Thus a rhythmic and rich verbosity existed as a form of polite address that, given a system of writing, might have been transmuted into literature.[22]

These activities, which we sanction in our own culture under the terms of arts and letters and to the practitioners of which we assign honour as creative artists, were existent in Aztec society. The status of these practices, however, was very different from their position in our own culture. Much of that area of our own life divided up into the infinite gradation of commercial, legal, and governmental pursuits fell within the span of the individual Aztec's normal social life. That energy and activity which we exhaust in religion, art, belles-lettres, and science were combined by the Aztecs in the observance of their religious requirements. An understanding of the nature of their religion and its position in Aztec life and social practice is fundamental to a realization of the nature of their culture.

Chapter 11   Religion

A brief survey of the Aztec Universe and the unpronounceable Gods and Goddesses who presided over it and ruled men's fate

Aztec religion, in purpose and practice, tried to attract those natural forces which are favourable to human existence and repulse those which are harmful. Ethical control and spiritual perfection fell within the province of social custom, so that the moral goals of our own religion were largely absent; the Aztec religion had no Saviour of mankind, no heaven or hell to reward or punish the consequence of human behaviour.[1]

The Aztecs and their forebears believed that the forces of nature acted for good or evil very much as does mankind, so that it was logical for them to personalize the elements as gods or goddesses. The process of worship entailed offering presents, uttering prayers, and performing symbolic acts to induce the divine powers to operate for the public benefit. The group intellect was mobilized, as it were, to sort out the processes of nature, find out how they acted, and devise magical procedures or rituals to win them to action favourable to man.

Nature operates in series of recurrences which give the effect of rhythms. Birth, maturity, and death follow relentlessly in human life; night succeeds day; the stations of the year rotate endlessly through spring, summer, autumn, and winter; the planets move in eternal sequence through the sky. Thus to discover what those rhythms were and follow their complicated but regular beat would, in Aztec philosophy, ensure the happy survival of the community. There was little thought of the perfection of the individual when vast powers hovered close, ready to destroy the whole people if it ceased its vigilant watch on nature. Thus rhythm and form became an essential part of worship and found their outlet in ritual and religion, art, philosophy, and science.

The growth of civilization, with the resultant ramification of social function and material equipment, led likewise to a more complex perception of the universe, expressed in the stratification of gods and goddesses and a specialization of their functions. This result led to a more intense observance of ritual, which consumed a great part of the material and intellectual product of the state.

Aztec religion was an outgrowth of the recognition and fear of natural forces and the attempt to constrain them. The process by which man defines these forces and grades them in order of importance is as much a part of the evolution of culture as art, mechanics, or social organization. The Aztecs developed a conception of the relationship of the supernatural forces to the universe that, given the precision of our method of thought, could have been developed into an imposing philosophy.

According to Aztec belief, the world passed through four or five ages, or Suns. Details differ, but the record on the great Calendar Stone may be taken as the official version in Tenochtitlan. The first era, Four Ocelot, had Tezcatlipoca as the presiding god, who, at the end, transformed himself into the sun, while jaguars ate up the men and giants who then populated the earth. Quetzalcoatl was the divine ruler of the second era, Four Wind, at the expiration of which hurricanes destroyed the world and men were turned into monkeys. The Rain God, Tlaloc, gave the world light in the third epoch, Four Rain, brought to a close by a fiery rain. Chalchiuhtlicue, 'Our Lady of the Turquoise Skirt', was a Water Goddess who presided appropriately over the fourth Sun, Four Water, wherein a flood came, transforming men into fish. Our present age, Four Earthquake, is under the control of the Sun God, Tonatiuh, and it will be destroyed, in time, by earthquakes.[2] (See Plate 50.)

While the versions vary from place to place, we seem to have a recapitulation of the great disasters from flood, volcanic eruption, hurricanes, and earthquakes that beset the communities of ancient Mexico. Also there is a reflection of the order in which the gods attained prominence in the local worship. In the history of the Mexicans there are references to struggles within single towns between the devotees of two cults, as to which would have the mastery.[3]

The universe itself was conceived in a religious rather than a geographic sense and was divided horizontally and vertically into areas of religious significance. The horizontal universe, possibly the older concept, recognized five directions, the four cardinal points and the centre. The Fire God, old and fundamental in Mexican religion,[4] controlled the central zone. The east was assigned to the Rain God, Tlaloc, and the Cloud God, Mixcoatl (Cloud Snake), and was a region of abundance. In this idea geography was combined with ritual, since the intensely fertile Vera Cruz coast plain is the actual source of the seasonal rains caused by the condensation of warm air when the Gulf of Mexico is exposed to the chill winds of the Central Plateau. The south was considered evil, possibly because of the arid zones south of Morelos and Puebla, but had as presiding deities gods associated with spring and flowers, Xipe (the Flayed One) (see Plate 60), and Macuilxochitl (Five Flower). The west, however, had a favourable significance, being the home of the planet Venus, the evening star, which was associated and even identified with Quetzalcoatl (Feathered Serpent), the God of Knowledge. The north was a place gloomy and awful, presided over by Mictlantecuhtli (Lord of the Dead), who, in one of those contradictions so frequent in Mexican theology, was sometimes connected with the south as well.[5] (See map, pages 6–7.)

The vertical world was divided into heavens and hells which had no moral significance, being merely overworlds and underworlds. The number of heavens varied up to thirteen and represented the dwelling places of the gods, according to their rank in the hierarchy, the original creator living in the topmost heaven, and so on down the scale. One of these heavens belonged to Tlaloc,[6] who received those who died by drowning, lightning, or other causes connected with water. One school of thought divided the heavens into east and west, according to the passage of the sun. The east was the home of warriors, whose death in battle or sacrifice nourished the sun, and the west the home of women who died in childbirth, thus sacrificing themselves in the bearing of potential warriors.[7] (See Plate 57, right.)

The rest of the dead passed to Mictlan, the underworld. They had to overcome several hazards before they could take up their life there, so they were equipped with charms and gifts for the journey, which took the sacred number of four days. The wayfarer had to travel between two mountains which threatened to crush him, avoid first a snake and then a monstrous alligator, cross eight deserts, surmount eight hills and endure a freezing wind which hurled stones and obsidian knives upon him. Then he reached a broad river which he crossed on the back of a little red dog, sometimes included in the grave furniture for the purpose. Finally arriving at his destination, the traveller offered gifts to the Lord of the Dead, who assigned him to one of nine different regions. Some versions make the dead spend a probationary period of four years in the nine hells before they take up their life in Mictlan, which was, like the Greek Hades, devoid of moral significance.[8]

The Aztecs, as we have said, conceived of their universe as extending horizontally outwards and vertically upwards and downwards. The world, as horizontally divided, implied the association of divine powers with the phenomena of geography and climate. This significance of direction is a familiar religious concept. The vertical arrangement of the heavens had rather more to do with rank and order than with a realization of natural phenomena. The hierarchy of the Christian saints, with its implicit recognition of position and authority, approaches closely to the point of view with which the Aztec peoples regarded their gods. Aztec and ritualized Christian worship have much the same attitude towards distinctions between philosophy and practice, and between the point of view of the instructed theologian and the humble worshippers.

At the head of the Aztec pantheon, in a theological sense, was a supreme and ineffable god, Tloque Nahuaque; but an active cult in his honour seems to have been restricted to a single temple, at Texcoco, which became a centre of religious philosophy under the stimulus of the great chief, Nezahualcoyotl. Ranking below this abstraction of divine power and far more widely recognized was a supreme couple, Tonacatecuhtli and Tonacacihuatl, 'Our Lord and Lady of Subsistence'. These gods were theologically important and fulfilled the functions of parenthood and origin for other divinities. They were not extensively worshipped, since their control of nature was remote. An equivalent being, Ometecuhtli, 'Lord of Duality', occupied an analogous position, resulting from priestly speculation as to the ultimate origin of the gods who controlled man's destiny. The Sun God, Tonatiuh, who also discharged the functions of a heavenly overlord, was, however, more closely associated with the active expression of Aztec religion. The daily appearance of the celestial orb, so infinitely important to the existence of all life, made sun worship an essential part of the Aztec religion.[9]

There were several gods who intervened in human affairs and were venerated above all others. Usually one of this group was the tutelary spirit of a community and had arrogated to him supreme powers. Such a god was honoured by the principal temple, synthesized the abstract position of the gods invented by the theologians, and partook of all the supreme powers exerted by the chief god of other communities. This group, without exception, was composed of sky gods.

Tezcatlipoca, the 'Smoking Mirror', sometimes appeared on the scene as an adversary of the Toltec divinity Quetzalcoatl, the 'Feathered Serpent'. He was widely worshipped, and his powers were shared by other chief gods. His attributes, as depicted in the sacred manuscripts, showed him to be protean, and they were often assigned to the tribal divinities of other places. A Mixtec manuscript, which emanates from the probable centre of the Tezcatlipoca cult, shows the same divinity presiding over the four directions but with a different colour in each instance. The powers and dress of this great god passed to local tribal divinities with the spread of Mixtec religion and the Tezcatlipoca cult to the Valley of Mexico. (See Plates 56b, 57, top; 61, top.)

The red Tezcatlipoca of the east took the name of Xipe, or Camaxtle, the tutelary god of Tlaxcala. Huitzilopochtli, the great War God of the Tenochca, assumed the functions and dress of the blue Tezcatlipoca of the south and was a Sun God as well, but his adversary and opposite divinity of the night retained the name Tezcatlipoca and was shown as the black Tezcatlipoca of the north. Quetzalcoatl was sometimes depicted as a white Tezcatlipoca, associable with the east as a morning star and the west as an evening star. Under the name 'Feathered Serpent' but with the attributes and powers of Tezcatlipoca, he presided over the destinies of Cholula. Tezcatlipoca, as god of a favourable region, as surrogate of the sun and as the chief god of the original cult, was the chief divinity worshipped at Texcoco.

Tlaloc, the Rain God, is an ancient god, going back at least to Teotihuacan times. His eye rings, his fangs, and the volute over his lips render him an easily recognized figure in the Mexican pantheon. At Tenochtitlan he shared the great temples with Huitzilopochtli, and his control of rain made the attraction of his powers essential to survival on the Mexican plateau. (See Plate 59, top left.)

Quetzalcoatl, the 'Feathered Serpent', God of Civilization and the planet Venus, seems to have been widely venerated but under different guises. In contrast to Tezcatlipoca, whose functions and appearance were assigned to various regional gods with different names, Quetzalcoatl had several forms shared by distinctive divinities. The sculptures of Teotihuacan and Chichen Itza show that a feathered snake was honoured, and the local records mention Quetzalcoatl and Kukulcan, Nahuatl and Maya names having the same meaning. At Tenochtitlan there is ample evidence of a serpent cult, but the records refer to Xiuhcoatl, 'Fire Snake', as well as to the standard sacred variety. The term Quetzalcoatl applies as well to a bearded god with a projecting mask, also called Ehecatl, the 'Wind God'. In parts of the Mixteca-Puebla area and the Valley, as we have seen, there is evidence that the 'white' Tezcatlipoca had the name 'One Reed', the date name synonymous with Quetzalcoatl.[10] (See Plates 22, 51; 59, top right.)

In addition to this confusion over Quetzalcoatl, the God of Civilization, the annals and myths tell of Quetzalcoatl, the great king, who civilized the Toltecs and left for the east to return again. The friars seized upon this myth as evidence that St Thomas the Apostle had visited Mexico and converted its inhabitants, who later slid back into pagan ways. Therefore, the friars, to justify the Conquest, made much of a blond god who, after taking leave of his people, promised to return from the east by sea. Yet the Quetzalcoatl of the Valley of Mexico manuscripts was never blond but usually black in beard and face paint, when he was not shown as the masked Wind God, Ehecatl.

As if the confusion between a man and a god of many guises were not baffling enough for the historian, we find to our dismay that the title Quetzalcoatl not only was given to a Toltec ruler, Topiltzin, but also was borne at Tenochtitlan by the chief priests who exemplified the learning of the time. Distinguished authority has supported the hypothesis that a Mexican named Quetzalcoatl went to Yucatan where he attained high office and absorbed the civilization of the Maya. Later he returned to Mexico and taught a version of the calendar, as well as many other useful arts, to the peoples of the plateau.[11] Others, more romantic, see in Quetzalcoatl an Irishman, Norseman, or even Atlantean, who popped into Mexico and spread sweetness and light. I, personally, believe that the introduction of superior culture elements and the creation of local arts as well might not only lead to the invention of a God of Civilization but also endow individual innovators with the name of that god. The conflicting data suggest to me that the name and concept did not originate in any one person but resulted, rather, from the experience of many peoples over a long period of time in explaining and honouring the introduction of those benefits which ensured their corporal and spiritual well-being.

The great gods of the sky played an important part in the duality of the Aztec world in which an eternal war was fought symbolically between light and darkness, heat and cold, north and south, rising and setting sun. Even the stars were grouped into armies of the east and the west. Gladiatorial combats, often to the death, expressed this idea in ritual, and the great warrior orders, the Eagle Knights of Huitzilopochtli and the Ocelot Knights of Tezcatlipoca, likewise reflected the conflict between day and night. This Sacred War permeated the ritual and philosophy of Aztec religion.[12] (See Plates 38, middle left; 39, 56b.)

While the great gods, the chief deities, tended to be associated with the heavens, there were many others who controlled growth and fertility. Often these gods had goddesses as wives or companions, as if the idea of reproduction of the male and female principles were dawning in Aztec theology. Tlaloc, the Rain God, held sway over growth and vegetation, and his companion Chalchiuhtlicue (Our Lady of the Turquoise Skirt) presided over lakes and rivers. This goddess was the centre of an important cult and is represented as a charming young girl beautifully dressed. Xipe (the Flayed One) symbolized spring, and his distinctive costume, a human skin, represented the new covering of vegetation with which the earth clothes itself each year. His priests, at the ceremonies in his honour, carried this symbolism into their costume by donning the skins of freshly flayed captives. (See Plates 26, top left; 59, top left; 61, middle left.)

The corn goddesses were young and lovely and probably derived from the old cult of the Pre-classic goddesses. Chicomecoatl (Seven Snake) was the Goddess of Crops and Subsistence, represented by corn, the staple food. Xilonen, 'Young Corn Mother', and Xochiquetzal, 'Flower Bird', were the embodied spirits of young growth and, by analogy, youth and the games. These had as male counterparts such gods as Centeotl, 'Maize God', Xochipilli, 'Flower Prince', and Macuilxochitl, 'Four Flower', whose functions, identified with growth, youth, and games, are almost synonymous. (See Plates 31; 54, top left; 57 bottom left.)

About the maguey plant revolved another cult embracing the goddess Mayahuel, who represented the plant and whose four hundred sons were associated with pulque. According to some accounts, the various styles of drunkenness were recorded in terms of these gods or their associated animal, the rabbit. Four hundred rabbits stood for complete drunkenness, while fifteen or twenty suggested mere conviviality. The chief of these pulque gods was called 'Two Rabbit', after his day in the almanac, and another, Tepoztecatl, was the tribal god of Tepoztlan, honoured by a temple placed high in the mountains of Morelos. (See Plate 56a.)

The gods of the earth and death were highly important, since growth takes place in the earth and the dead are received there. The sun on rising seems to be born in the earth and at its setting to be hidden by it, thus passing apparently to the world of the dead. The gods and goddesses associated with the earth had significance for the solar cults as well as for growth and fertility.

Tlaltecuhtli, 'Lord of the Earth', was depicted as a male monster of horrifying aspect, partaking of the attributes of a toad and an alligator. His open mouth could consume even the sun, since the setting sun passed into the earth, according to Aztec astronomical ideas. The goddesses, however, seem to have been worshipped more extensively, and the clay images made in their honour also continued in unbroken line the tradition of the Pre-classic figurines. Coatlicue (Our Lady of the Serpent Skirt) was the mother of the gods in their stellar aspect but also was honoured as the mother of Huitzilopochtli. (See Plates 52, 53.) The measure of her importance may be gauged by the great statue of her in Mexico which is a master-piece of sacerdotal art and undoubtedly had a temple to itself. Coatlicue was also represented as a mother carrying a child in her arms. In this guise her function as a mother goddess brought her image into almost every home in the Valley. Tonantzin (Our Mother), which may have been an aspect of this same goddess or of Cihuacoatl (Snake Woman), had a temple at Tepeyac, now the site of the shrine to the Virgin of Guadalupe, and her cult was transferred to the Virgin by the early missionaries, an act exemplifying their intelligent pro-cedure in evangelizing the Aztecs. A goddess, Tlazolteotl (Eater of Filth) (see Plate 55), was extensively worshipped and was also synonymously known as the 'Mother of the Gods'. Primarily an earth-goddess, she, alone of the goddesses, had a moral significance, since in eating refuse she consumed the sins of mankind, leaving them pure. A rite of confession developed in her cult.

Standing out from the numerous divinities associated with death were Mictlantecuhtli and Mictecacihuatl (Our Lord and Lady of the Region of Death). They wore masks made from human skulls, and their ornaments were either human bones or representations of them. They presided over the northern regions and also ruled the hells below the earth. Theirs was no punitive function, for all who died, save in war or sacrifice, childbirth or drowning, passed upon death to their domain. (See Plate 53, bottom left.)

This incomplete description of the gods and goddesses who thronged the Aztec pantheon gives an idea of their variety of purpose and character, outlined more fully in Table 7. For an individual to try to do honour to so many gods could result in an insupportable situation. Yet even the modern Navajos pass a third of their time in ceremonial activity, and they do not have half the economic wealth of the Aztec peoples. While the ancient Mexicans extended their ceremonialism to greater lengths than do the most ritualized Christian sects, the relationship between the Aztecs and their gods and the Christians and their saints is not so very dissimilar, different as are the ultimate concepts of the two religions.

The priests gave guidance and prescribed the ceremonies, and the worshippers gave heed to those especial divinities upon whose patronage their life directly depended, much as a devout Catholic selects certain saints for veneration above the list of those whose days are recorded on the calendar. In the same way an individual Aztec god may have his counterpart in the patron saint of country, town, or craft. The Aztec, however, thought of his gods as having strong material powers, and their spiritual aspect counted little with him.

The ritual of Aztec religion was as complex as the theology. The organization of the priesthood followed the pyramided structure of the social order, but the ceremonies were worked out in accordance with the ritualistic requirements of the calendar and the seasons. In the following chapter we shall describe the priesthood, the ceremonies, and also the Aztec methods of counting, recording, and using time.

Table 7. PRINCIPAL MEMBERS OF THE AZTEC PANTHEON, THEIR CHARACTER AND SPHERES OF WORSHIP

	Month	Week	Day	Day Hour	Night Hour
GREAT GODS					
Huitzilopochtli, Hummingbird Wizard, War and Sun God, chief god of Tenochtitlan	5* 9 15				
Tezcatlipoca, Smoking Mirror, chief god of pantheon, solar attibutes, chief god of Texcoco	5 12	13	8	10	
Quetzalcóatl, Feathered Serpent, God of Learning and of Priesthood, chief god of Cholula, and Xochicalco, also important at Tula, frequently shown as Ehécatl, the Wind God		2	2	9	
CREATIVE DEITIES					
Tloque Nahuaque, Lord of the Close Vicinity, creative spirit, theological abstraction					
Ometecuhtli, Lord of Duality, and his wife Omecíhuatl					
Tonacatecuhtli, Lord of Our Subsistence, Creator God, chief of the gods	1	1			
Tonacacíhuatl, Lady of Our Subsistence, wife of the above					
FERTILITY GODS					
Tlazoltéotl, Goddess of Dirt, Earth Mother, worshipped under many synonyms	11	13	14	5	7
Teteoinan, Mother of the Gods, synonym of Tlazoltéotl					
Ixcuina, Four Faces, synonym of Tlazoltéotl					
Toci, Our Grandmother, synonym of Tlazoltéotl					
Chicomecóatl, Seven Snake, Corn Goddess, ancient goddess dating from Pre-classic times	4 11				
Cihuacóatl, Serpent Woman, Earth Goddess, ruling childbirth and death thereby					
Tonantzin, Our Mother, synonym of Cihuacóatl					
Coatlicue, Serpent Skirt, Earth Goddess, associated with spring, mother of Huitzilopochtli					

* The numbers refer to the *Tonalamatl* of the *Codex Borbonicus*. Those in parentheses refer to variations found in the *Tonalamatl Aubin* and the *Codex Telleriano-Remensis*.

	Month	Week	Day	Day Hour	Night Hour
Centéotl, Corn God, son of Tlazoltéotl, husband of Xochiquetzal, important				(12)	
Xochiquetzal, Flower Feather, Goddess of Flowers, of Craftsmen, important		19	20	(7) (13)	4
Xochipilli, Flower Prince, God of Pleasure, Feasting, Frivolity			11	(3)	
Macuilxóchitl, Five Flower, synonym of Xochipilli				7	
Xipe, Our Lord, the Flayed One, God of Seedtime and Planting, the red Tezcatlipoca, highly important	2	14	15	(11) (4)	
Xilonen, Young Maize Mother, Goddess of the Young Corn	8				
Ilamatecuhtli, the Old Princess, a goddess of ancient times, related to corn and the earth	17			13	

GODS OF RAIN AND MOISTURE

	Month	Week	Day	Day Hour	Night Hour
Tláloc, He Who Makes Things Sprout, Rain God, very important	6 13 3 1 16	7	7	8	(8) 9
Tlaloques, minor rain gods, children or brothers of Tláloc, a plural synonym					
Chalchiuhtlicue, She of the Jewelled Robe, Water Goddess, very important	1	5	5	3	6
Huixtocíhuatl, Salt Woman, Goddess of Salt and of the Dissolute	7				
Naápatecuhtli, Four Times Lord, one of the Tlálocs					
Ehécatl, Wind, Wind God, a frequent guise of Quetzalcóatl					

FIRE GODS

	Month	Week	Day	Day Hour	Night Hour
Xiuhtecuhtli, Lord of the Year, Fire God, a divinity of ancient times, important	18 10	20 9	9	(7) 1	1
Huehuetéotl, Old God, a synonym of Xiuhtecuhtli					
Chantico, In the House, goddess associated with the hearth and volcanic fire		18	19		

PULQUE GODS

	Month	Week	Day	Day Hour	Night Hour
Mayahuel, She of the Maguey Plant, Goddess of the Maguey and also of Fertility		8	8		
Patécatl, He from the Land of Medicines, God of Medicine, husband of Mayahuel		11	12		

	Month	*Week*	*Day*	*Day Hour*	*Night Hour*

Ometochtli, 'Two Rabbit', to whom the game of *patolli* was dedicated

Tepoztécatl, god of Tepoztlan, said to have been born of a virgin

Tezcatzontécatl, Straw-Covered Mirror, an important pulque god, identifiable with the Chacmool figures in stone

Centzon Totochtin, Four Hundred Rabbits, the many pulque gods

PLANETARY AND STELLAR GODS

Tonatiuh, the Sun, Sun God with intimate connexions with Huitzilopochtli and Tezcatlipoca — Day Hour 4

Piltzintecuhtli, Young Prince, Synonym of Tonatiuh — Day Hour 3

Metztli, the Moon, Moon God, sometimes identified with Tezcatlipoca

Tecciztécatl, He from the Sea Snail, synonym of Metztli — Month 6, Week 6, Night Hour (5)

Mixcóatl, god of the Chichimecs, Cloud Serpent, God of Stars and of Numbers — Month 14

Camaxtle, god of Tlaxcala, another name for Xipe

Itzpapálotl, Obsidian Knife Butterfly, stellar and also agricultural goddess — Month 15, Week 16

Tlahuizcalpantecuhtli, Lord of the House of Dawn, Venus, the morning star, variant of Quetzalcóatl — Week 9, Night Hour (1) (12)

Coyolxauhqui, Painted with Bells, Moon Goddess, sister of Centzonhuitznáuac

Centzonhuitznáuac, 400 Southerners, star gods of south

Centzon Mimixcoa, 400 Northerners, star gods of north

Tzitzimime, Monsters Descending from Above, stellar gods

GODS OF DEATH, EARTH

Mictlantecuhtli, Lord of Region of Death, God of Death — Month 10, Week 10, Day 11, Day Hour 5

Mictecacíhuatl, Lady of Region of Death, wife of Death God

189

	Month	Week	Day	Day Hour	Night Hour
Tepeyolohtli, Heart of the Mountains, Mountain God, Jaguar God		3	3		8
Tlaltecuhtli, Lord of Earth, earth monster, personification of earth in contrast to sun				2	
Teoyaomiqui, God of Dead Warriors, a specialized Death God				6 (6)	
Huahuantli, the Striped, synonym of Teoyaomiqui					

VARIANTS OF GREAT GODS

	Month	Week	Day	Day Hour	Night Hour
Itztli, Stone Knife, a surrogate of Tezcatlipoca in guise of sacrificial knife			20		2
Itzlacoliuhqui, Carved Obsidian Knife, another variant of Tezcatlipoca		12 (13)			
Paynal, the Hasty, messenger of Huitzilopochtli					
Yacatecuhtli, Lord Who Guides, God of Travelling Merchants	15 12				
Chalchiuhtotolin, Jewelled Fowl, variant of Tezcatlipoca		17 (18)			
Yáotl, Enemy, synonym of Tezcatlipoca				(5)	

OTHER GODS

	Month	Week	Day	Day Hour	Night Hour
Xólotl, Double, Monster God, twin of Quetzalcóatl		16	17		
Ixtlilton, Little Black Face, God of Health and Cures from Ills				(2)	
Cihuateteo, Goddesses, witches, spirits of women dead in childbirth					
Huehuecóyotl, Old Coyote, back-biter or mischief-maker, god of Otomi		4	4		

Chapter 12   Ritual

In which are summarized the nature of the
Religious Organization, the Feasts, and the relationship between ritual, calendar, and writing

Religion was a general group activity necessary for the social
and economic safekeeping of the people, and the priesthood
was a highly important force in the direction of the communal life. In the early simple societies there were two executive chiefs, one for war and one for religious affairs. We do
not know whether the priesthood comprised laymen who
performed the ritual acts of specific ceremonies or whether it
was an established group whose whole life was devoted to
religious ends. It is probable that selected individuals originally
carried out the religious duties of the community in addition
to their civil obligations, but as Aztec culture became more
elaborate, the complexity of their functions moulded them
into a body of permanent officials.[1]

In Tenochtitlan the Chief of Men and the Snake Woman
had double duties in respect to civil and religious affairs, the
former actively leading the services and the latter supervising
the temples, the form of the rites, and the internal affairs of the
priesthood. Two high priests directed cult activities in honour
of the War God, Huitzilopochtli, and the Rain God, Tlaloc,
the chief divinities worshipped in this city. They were called
Quetzalcoatl-Totec-tlamacazqui and *Quetzalcoatl-Tlaloc-tlama-
cazqui*. The name Quetzalcoatl was given them perhaps as an
honourific title in memory of the God of Civilization and
Learning, who was the archetype of the priestly ideal. The
second names refer to the gods of the respective cults, and the
third word means priest. Ranking below these two officials
was a third, *Mexicatl-Teohuatzin*, who, like a vicar-general,
supervised general religious business in the city-state and

conquered towns. Two assistants looked after the instruction in the schools for citizen-warriors and for priests, and other officials supervised the pulque ceremonies.[2]

Next in rank were the priests who were in charge of the worship, temple, and ritual of each specific god or goddess and who, in the ceremonies, assumed the dress of the divinity, impersonating him on earth. They, in turn, had a host of assistants who were supplemented by aspirants to the priesthood, the bottom of the hierarchical scale. There seem to have been priestesses as well, and schools for their instruction were established in connexion with certain temples. As might be expected as an accompaniment of a highly ritualized religion far above the comprehension of the masses, there was an active practice of magic carried on by male and female witch doctors. Undoubtedly many of these unsanctioned rites were rooted in the more primitive stages of the Aztec development; and in modern times, although the formal Aztec religion has been almost completely eradicated, the indigenous population continues many of the old magico-medical practices.

The priests, however, directed the intellectual life of the group. They elaborated cult ritual and so instilled the realization of the power and proximity of the gods into the minds of the people that even their arts were dedicated chiefly to religious expression. The complicated astronomic and mathematical computations that kept the solar and religious calendars in harmony with the passage of the seasons were also the province of the priesthood. The priests arrayed the dancers, who, depicting mythological events, performed a type of mass drama. Aztec life under hierarchical direction became a pattern of rhythmic ritual, and this continued ceremony served the more firmly to establish the priests as interpreters of the divine order. One has the impression that the priests never overtly showed their temporal power. Situated as they were, with the instruments for interpreting the divine will in their own hands, they had to follow the exactions of ritual far more exigently than did the masses. Were one to choose a single word to describe Aztec government, it would be theocracy. The gods ruled; the priests interpreted and interposed, and the people obeyed, not the priests, but the rhythm of action whereby the gods lived. (See Plate 58, bottom left.)

At the core of the religion stood the calendar, which was arranged in two divisions: a ritualistic succession of days, the *tonalpohualli* (Tables 8–13), and a solar calendar (Table 14), divided into eighteen twenty-day months and a five-day unlucky period, in which the months' names related to crops and indicated the agricultural origin of this time count. A combination of the two systems permitted the numbering of years, which were counted not on an infinite scale, as with us, but in terms of a fifty-two-year cycle.[3]

The *tonalpohualli*, sometimes erroneously referred to as *tonalamatl*, after the book in which it was recorded, was a sacred almanac. It covered a period of 260 days, the significance of which may have been magical or possibly of an astronomical origin, as yet unexplained. It was composed of the twenty day names of the Aztec month, combined with the numbers one to thirteen (Table 8). Whenever the sequence of numbers ended, the series was repeated, and the same arrangement held true for the list of days. Thus the fourteenth day of the twenty in the list received the number one, and so on up to seven for the twentieth day. Then when the series of day names recommenced the first name was numbered eight. By this means within the 260-day period every day was distinguished by the combination of one of twenty names with one of thirteen numerals. At the close of each period another began immediately, as is shown on Table 8.

This sacred period was further divided into twenty weeks of thirteen days each (Table 9). Every week began with the number one and the day name which came up according to the rotation of the sequence. Thus within the *tonalpohualli* period no day in one week could be confused with that of another, since the name and associated number precluded repetition.[4]

A god or goddess presided over each of the list of twenty days (Table 10) and over each of the twenty 'weeks' (Table 11). The gods of the weeks followed the same order as the day gods, with this exception, that the god of the eleventh day was dropped from the list, moving the remainder in order up one place each. The resultant vacancy in the twentieth week, was filled by two divinities who exercised joint control. Sometimes there was a further refinement whereby

Table 8. DAY NAMES AND NUMBERS OF THE AZTEC MONTH

1	Cipactli (Mythical Water Monster, Crocodile, Alligator)	
2	Ehécatl (Wind)	
3	Calli (House)	Year Name
4	Cuetzpallin (Iguana Lizard)	
5	Cóatl (Snake)	
6	Miquiztli (Death's-Head)	
7	Mázatl (Deer)	
8	Tochtli (Rabbit)	Year Name
9	Atl (Water)	
10	Itzcuintli (Dog)	
11	Ozomatli (Howling Monkey)	
12	Malinalli (Grass)	
13	Acatl (Reed)	Year Name
1	Océlotl (Ocelot)	
2	Cuauhtli (Eagle)	
3	Cozcaquauhtli (Vulture)	
4	Ollin (Motion, Earthquake)	
5	Técpatl (Flint Knife)	Year Name
6	Quiáhuitl (Rain)	
7	Xóchitl (Flower)	
8	Cipactli	
9	Ehécatl	
10	Calli	Year Name
11	Cuetzpallin	
12	Cóatl	
13	Miquiztli	
1	Mázatl	
2	Tochtli	Year Name
	Etc., etc.	

Table 9. TONALPOHUALLI: SEQUENCE OF DAY NAMES, NUMBERS, AND WEEKS

Day													
	I												
Crocodile	**1**	8	2	9	3	10	4	11	5	12	6	13	7
												XVIII	
Wind	2	9	3	10	4	11	5	12	6	13	7	**1**	8
										XV			
House	3	10	4	11	5	12	6	13	7	**1**	8	2	9
								XII					
Lizard	4	11	5	12	6	13	7	**1**	8	2	9	3	10
						IX							
Serpent	5	12	6	13	7	**1**	8	2	9	3	10	4	11
				VI									
Death's-Head	6	13	7	**1**	8	2	9	3	10	4	11	5	12
		III											
Deer	7	**1**	8	2	9	3	10	4	11	5	12	6	13
													XX
Rabbit	8	2	9	3	10	4	11	5	12	6	13	7	**1**
											XVII		
Water	9	3	10	4	11	5	12	6	13	7	**1**	8	2
									XIV				
Dog	10	4	11	5	12	6	13	7	**1**	8	2	9	3
							XI						
Monkey	11	5	12	6	13	7	**1**	8	2	9	3	10	4
					VIII								
Grass	12	6	13	7	**1**	8	2	9	3	10	4	11	5
			V										
Reed	13	7	**1**	8	2	9	3	10	4	11	5	12	6
	II												
Ocelot	**1**	8	2	9	3	10	4	11	5	12	6	13	7
												XIX	
Eagle	2	9	3	10	4	11	5	12	6	13	7	**1**	8
										XVI			
Vulture	3	10	4	11	5	12	6	13	7	**1**	8	2	9
								XIII					
Motion	4	11	5	12	6	13	7	**1**	8	2	9	3	10
						X							
Flint Knife	5	12	6	13	7	**1**	8	2	9	3	10	4	11
				VII									
Rain	6	13	7	**1**	8	2	9	3	10	4	11	5	12
		IV											
Flower	7	**1**	8	2	9	3	10	4	11	5	12	6	13

the nine gods and goddesses succeeded each other in governing the nights of the *tonalpohualli*, or sacred period (Table 13). Finally thirteen of these gods influenced the thirteen stations of the Aztec day (Table 12), and nine held sway over the night hours (Table 13). The names and characters of these divinities are set forth in the accompanying tables.

The array of gods had to be placated and honoured at the appropriate time by the priesthood; but the individual, before embarking on an undertaking, could find out the proper divinity to appease on the date of that undertaking. It is im-

Fig. 24. Aztec day signs from Codex.

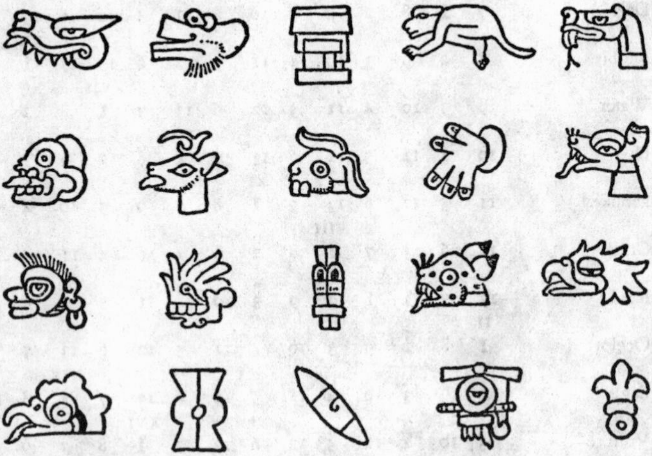

Cipactli Crocodile	*Ehecatl* Wind	*Calli* House	*Cuetzpallin* Lizard	*Coatl* Serpent
Miquiztli Death's-Head	*Mazatl* Deer	*Tochtli* Rabbit	*Atl* Water	*Itzcuintli* Dog
Ozomatli Monkey	*Malinalli* Grass	*Acatl* Reed	*Ocelotl* Ocelot	*Cuauhtli* Eagle
Cozcaquauhtli Vulture	*Ollin* Motion	*Tecpatl* Flint Knife	*Quiahuitl* Rain	*Xochitl* Flower

196

probable that the ordinary communicant daily honoured each god any more than a Catholic layman prays daily to each saint in the calendar. He did reverence in terms of his own spiritual and actual necessity.

A number of the *tonalamatl* have survived. These reference books for priestly guidance are made of paper beaten from the

Table 10. DAY GODS OF TONALPOHUALLI

Day	God	Name and Nature
1. Crocodile	Tonacatecuhtli	Lord of Our Subsistence, a Creator God
2. Wind	Quetzalcóatl	Feathered Serpent, Sky God, God of Learning
3. House	Tepeyolohtli	Heart of Mountains, an Earth God
4. Lizard	Huehuecóyotl	Old Coyote, Mischief-Maker
5. Snake	Chalchiuhtlicue	Lady of the Jewelled Robe, Water Goddess
6. Death's-Head	Tecciztécatl	He from the Sea Snail, Moon God
7. Deer	Tláloc	He Who Makes Things Sprout, Rain God
8. Rabbit	Mayahuel	She of the Maguey Plant, Pulque Goddess
9. Water	Xiuhtecuhtli	Lord of Year, Fire God
10. Dog	Mictlantecuhtli	Lord of Region of Dead, Death God
11. Monkey	Xochipilli	Flower Prince, God of Spring and Flowers
12. Grass	Patécatl	He from the Land of Medicines, God of Medicine
13. Reed	Tezcatlipoca or variant like Itzlacoliuhqui	Smoking Mirror, a Great God, cf. Gods of Weeks Carved obsidian Knife
14. Ocelot	Tlazoltéotl	Goddess of Dirt, Earth Mother
15. Eagle	Xipe	Our Lord, the Flayed One, God of Seedtime
16. Vulture	Itzpapálotl	Obsidian Butterfly, a Stellar Goddess
17. Motion	Xólotl or variant	Double, Monster God
18. Fling Knife	Tezcatlipoca or Chalchiuhtotolin	Smoking Mirror, Great God, Jewelled Bird, a Week God
19. Rain	Chantico	In the House, Goddess of Hearth Fire
20. Flower	Xochiquetzal	Flower Feather, Goddess of Flowers

Table 11. GODS OF TONALPOHUALLI WEEKS

Week Beginning	God	Name
1 Crocodile	Tonacatecuhtli	Lord of Our Subsistence, a Creator God
1 Ocelot	Quetzalcóatl	Feathered Serpent, a Sky God
1 Deer	Tepeyolohtli	Heart of the Mountains, an Earth God
1 Flower	Huehuecóyotl	Old Coyote, Back-biter, old Otomi tribal god
1 Reed	Chalchiuhtlicue	Lady of the Jewelled Robe, Water Goddess
1 Death's-Head	Tecciztécatl	He from the Sea Snail, Moon God
1 Rain	Tláloc	He Who Makes Things Sprout, Rain God
1 Grass	Mayahuel	She of the Maguey Plant, Pulque Goddess
1 Snake	Xiuhtecuhdli	Lord of the Year, Fire God
1 Flint	Mictlantecuhtli	Lord of the Region of the Dead, Death God
1 Howling Monkey	Patécatl	He from the Land of Medicines, God of Medicine
1 Lizard	Itzlacoliuhqui	The Carved Obsidian Knife, God of Cold
1 Motion	Tlazoltéotl	Goddess of Dirt, Earth Goddess
1 Dog	Xipe Totec	Our Lord the Flayed One, God of Seed-time
1 House	Itzpapálotl	Obsidian Butterfly, a Stellar Goddess
1 Vulture	Xólotl	Double, Monster God
1 Water	Chalchiuhtotolin	Jewelled Fowl, variant of Tezcatlipoca
1 Wind	Chantico	In the House, Goddess of Hearth Fire
1 Eagle	Xochiquetzal	Flower Feather, Goddess of Flowers
1 Rabbit	Xiuhtecuhtli and Itztli	Lord of Year, Fire God; Stone Knife, God of Obsidian Knife

Table 12. GODS OF THE DAY HOURS AND THEIR ASSOCIATED BIRDS

Day Gods	Name	Associated Bird
1. Xiuhtecuhtli	Fire God	White Hummingbird
2. Tlaltecuhtli	Lord of Earth, the Earth Monster	Green Hummingbird
3. Chalchiuhtlicue	Water Goddess	Falcon
4. Tonatiuh	The Sun, Sun God	Quail
5. Tlazoltéotl	Earth Mother	Eagle
6. Teoyaomiqui	Warrior Death, Death God	Screech Owl
7. Xochipilli	Flower Prince, God of Flowers	Butterfly

Day Gods	Name	Associated Bird
8. Tláloc	Rain God	Striped Eagle
9. Quetzalcóatl-Ehécatl	God of Learning	Turkey Cock
10. Tezcatlipoca	Great God	Horned Owl
11. Mictlantecuhtli	Death God	Guacamaya
12. Tlahuizcalpante-cuhtli	Lord of the House of Dawn, Venus God, variant of Quetzalcóatl	Quetzal
13. Ilamatecuhtli	Old Princess, ancient Earth Goddess	Parrot

Table 13. GODS OF THE NIGHT HOURS AND THEIR ATTRIBUTES IN DIVINATION

Night Gods	Name	Significance
1. Xiuhtecuhtli	Fire God	Good
2. Itztli	God of Obsidian Knife	Bad
3. Piltzintecuhtli	Lord of Princes, Sun God	Good
4. Centéotl	God of Corn, Corn God	Indifferent
5. Mictlantecuhtli	Death God	Bad
6. Chalchiuhtlicue	Water Goddess	Indifferent
7. Tlazoltéotl	Earth Mother	Bad
8. Tepeyolohtli	Earth or Jaguar God	Good
9. Tláloc	Rain God	Good

bark of the amate or wild-fig tree, although some post-Conquest copies were composed of European paper. An ancient book consisted of a long paper strip which was prepared and coated to take paint and subsequently folded screen-wise to permit easy handling. Occasionally only one but usually the two open pages were devoted to each week. A large coloured drawing depicted the divinity controlling the week, and other figures represented subsidiary gods and objects connected with their worship, such as thorns, incense burners, altars, and the like. The rest of the space was ruled off into squares, in which were painted the requisite thirteen

199

day names and numbers, the gods and goddesses associated with each, and occasionally their *nahuals*, the bird or animal forms which the divinities could assume. Obviously only the initiate could make use of this information, which existed in the form of pictures without an explanatory text. However, it is the great good fortune of Mexicanists that some of the friars after the Conquest annotated a few of these manuscripts according to the explanation of Indian informants.[5] (See Plate 59, bottom.)

The great Aztec ceremonies, however, took place in accordance with the solar year, composed of eighteen months of twenty days and a five-day period which was considered unlucky (Table 14). The months had names having to do with farming, and the days of the month were distinguished by numbers, in addition to their *tonalpohualli* name and number described above. Years were identified in terms of the two methods, since they were named for the *tonalpohualli* day on which the year began.[6]

Only four of the twenty day names could begin the year, as a simple mathematical calculation will prove. Three hundred and sixty-five (the number of days in a year) divided by twenty (the total of the day names) leaves a remainder of five. Thus of the twenty day names only four can begin the year. House, Rabbit, Reed, and Flint Knife must always recur as New

Table 14. THE SOLAR YEAR, THE EIGHTEEN MONTHS AND CEREMONIES

Months, seasonal character, approximate Gregorian dates, presiding gods, and chief ceremonies

    I Atlcoualco (want of water), ceasing of rain [12 Feb.–3 Mar.]. Chal-chiuhtlicue and Tlálocs. Ceremonies for rain; child sacrifice; Xipe sacrifice with blunt weapons.

   II Tlacaxipeualiztli (boning of men), seedtime [4 Mar.–23 Mar.]. God Xipe. Impersonation of Xipe by priests wearing skins of captives; dances by priests wearing human skins; agricultural dances.

III Tozoztontli (short fast), rain desired [24 Mar.–12 Apr.]. Coatlicue and Tlálocs. Child sacrifice to Tlálocs to bring rain; end of Xipe rites which sometimes held over a month.

IV Huei Tozoztli (long fast), worship of new corn [13 Apr.–2 May]. Centéotl and Chicomecóatl. Ceremonial bloodletting; decoration of house altars with corn plants; young girls' ceremony with blessing of seed corn.

V Tóxcatl (dry or slippery), rainy season begins [3 May–22 May]. Tezcatlipoca and Huitzilopochtli; god-impersonation ceremonies for either or both great gods (p. 206); scarification of children.

VI Etzalqualiztli (bean porridge), rain desired [23 May–11 June]. Tlálocs. Ceremonial robbing; rain ceremonies; fertility rite, drowning boy and girl in canoe filled with hearts of sacrificial victims.

VII Tecuhilhuitontli (little feast of princes), rain desired [12 June–1 July]. Huixtocíhuatl. Ceremony of salt-workers, who leeched product from lake; women's dance with sacrifice of priestess impersonating goddess.

VIII Hueitecuhilhuitl (great feast of rulers), adoration of ripening corn [2 July–21 July]. Xilonen. Feast for Goddess of Young Corn; eight-day feast; women wear hair loose as sympathetic magic; sacrifice of slave girl impersonating goddess; after sacrifice people can eat new corn.

IX Tlaxochimaco (birth of flowers), first flowering [22 July–10 Aug.]. Huitzilopochtli. Feasts on turkeys and corn-meal cakes in honour of the god; great dance with both sexes taking part and men even touching the women; merchants' feast, honouring their patron god Yacatecuhtli.

X Xocotlhuetzi (fall of the fruits), heat for ripening [11 Aug.–30 Aug.]. Xiuhtecuhtli (Huehuetéotl). Furnace sacrifice (p. 205); competitive climbing of high pole by young men to win special insignia at top.

XI Ochpaniztli (month of brooms), refreshment of Earth Mother [31 Aug.–19 Sept.]. Tlazoltéotl or Teteoinan (Toçi). Sacrifice of woman impersonating Goddess of Ripe Corn; efforts to avoid sorrow by buffoonery, sympathetic magic to avoid rains at harvest; review of warriors and distribution of insignia of rank; drills and mock combats of Eagle and Ocelot Knights.

XII Teotleco (return of the gods), harvest [20 Sept.–9 Oct.]. Tezcatlipoca. Ceremonies honouring the return of the gods to the earth; Tezcatlipoca first to come; two absent, Xiuhtecuhtli, too old to travel, Yacatecuhtli, merchant wandering off beaten track; ceremonial drunkenness and furnace sacrifice.

XIII Tepeilhuitl (feast of the mountains), rain [10 Oct.–29 Oct.]. Tlálocs Ceremonies for mountain rain gods, an aspect of Tlálocs; use of wooden snakes and figurines covered with amaranth paste; sacrifice of four women and a man with subsequent ceremonial cannibalism.

XIV Quecholli [bird, quail(?)], rain [30 Oct.–18 Nov.]. Mixcóatl. Making of weapons; general penance of four days; licensed old people abstain from liquor and husbands from their wives; ceremonial hunt with sacrifice of game and ceremonial feasting on the hill.

XV Panquetzaliztli (feast of the flags), winter solstice [19 Nov.–8 Dec.]. Huitzilopochtli. Festivals honouring War God; mock or staged combats; imprinting of hand impressions by captives.

XVI Atemoztli (fall of the waters), rain [9 Dec.–28 Dec.]. Tlálocs. Vigils and offerings to household gods; winter solstice at time of Conquest; erection of poles with paper streamers coated with rubber.

XVII Tititl (severe weather), season of serenity [29 Dec.–7 Jan.]. Ilamatecuhtli. Sacrifice of woman impersonating goddess; sympathetic magic to bring rain by weeping, through children crying on first day of month and men and children beating women with straw-filled bags to make them cry.

XVIII Izcalli (resuscitation), toasting of corn supply [18 Jan.–6 Feb.]. Xiuhtecuhtli. Ceremonial hunt; killing of captives every four years; killing of birds and arrow sacrifice at Cuauhtitlán.

Nemontemi (five unlucky days) [7 Feb.–11 Feb.].

Year's Day, since they are the third, eighth, thirteenth, and eighteenth days in the list, thus being separated from each other by five numbers. In that thirteen, the quantity of numbers available divides into 365, with a remainder of one, the number of the day increased by one each new year. Thus the years were numerically distinguishable – 1 Rabbit, 2 Reed, 3 House, 4 Flint Knife, 5 Rabbit, and so on, until the thirteen numbers and four day names began to repeat themselves, which occurred after fifty-two (13×4) years. This is the mathematical reason for the Aztec cycle or major time unit, and in the Valley of Mexico they did not go further and distinguish between cycles except indirectly. In consequence there is the same sort of confusion in referring to events as would result were we to designate years within the century without distinguishing the number of centuries before or after Christ. Thus the discovery of America would be recorded as 92 and the Declaration of Independence as 76, and only a detailed knowledge of history would enable us to fix the events in their proper relationship to the fifteenth and eighteenth centuries. (See Plates 62, top left; 63.)

The lag between the calendric and the solar year, for which we compensate by adding a day every four years as the twenty-ninth of February, was difficult to adjust by Aztec standards since so much of the time count hinged on the orderly mathematical sequence of days. Some authorities believe that the Aztecs let the calendar drop behind, others that compensation was made during the unlucky period of five days. A third suggestion interprets the celebration of a feast held every eight years as a sign that a dateless day was introduced, unrecognized in the *tonalpohualli* of the year but honoured with special rites.[7] (See Plate 58, bottom left.)

However the matter of the leap year was settled, the close of one cycle and the beginning of a new one was celebrated with great pomp each year with Two Reed chosen as the first day of each cycle for some ritualistic reason. In the Mixteca-Puebla area the *tonalamatls* show evidence that the priests observed the planet Venus and took note of a Venus Year of 584 days. At the end of two cycles (104 years) there was a tremendous ceremony of great ritualistic significance, for at the same time as the beginning of a Venus count, a solar count, a fifty-two-year cycle, and a *tonalpohualli* all coincided. That four mystical rhythms, affecting such diverse aspects of the universe and the gods that dwelt therein, could meet must have produced great satisfaction and occasioned the utmost rejoicing among people for whom pattern and form had such great significance.[8]

Although the Valley of Mexico Aztecs did not use the Venus count they celebrated the cyclical change with the utmost ceremony. They thought of the change from one cycle to another as the death of one life and the beginning of a new one. The realization that nature could withhold the continuance of their existence endowed the ritual with profound solemnity. The New Fire Ceremony was symbolized by the extinction of the old altar fire, which had burned perpetually for fifty-two years, and the kindling of a fresh one in token of the new grant of life.[9] (See Figure 20).

During the five useless days (*nemontemi*) of the final year the people let their fires go out and destroyed their household furniture. Fasting and lamentation were the order of the day while the populace awaited catastrophe. Pregnant women were shut up in granaries, lest they be changed into wild animals, and children were marched up and down and kept awake, for fear that sleep on that fatal evening would result in their turning into rats.

At sunset the priests, in solemn panoply, representatives of the whole array of the Aztec pantheon, ascended the Hill of the Star, anciently known as Huixachtecatl. This extinct volcanic crater rises abruptly from the Valley floor and is visible from almost every quarter of the Valley of Mexico. From the temple on its summit the priests anxiously scanned the heavens as the night wore on, awaiting the hour when a certain star or stars, Aldebaran or the Pleiades, reached the centre of the heavens and gave the sign that their world would continue.

At the very moment when these stars passed the meridian the priests seized a wooden fire drill and kindled a new fire in the open breast of a victim freshly slain for the purpose. The populace – priests, chiefs, and commoners – thrilled to a great happiness. Runners lit torches from the new fire and rekindled the altars in the temples of every town and hamlet, whence the people bore the flames to their hearths. Like fireflies the darting torchbearers sped through the night, bringing the promise of a new life to every man, woman, and child. With the dawn, more than ever gracious in its fulfilment of a nation's piety, the populace rallied, renovating their temples, refurbishing their houses, and making new utensils for temple and household use. There was feasting on special food, and sacrifice, both by personal bloodletting and the immolation of captives, betokened the measure of popular gratitude.

Another striking ceremony fell on the day Four Earthquake (or Motion), the sign of the present age, and symbolized the passage of the sun through the heavens. At dawn a captive dressed as the Sun God, Tonatiuh, ascended to the platform in front of the temple. Four priests spreadeagled the victim, and a fifth opened his breast to tear out the heart as an offering to the god. The populace then feasted until noon, gashing their ears and parts of their bodies with blades of obsidian. In the afternoon the Eagle and Tiger Knights, votaries of the solar cult, took part in a dance dramatizing the sacred war wherein the sun is slain, to be reborn the following day. The dance culminated in a gladiatorial sacrifice. Selected Eagle and Tiger Knights, armed with real weapons, slew a captive warrior, chosen for his military distinction, who was tethered to a circular stone representing the sun's disc and who defended himself with dummy weapons only.[10] (See Plate 60, top right, bottom.)

A curious type of sacrifice took place in connexion with the worship of the god Xipe, and may be the origin of the arrow sacrifice which is performed in honour of the morning star by the Pawnee of our Western plains. In the Mexican rite the victim was lashed to a scaffold, and priests, using bows or *atl-atls*, shot him to death.[11]

The Aztecs performed a hideous ceremony in honour of the Fire God, Huehueteotl. Prisoners of war and their captors took part in a dance in honour of the god, and the next day the captives ascended to the top of a platform, where a powder, *yauhtli* (Indian hemp), was cast in their faces to anaesthetize them against their ghastly fate. After preparing a great fire, each priest seized a captive and, binding him hand and foot, lifted him on to his back. A macabre dance took place around the burning coals, and one by one they dumped their burdens into the flames. Before death could intervene to put an end to their suffering the priests fished out the captives with large hooks and wrenched the hearts from their blistered bodies.[12]

In contrast to the callous brutality of the fire sacrifice, the ceremony in honour of the god Tezcatlipoca was strikingly dramatic, tinged with the pathos with which we view the taking of a life. The handsomest and bravest prisoner of war was selected a year before his execution. Priests taught him the manners of a ruler, and as he walked about, playing divine melodies upon his flute, he received the homage due Tezcatlipoca himself. A month before the day of sacrifice four lovely girls, dressed as goddesses, became his companions and attended to his every want. On the day of his death he took leave of his weeping consorts to lead a procession in his honour, marked by jubilation and feasting. Then he bade farewell to the glittering cortege and left for a small temple, accompanied by the eight priests who had attended him throughout the year. The priests preceded him up the steps of the temple, and he followed, breaking at each step a flute which he had played in the happy hours of his incarnation. At the top of the platform the priests turned him over the sacrificial block and wrenched out his heart. In deference to his former godhood his body was carried, not ignominiously flung, down the steps; but his head joined the other skulls spitted on the rack beside the temple.[13] (See Plates 56b, 61, top.)

Every one of the great monthly sacrifices had a dramatic significance, and a list of the principal feasts, the gods they honoured, and the month of their occurrence is set forth on Table 14. Several authors have availed themselves of Friar Sahagún's matchless descriptions to set forth the elaborate rituals which we have lightly sampled here. The elements of time, training, and elaborate preparation of costume, it can be readily seen, must have absorbed a large part of the resources of the state. The tentacles of ritual extended throughout all public activities, so that even games and sports were transformed into acts of religious meaning, although the participants undoubtedly derived a great deal of fun from their performance.

The ball game, *tlachtli*, was such a game, played in a court shaped like the capital letter 'I'. Walls extended on either side of the stem of the 'I', and in the middle of each a stone or wooden ring was set vertically, in contrast to the horizontal position of a basketball hoop. The players tried to pass through this ring a hard rubber ball, which they could only strike with their elbows, hips or legs. There must have been some other method of scoring than by goals alone, since these, very naturally, were of rare occurrence – so much so that, in the event of one, players and backers had the right to snatch the wearing apparel of their adversaries. The game was played far and wide, courts having been found from the Republic of Honduras to south-eastern Arizona. It has a special interest for us in that the first description of rubber, so important in our modern economy, was when Oviedo, in the sixteenth century, wrote of the game and the ball used by its players.[14] (See Plate 57, bottom left; Figure 26.)

There were also games of chance which were played with a semi-sacred significance. One such game, *patolli*, utilized a board shaped like a cross, with spaces ruled in the arms, not unlike a version of the old-fashioned parchesi of our childhood. Macuilxochitl, Five Flower, the god of all games, was sometimes portrayed in connexion with players of *patolli* as was Ometochtli.[15]

Another important entertainment involved the erection of a high pole at the top of which a revolving platform was socketed. Men dressed as gods or the birds into which the gods transformed themselves and, fastened by ropes wound around the platform, leaped off into space. As they did so the ropes, unwinding, rotated the platform and gave the effect of flight to the circling performers. Each turn brought the bird-men nearer to the ground, and they were wont to alter their centre of balance and adjust their wings, producing the effect of the rise and fall of soaring birds. This modest application of the principle of gliding must have created a spectacle of colour and beauty. The ceremony is still performed in parts of Mexico, and the Volador, or flying place, of Tenochtitlan was located where the Supreme Court building now stands in Mexico City.[16]

The application of human sacrifice to the most simple ceremonial act of thanksgiving offers a grisly contrast to the spirit in which these rituals were carried out. However, social and religious behaviour are calculated to preserve human existence and ensure man's well-being, regardless of how warped the methods may become. It follows that the idea of sacrificing precious possessions to attain such ends would lead to the offering of the most precious gift of all, human life, since that is what man most ardently strives to keep intact. Thus instances of human sacrifices keep cropping up in the world's religious systems, and we preserve in our own culture the concept of martyrdom, achieved by voluntary or involuntary means, as an act of virtue. The very beautiful example of the Saviour transmutes to the highest spiritual plane this idea of sacrifice for the good of humanity.

The Aztecs did not reach this spiritual level, but the symbolism of their sacrifice has, none the less, its own barbaric beauty. They reasoned that for man to survive, the gods who permit his existence must also live and wax strong. These gods, however, received their best nutriment from the most precious of offerings, the hearts of men. Thus a vicious circle became established which led to sacrifice on an increasing scale. The gods manifested their favour and their strength to the Aztecs by letting them prosper, but the Aztecs, on their part, had to sacrifice hearts to the gods to maintain their good will. A good part of the state's prosperity emanated from military success, so that the most acceptable sacrifices were the hearts of adversaries, which were the hardest to acquire since prisoners could not be taken without military victory. A martial success, on the other hand, could only be achieved through the exercise of divine favour. Thus sacrifice led to war and war back to sacrifice, in an unending series of expanding cycles. The effect that this practice had on foreign affairs we shall describe in the next chapter. (See Plate 60, top.)

War captives were the most esteemed offering, and the braver and higher in rank, the more valuable they were. Slaves were killed for minor ceremonies, and in rare instances women and children were slain in fertility rites to ensure growth in plants by the powers of sympathetic magic. Ceremonial cannibalism was sometimes practised, in the belief that the eater could absorb the virtues of the eaten, but this rite cannot be considered a vice. The letting of one's own blood was another way to ensure divine favour, and people did horrible self-penances such as mutilating themselves with knives or drawing through their tongues a string on which were threaded maguey spines. The higher the social position of the individual and the more he consequently knew of ritualistic observance, the more arduously he performed the fasts, penances, and tortures imposed by the religion. The priests, therefore, were strongly cognizant of their social responsibility and by the rigour of their own lives strove to ensure the well-being of the society.[17] (See Plate 61, bottom right.)

The picture writings of the Aztecs take human sacrifice and penance as a matter of course but seldom indicate the number of victims. Indeed, only one such manuscript records the monthly ceremonies, and a post-Conquest copy of another reveals a sacrifice of twenty thousand people at the dedication of the enlarged great temple of Mexico. The Spanish accounts and those of the educated Indians agree, but whether Christian piety induced exaggeration, and how much, it is difficult to ascertain at this time and age. The Conquistador who counted thousands of skulls on the skull rack in Tenochtitlan apparently confirms these other statements, which the great humanitarian and Indian-lover, Las Casas, discounted in his special pleading for decent treatment of the indigenous population of New Spain.[18]

The priesthood, beside performing these bloodcurdling acts, had other more pacific duties; they also instructed youth in the mysteries of writing and keeping records. Aztec writing was pictographic and was arriving at the stage of syllabic phonetics, which is an important part of the hieroglyphic writing of Egypt. There was no alphabet, but a picture of an animal or thing could be combined with the picture of another animal or thing to give a third meaning in terms of its sound value, much like our method of rebus writing. We could write: 'I can be hospitable', in terms of the sounds given to pictures of an eye, a tin can, a bee, a horse, a hole in the ground, and a table. The Aztecs wrote the name of their capital by drawing stone *tena* from which sprouted a nopal cactus, *nochtli*, or the town Pantepec, by drawing a flag, *pantli*, on a conventionalized hill, *tepec*. Colour, position, puns, and abbreviations all contributed to recording sounds by this means. Conventionalized signs, like footprints to show travel or movement, a shield and club for war, a bundled corpse for death, gave simple connotations of action.[19] (See Figure 25.)

Aztec writing offered no way of making general statements or expressing abstract ideas. Yet the full accounts of historical events, set down after the Conquest in Spanish or Nahuatl, indicate that oral traditions, possibly learnt as a chant or saga, supplemented these ideographic records.

Their numerical system was vigesimal. The Aztecs counted by twenties where we count by tens. They indicated quantities up to twenty by the requisite number of dots, although in the Mixteca this method was abridged by using bars to represent groups of five. The Aztecs used a flag to indicate twenty, repeating it for quantities up to four hundred, while a sign like a fir tree, meaning numerous as hairs, signified four hundred (20×20). The next unit, eight thousand ($20 \times 20 \times 20$),

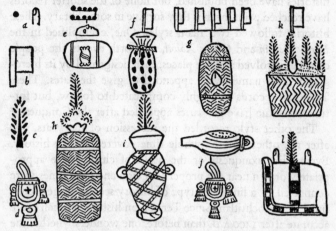

Fig. 25. Aztec numbers and methods of enumeration

(*a*) one, a dot or finger. (*b*) twenty, a flag. (*c*) four hundred, a sign denoting hairs. (*d*) eight thousand, a bag. (*e*) ten masks of precious stone. (*f*) twenty bags of cochineal dye. (*g*) one hundred bags of cacao. (*h*) four hundred bales of cotton. (*i*) four hundred jars of honey of tuna. (*j*) eight thousand leaf-bundles of copal gum. (*k*) twenty baskets each containing one thousand six hundred ground cacao nibs. (*l*) four hundred and two cotton blankets of this type.

was indicated by a bag, referring to the almost innumerable contents of a sack of cacao beans. (See Figure 25.)

A post-Conquest manuscript shows devices that may not have been of native origin but European adaptations of the Aztec system. For example, fractions are shown by blacking in segments of a quarter, a half, or three quarters of a disc. Similarly fives and multiples of five are indicated by colouring the requisite spaces in the flag of the sign for twenty, and hundreds by showing the proportionate lines in the four-hundred symbol.[20]

Aztec histories consisted of annals of ancient times, contemporary events, year counts, accounts compiled yearly, specific records for each year, books of each day, and day-by-day counts or diaries.[21] Some of the ancient and contemporary histories have been published, but none of the shorter records have reached print, even if they survive in some library. These histories followed two main styles. One, exemplified in the *Mapa Tlotzin* and *Codex Xolotl*, sets forth events, the people or tribes involved and the places, each designated by its hiero-glyph. Year names were appended to give the dates. These Texcocan records are highly complicated to follow, but for-tunately some have glossaries appended after the Conquest.[22]

The other style recorded the succession of the years, one after the other, for the whole time covered by the history. Events, like conquests or the death of chiefs, were appro-priately drawn near the proper year sign and sometimes were connected by a line. This type of history seemed largely con-fined to Tenochtitlan. Since Tenochcan history is much more accurate after 1400 A.D. than before, one wonders whether the destruction of the books, ordered by Itzcoatl, did not really pave the way for a new style of writing.[23] (See Plates 62, top; 63.)

In addition to the histories and the sacred almanacs tribute records were kept. These are most useful to the modern stu-dent, for the names of the towns are inscribed in one column, while the rest of the page records the amount of gold, orna-ments, or cloth that was paid in as tribute. Since the geogra-phical location of most of these towns is known, the chief products of each area can be determined. Other records showed lines of descent, lands occupied, and other data essen-tial to family economics.[24] (See Plates 62, bottom right; 64.)

Fortunately, after the Conquest the Spaniards utilized the native methods of writing as well as their own in civil records, such as tax rolls, lawsuits, and the like, so that the Indians could understand the Spanish legal code and present their complaints.[25] Friar Nicolas Tester even made an attempt to shift the picture writing over to syllabic writing – the effect of the Lord's Prayer in Aztec glyphs is startling.[26] This was too cumbersome a plan and was soon abandoned for the recording of Nahuatl words in Roman characters. However, it is due to this usage of Aztec pictographs that so much survives of the records, many of which, with their oral accompaniment, were copied into Roman characters both in Spanish and Nahuatl. From these we derive such knowledge as we have of Aztec history and customs. (See Plate 42b.)

The drawback of picture writing is its rigidity and its uselessness for the expression of abstract ideas. The cyclical count created great confusion as to the particular cycle in which an event took place. Exact and careful drawing was essential for the glyphs, and a slurred line might result in a totally different reading. However, the worst feature of Aztec history is its provincialism, for the scribes saw things only in terms of their own group and took no heed of internal events in other communities. The picture writings show how communal interests extended vertically, as it were, from the people to the pantheon. There is no reflection of a horizontal interest outward to the lives and occupations of other peoples. The attitude of the Aztec communities to foreign affairs merits a chapter in itself.

Chapter 13   Foreign Affairs and War

The relationships of Aztec communities to each
other in peace and war, the nature of the Aztec
domain and methods of military organization
and warfare

The community or group was the centre of the political and
economic life of theAztecs. Existence depended on the favour
of the gods, who participated directly in the people's fortunes,
so that the degree of elaboration of the ceremonial structures
was an accurate gauge of the state's prosperity. A man's
position in the civil life of the community had a corresponding
level in the hierarchy, since conspicuous fulfilment of civil
obligations entailed an equal attainment in piety and observance of ritual. The basic design for living was a communal
agriculture. The early tribal existence had sought to achieve
this pattern by avoiding other peoples and finding new land
to settle. There is an essential affinity between agriculture and
political isolation, just as commerce and manufacture require
successively broader political contacts and more complicated
political structure.[1]

In the early history of the Valley of Mexico there appears to
have been a series of small isolated settlements which carried
on a vague process of exchange. The civilization of Teotihuacan seems to have attained uniform development over a
wide area spread by a population which gradually filled up
unoccupied territory. There was little to suggest war or conquest at first. There seems rather to have been a loosely knit
group of civilizations held together by religious and cultural
ties and the coming and going of merchants. With the establishment of the Toltec empire the character of the Valley was
transformed. Formerly, groups had slowly grown in numbers until dense occupation of a previously unpopulated
territory took place. But in the Chichimec period men were

driven from their home territories by various factors, of which overpopulation may have been one, vague unrest another, and set out in search of new land. While the goal of each group of immigrants may well have been to settle and farm in peaceful isolation, the very process of movement must have brought war and consequent readjustments in the social organization.

Throughout Chichimec times and into the Aztec period as well, the political unit was a group, dwelling in its own village or city, supported by its own land. Even though such a group might grow to thousands of members, the village become transformed into a city-state, and the communal lands cease to support the population, no real shift in political organization took place. No leader developed the concept of empire so successfully applied by the Incas of Peru. The group experience of the Indians was to colonize new land but, with perhaps the sole exception of Peru, never to incorporate, through conquest, weaker communities into their own state.

However, when the group became too unwieldy to migrate *en masse*, an adjustment had to be made between population and food supply. One method was for part of the population to break away and join another community whose economic resources were relatively unexploited. As an illustration we have the case of the Chimalpanecs and the Culhuas, who joined the nascent community of Texcoco to the vast benefit of its material and intellectual culture.[2] (See Figures 20, 24.)

The more usual means of adjusting food supply to population was the exaction of tribute from richer and weaker neighbours. Quinatzin of Texcoco instituted the system first in the northern Valley in the early fourteenth century, and it is an interesting point to speculate as to whether or not the Chimalpanec immigrants suggested this as a practice found successful in their homeland. Quinatzin, by force of arms or by persuasion, induced a number of towns to turn over to him supplies of various sorts. The local chiefs recognized him as an overlord but maintained a complete political independence. He, in turn, granted the vassal chiefs the full measure of his military support. Yet these vassals had no sense of loyalty and were quite ready to revolt or transfer their allegiance to a stronger suzerain.[3] (See Plate 41, top.)

When Tezozomoc of Azcapotzalco saw his tribe develop to the point where it had to expand he found the southern Valley overpopulated, so that he had to challenge the power of Texcoco. His first move was to create disaffection in the vassal states, after which he could move against his rivals with good hope of military success. Yet so light was Tezozomoc's tenure of control that it was relatively easy for the conquered peoples to combine later and wreck his domination.

Alliances like that formed by Texcoco, Tenochtitlan, and Tacuba were so very rare that much is made of this combination as an example of the excellence of Aztec statecraft. It would seem that the division of spoils, two parts each to the larger states, and one part to Tlacopan, was in force only for that campaign. Later Texcoco and Tenochtitlan undertook wars for their mutual advantage, but there was constant intrigue in the hope that one of the two could overcome the other and derive the full benefits of the booty taken. By the mid-fifteenth century both Tenochtitlan and Texcoco had grown to the point where they had to have additional supplies or else starve, so, because of this common necessity, the alliance endured fairly well.[4]

Despite their common background of language, thought, religion, custom, and material culture, the Aztecs had no sense of unity. Tenochtitlan and Tlaltelolco, both of which are within the city limits of modern Mexico, existed side by side in complete independence for many years; not until 1473 did the Tenochcas make up their minds to conquer their neighbours. Each town and hamlet was sufficient unto itself, and its members felt no larger loyalty. In modern Teotihuacan this feeling still persists, and the members of one *barrio*, or ward, look upon those of the adjacent one as a congregation of the most horrible criminals. Not even the Spanish siege of Mexico brought unity to the Aztecs, and the Texcocans blithely joined the invaders to exterminate their former ally Tenochtitlan.

Although community was potentially hostile to community, individuals could move freely about the countryside. Trade in simple commodities was carried on extensively from early Pre-classic times. In the Aztec period the travelling merchants became a special class, and their security of body and property, preserved at first for the advantages which each town could derive from their wares, was guaranteed by the force of Aztec arms.[5] Pilgrims going to worship at special shrines had free and unmolested passage; and a suggestion that such journeys were made in the distant past is given by the Pre-classic figurines of foreign origin. One site especially, Tetelpan, produced so great a variety of idols from such a wide area that it must have been an important religious centre in Pre-classic times. However, neither trade nor religion broke down the sense of communal and political independence in Central Mexico. (See Plate 35; Figure 25.)

Foreign relations centred round war, which, we have seen, was an important part of Aztec economy and religion. The same confusion of motives that we find in our modern culture affected the reasons for military action. We wage war for economic, territorial, and political advantages and, while condemning the practice in our adversaries, justify our own participation by saying that we are fighting for freedom, to liberate someone, to extend civilization, or to ensure peace. Soldiers on our own side are brave and attain glory, preserve our social virtues, and sacrifice themselves for the public well-being. Those on the other side are aggressors, agents of evil, and cowardly knaves. The Aztecs made war for defence, revenge, and economic motives, which were inextricably confused with the need for the sacrificial victims requisite for proper adoration of their gods. Thus in warfare the great aim was to take captives, but behind this religious goal lurked the less holy urges of political and economic expediency.

The captive himself attained social status, since he went to a special warrior's heaven. A redoubtable Tlaxcalan chief, named Tlahuicol, was singled out for sacrifice to the sun and fought so successfully with his dummy weapons that he killed some of his adversaries and wounded a number of the others. He was pardoned and offered a chieftaincy in the Tenochcan army. Tlahuicol, however, rejected his pardon and gladly underwent sacrifice for the greater honour and glory in that death. This story illustrates the attitude of the individual warrior, which is not unlike that of the medieval knight or career soldier in our own culture.[6]

The Aztec reasons for fighting and their social and moral sanctions for war were not so very different from our own, except that we have many more, due to our superior rationalizations. The Aztec military technique, however, was definitely inferior, since it was not so completely developed a social tool as it is in our own culture. The basic organization of the army required the participation of every able-bodied man under the direction of the war chief. However, as Aztec society grew more intricate and greater numbers of warriors took the field, the military structure became more rigid.

The unit of organization was an aggregation of twenty men, several of which were combined into larger bodies of two to four hundred, roughly corresponding to our platoons and companies. Special detachments of from four to six men, who did scouting and raiding, operated much as do the squads of our own military system. The clan commander marshalled the larger bodies, much as a colonel handles his regiment. The clan troops were banded together in four divisions under the heads of the four municipal quarters, and the tribal war chiefs had the supreme command. In a very numerous army the troops from a given quarter, or *barrio*, were sometimes divided into brigades, composed of the forces from two or three clans.[7]

The high tribal officers, the war chief, the chiefs of the quarters, and the clan chiefs commanded the larger bodies. The ordinary chiefs and members of the warrior orders, the Knights of the Eagle and the Tiger and of a third infrequently mentioned order, the Arrow, according to their particular ability, took over the lesser units. In other words, the executive officials of the community in peacetime became its military officers in time of war. There was no distinction made between the civil and military offices, since the group operated as an entity in both peace and war, and standing armies did not exist. (See Plate 34, bottom left.)

The soldiers were the able-bodied men of the community. The *telpuchcalli*, houses of youth, through which boys passed at the age of fifteen for formal instruction in the duties of manhood, taught them the usage of different weapons. Drill, in the sense of the accurate movements of modern troops, did not exist, but the great monthly ceremonies called for military demonstrations in which warriors showed their abilities and performed sham manoeuvres. Each recruit followed an experienced warrior in battle, much as a medieval squire served an apprenticeship to a knight in full standing.

The chief offensive arms were wooden clubs, edged with sharp blades of obsidian, and the javelin, hurled by means of the *atl-atl*. Bows and arrows were used, but the heavier javelins were preferred for the close fighting of Aztec warfare. Slings and spears were weapons favoured by some. For defensive armour shields of wickerwork covered with hide were most commonly in use, and some were elaborately painted or covered with feathers. The Aztecs also developed a body armour of quilted cotton, soaked in brine, which covered the whole body like an old-fashioned union suit. This was so effective a protection against clubs and missiles that the

Spaniards rapidly adopted it, extolling it as cooler and lighter than steel armour.[8] Some warriors wore wooden helmets, which were elaborately carved to represent the insignia of the military orders. These had decorative rather than defensive values and added to the richness of costumes worn by the maturer warriors. A warrior had the right to elaborate his dress in accordance with his prowess, and the great chiefs wore attached to their backs immense frames covered with feathers. Tribes, and even clans, wore special insignia, so that friend could be distinguished from foe and chief from common warrior. The term uniform could hardly be used, since the rich variety and indulgence in individual fancy produced a kaleidoscopic effect in the motley array of bright colours and strange forms.[9]

To supply these forces was a very considerable task. Each quarter of the town had its *tlacochcalco*, or house of darts, an arsenal where the military supplies were stored. This was situated near the chief temple, the lofty sides of which made it a natural strong point. At a call to arms the clan leaders could rapidly assemble their men and equip them at these rallying points, which were also centres of the religious and social life of the community.[10]

An offensive campaign was a more serious undertaking. Having no beasts of burden, the warriors had to carry their own food with them. Due to the governmental system, wherein each town was independent, the armies did not dare live off the country for fear of inciting revolt and also because most communities lacked the food to sustain a large body of men. Thus, prior to a war, negotiations had to be made whereby supplies could be concentrated and allies brought together at a point as near as possible to the zone of attack. Usually a single battle decided the issue, since the attacking force could not maintain itself in the field for more than a very few days. The calculations necessary to fight a war two or three hundred miles away in Oaxaca, say, were highly complex, and much of the Aztec force on such a campaign must have been composed of local tribesmen, stiffened with a *garde d'élite* of Tenochcas and Texcocans.

Owing to this difficulty in respect to transport, siege operations were virtually impossible, so that formal fortifications were rare. Some towns were built in very strategic locations, high on a mountainside or in the bend of a river, having access restricted to a narrow neck of land. Tenochtitlan, owing to its situation on the lake, was a natural fort. The causeways were penetrated by canals at intervals, so that removal of the portable bridges created natural barriers. The flat rooftops offered good points from which to harry the enemy in the street below, and the many temples were strong points difficult to reduce. (See Plate 36, top.)

Miles of defensive walls surrounded a site in Tlaxcala, where a ditch backed by a wall enclosed an area of several square miles. At Huexotla, a fief of Texcoco, a wall at least fifteen feet high still exists and must have had a strong defensive value, although its ostensible purpose was to enclose the area about the main temple. Xochicalco is situated on a high hill which was intensively terraced, and it was further strengthened by a wide ditch cut through the point of easiest access. Sometimes a site was chosen between two ravines which made impassable obstacles to an attacking force. However, while defensive *purposes* were often taken into account in building towns, strictly defensive *works*, in the nature of fortifications, were seldom undertaken.[11]

Open fighting, the difficulty of keeping up extended campaigns, and the informal character of the military force were factors which stultified the development of tactics or strategy. In battle the howling mob which represented the collective strength of one group tried to rout the yelling horde of their adversary, and the first to run lost the battle. Captives were taken, tribute imposed, the temple burned, and the defeated group was then left alone again.

To attain victory more easily surprise attacks, sometimes implemented by a little treachery, were instituted. However, the cumbrous process of getting an army on to the field of battle usually prevented this favoured method of warfare. More often the Tenochcas and their allies would feint with a screen of warriors, who would be easily repulsed in a pretended rout. The main body would wait in a place of concealment until the pursuing enemy came into view, whereupon they would charge out and demolish them. Losses were chiefly felt in the number of captives taken, since these short hand-to-hand combats were not very damaging to the manpower of either side. The capture of a chief or the recognition of a sign of evil portent was sufficient to demoralize an army and, despite their bravery and constant experience in warfare of this type, the Aztecs were little fitted to resist soldiers trained in European techniques.

There was rather more opportunity for strategy than for battle tactics. Considerable planning, as we have said, was necessary to move troops upon the field of battle. The Aztecs won campaigns in Oaxaca, Puebla, western Mexico, and along the Vera Cruz coast, as far north as Tamaulipas. Having to move step by step and to intimidate or win over town after town, they needed patience and knowledge of geographical and political conditions. One reason for the honour in which merchants were held was the information of this character which they could furnish from their travels.

The triple alliance was a typical example of Aztec strategy. Nezahualcoyotl wanted to restore the hegemony of Texcoco and destroy Tezozomoc's Tepanec power, the centre of which was Azcapotzalco. The two towns were separated by the Lake of Mexico. To move troops overland would have required several days; to move them across the lake in canoes would have meant having a landing base on the western shore. Nezahualcoyotl, therefore, induced Tlacopan and Tenochtitlan, which were at the back door of Azcapotzalco and tributary to it as well, to declare war. Thus he had a base at which to land his canoes filled with troops, and while his allies engaged the enemy strongly in this quarter, the Texcocan chief had time to bring reinforcements round the lakes by the overland route to attack another point.

The town of Chiconauhtla offers another example of these simple strategic ideas. This settlement dominated the straits through which the northern lakes of Zumpango and Xaltocan empty into Lake Texcoco. The people here could destroy any force in canoes moving east against Texcoco or west against Azcapotzalco. Their forces also could make a flank attack on land armies skirting the lakes against either of those two objectives. Early in the thirteenth century Chiconauhtla became a fief of Texcoco and participated, as a sort of guardian of the western marches, in campaigns against rebellious western peoples and in the great war with Tezozomoc. Later it seems to have become part of the Tenochtitlan chain of vassal towns, and its chief had the honour of sharing a royal apartment in Montezuma's palace with the rulers of far more important city-states. To confirm this documentary evidence excavation of the site reveals, in the quantity and quality of the material culture surviving, evidence of participation in trade and booty far in excess of the apparent size and importance of the town.[12] (See map, page 6; Plates 40, top; 41, top; 42a.)

The purely economic and military aspects of war are as crude, when judged by our modern technical standards, as the rest of the purely mechanical aspects of Aztec life. On the other hand, the ritualistic conception of war as the earthly re-enactment of the titanic struggle between opposing forces in nature has a quality almost sublime. The political and economic frictions that brought about conflict were welcomed by the warriors as an opportunity to vibrate to the deep rhythms of nature, rhythms which met in a celestial antiphony in the Sacred War which the Sun fights each day as he, by his own death and sacrifice, ensures the life of man.

The War of Flowers was undertaken to satisfy this yearning when no active campaign was in progress. In this incongruously named ceremonial combat the best warriors from several states met in a very real battle, so that feats of arms could be accomplished and captives taken to satisfy the hunger of the gods. One famous War of Flowers was repeated for several years, and the cream of the fighting men of Texcoco, Tenochtitlan, and Tlacopan vied with the might of Cholula, Huexotcingo and Tlaxcala. If a warrior were captured he met the most glorious of deaths in direct sacrifice to the Sun. If he lived he gained renown. If he were slain, he was cremated, an honour reserved only for fighting men, and passed on to the special heaven where warriors dwell.[13]

Such warfare had no place in a conflict with Europeans, but, when reduced to fighting for their bare lives against the Spaniards, the Aztecs put up one of the most desperate defences in history. It was the last sacrifice, in which Aztec civilization offered up its very existence in an effort to survive. Aztec culture achieved, with Stone Age tools, a civilization patterned to balance the life of man against the dimly perceived forces of the universe. Its downfall was inevitable when confronted with that inexorable European world of steel, objective reasoning, and a religion adjusted to meet such totally different concepts as the demands of the powerful and the needs of the weak.

We cannot tell what Aztec civilization might have become. Like all the nations of the past, and of the present too, which have flourished and ultimately withered in death, the Aztecs nurtured within themselves the seeds of their own destruction. But before we turn from their remote splendour to the preoccupations of our modern life let us catch two last glimpses of Aztec civilization: one of the city of Tenochtitlan as the Spaniards first saw it, the other of the Aztecs in their ultimate war, profane and deadly on this final occasion.

What the Spaniards saw when they entered this
great Aztec Capital

The history of the Aztecs and their forebears is the most complete record we have of the growth of any Indian civilization.
Their conquest was the greatest feat in the European occupation of the American continent. The Aztecs were at their
zenith in 1519, when Cortés and his four hundred men first
landed, and a description of Tenochtitlan, taken from the
contemporary records of the conquerors themselves, will
show us something of the external character of Indian civilization in America.[1]

Bernard Díaz del Castillo, who left the most personal
record of the Spanish Conquest, tells how his comrade-in-
arms on first beholding Tenochtitlan, the ancient Mexico
City, exclaimed, 'It is like the enchantments they tell of in the
legend of Amadis! Are not the things we see a dream?'

This is lyric language from hard-bitten men-at-arms, whose
chief avocations, while engaged in converting the heathen,
lay in acquiring booty and enjoying the charms of dusky
Dulcineas. Yet in contrast to the drab towns and tawny hills
of Spain, Tenochtitlan must have appeared a paradise, for its
green gardens and white buildings were set in the midst of
blue lakes, ringed by lofty mountains. 'Gazing on such wonderful sights,' wrote Bernal Díaz, 'we did not know what to
say or whether what appeared before us was real, for on one
side in the land there were great cities and in the lake ever so
many more, and the lake itself was crowded with canoes, and
in the causeway were many bridges at intervals, and in front
of us stood the great City of Mexico, and we ... we did not
even number four hundred soldiers.'[2]

Although socially and governmentally Tenochtitlan was

distinctly Mesoamerican, outwardly it appeared the capital city of an Old World empire. A bird's-eye view would have revealed an oval island connected with the mainland by three causeways which converged at the centre of the city. These roads were cut by waterways over which removable bridges extended. The edges of the island were fringed by the green of the 'floating gardens', while at the centre the shiny white of the houses predominated, and the verdure was reduced to tiny green squares in the patio gardens. Thrust above the quadrate masses of the rooftops loomed the various clan temples, each set on its platform in the form of a truncated pyramid. The city had few streets or open spaces but was gridded with canals crossed by portable bridges. The two principal plazas were those of the Temple of Tlaltelolco and of the religious centre of Tenochtitlan proper, open spaces which gave a welcome relief from the pyramids and official palaces clustered about them. There must have been a curiously living quality about this grouping, the temples seeming to ride like horsemen among the serrated ranks of the houses. (See Plate 36, top.)

Were a visitor to traverse Tenochtitlan from south to north, he would have been struck by the rich variety of sights. Approaching along the causeway, the traveller of that time passed first between expanses of open water. Then gradually tiny islands of green appeared, made of masses of mud dredged up from the bottom of the shallow lake and held in place by wickerwork. White-clad farmers dexterously poled their tiny dugouts through the maze as they went about the cultivation of their gardens. These irregular islets merged gradually into a more orderly grouping where the accumulation of soil had become stabilized as the roots, striking downward, had established anchorage in the lake bottom and created solid ground. This artificially made land reduced the open water of the lake to mere canals. (See Plate 36, bottom.)

Save for the broad causeways, there were few roads; and

along the canals the traveller saw, in increasing numbers, boat-loads of produce headed towards the city. Here and there among the green of the crops and trees he caught glimpses of thatched roofs and wattled walls, the huts of the farmers. Then adobe walls of more substantial dwellings began to encroach on the gardens, and the waters of the lake shrank to a canal following the roadway. The adobe walls gave way to the fronts of more pretentious houses plastered white or washed with powdered pumice, a dull, rich red. Now the visitor could realize how the city expanded through the successive creation of artificial islands which bore first a crop, then a modest hut, and finally became integral with the masonry of the city proper.

The causeway had now changed from a simple means of communication into a principal street with all its social complexity. Since canals took the place of roads, space for a saunter was so rare that the causeways were as much recreation grounds as arteries of traffic. Thus people out to see the sights, people on errands, people on their way to the myriad functions of religious import, swallowed up the long lines of trotting carriers who, bowed under their burdens, went to the city with produce and tribute or left with goods for barter. Not a wheel turned nor pack animal neighed; transport was on the backs of men or in the bottoms of boats.

Outside the city limits the monotony of ant-like columns of laden folk had been but rarely relieved by the passage of a civil functionary, all pomp and feathers, or by a stern merchant with a handful of fighting men, followed by a chain of apprentices, showing the whites of their eyes as they peered from under the press of their headbands. Now could be seen clan leaders, wearing rich mantles and sniffing flowers as they watched the milling crowd, and black-robed priests whose ears were shredded and whose hair was matted with the blood of self-inflicted penance. There was little sound, little hurry, save for the carriers trotting to reach relief from their burdens. There was an intense vitality, none the less; that of a multitude of units participating in complex action, knowing each its allotted part but never the substance of the whole. (See Plates 33–5.)

A glance into the doorway of a house gave welcome relief from the cold-blooded, almost insect-like quality of life outside. A shaded patio was flanked by buildings whose interiors were cool and spacious. Mats and straw cushions on the polished red of the cement floor welcomed the visitor to repose, while the rhythmic clap of hands and the scrape of stone on stone told that tortillas were being made and corn meal ground in a kitchen at the back. Seated in a corner, an elderly man was talking to two small boys, whose serious faces showed that, already conscious of their participation in the common life, they heeded their uncle's precepts as to conduct befitting boys and men. A fat little girl squatting in the doorway vainly tried to imitate with her stubby fingers and toy implements the graceful movements of her mother as she produced fine threads by the cunning manipulation of her spindle. Lolling on a cushion, a young man idly smoked a cigarette in a cane holder as he picked throughtfully at the scarcely healed lobe of his ear, tattered by penitential bloodletting with cactus spine and obsidian blade.

A fiesta was going on in another house, and one heard the rich vibration of wooden drums and the high squeal of reed flutes. The patio was full of people, gay in the bright colours of their holiday clothes, and the air was heavy with the cloying scent of lilies. The sharp smells of rich sauces cunningly mixed from many peppers embroidered this odour, and occasionally a light breeze wafted the cool, mystic scent of incense. Somebody was celebrating his birthday, since in the background one saw a painted figure adorned with amate paper, representing the god who presided over that event. A little apart from the feasters, who partook of their entertainment with dignified pleasure, was a group of old men whose clownish gestures and burlesque solemnity could be easily associated with the cups of pulque that a slave was industriously filling for them. Not for nothing had these elders passed through the rigid self-denial of young manhood; they were permitted alcoholic indulgence in their old age whenever a feast came to pass. A last backward glance revealed the musicians, garlanded with flowers, blowing their flutes and conch shells, while one man beat the head of a cylindrical drum and another the wooden tongues in the side of the two-toned *teponaztli*.

Farther up the street the priests seemed to increase in number. More individuals wore the trappings of high office, such as nodding panaches of quetzel plumes and cloaks, the designs of which were worked in feathers like the personal insignia on their circular shields. Evidently the visitor was near the centre of the town, and presently the causeway ended in a great open square, where the temples rose above the majestic planes of their pyramidal foundations. In the hard bright light of early afternoon, heat waves joined the smoke of incense in rendering indistinct and unearthly the outlines of the temples.

The short black shadows suggested unspeakable things. Was it imagination or reality, that sickening smell of a filthy butcher shop, that hung in the air in revolting contrast to the immaculate pavement of the temple courtyard? Imagination is too personal and egocentric a sensation for an Indian community, and the great block of the skull rack gave an answer only too firmly founded on fact. Thousands of skulls threaded on poles, were piled up in orderly symmetry, and the black cavities of their orbits and nasal apertures suggested the marks on infernal dice. Undisturbed by this monument to human sacrifice, a few young men were practising in a ball court near by. They thrust at a solid rubber ball with agile hips and elbows, in an effort to drive it through the rings set transversely into the long side walls of the court.

A circular stone placed a short distance away was the scene of a most cruel game. Here, on certain ceremonial days a tethered captive was forced to defend himself with a wooden club against the onslaught of an adversary whose weapon was set with razor-sharp obsidian blades. Usually he was killed in the most honourable of deaths, that of sacrificial victim to the Sun God, Tonatiuh, but sometimes he would resist so successfully that he gained a pardon. Other disc-shaped stones were placed about the plaza. One, thirteen feet in diameter, was set vertically on a special platform. Carved with a consummate mastery of design, it represented the symbolic history of the world. Another disc, set flat, was hollowed in the centre so that hearts wrung from war captives might be burned to nourish the great gods. This was carved on its surface and edge to commemorate the many conquests of War Chief Tizoc, who was shown dressed as a god, with his captives before him.

In another part of the plaza a sacrifice was to be made. Before a small temple dedicated to one of the myriad Aztec gods a group was gathered, some in the gay panoply of merchants and others wearing the sinister black of the priesthood. A tightly pinioned slave stood in their midst and looked unseeingly before him, resignation, not fear, on his face. The priests rushed him up the steep steps of the temple, followed by the merchants at a more leisurely pace. Two priests seized the slave by either arm, forcing him backwards, while two others pulled his legs from under him until his body curved, belly upwards, over the altar. A fifth priest ploughed his flint knife in a long sweep from the breastbone to the base of the stomach and, reaching into the aperture, with a dexterous twist tore out the heart. This he burned, while it was still throbbing, in a carved stone vase, while the merchants, swinging long ladles of smoking incense, chanted their thanks for a safe and profitable excursion into the hot country. (See Plate 60.)

230

Paying only the most cursory attention to this pious little scene, knots of chiefs were converging on a large building at a corner of the plaza. The war chief, Montezuma, was planning an attack on a neighbouring town, remiss in its tribute payment, so there must be a gathering of clan leaders to prepare for war. Adorned with helmets like the heads of jaguars, eagles, and wolves, girt with armour of quilted cotton brocaded in many colours or embroidered with feathers, their faces set with nose and lip ornaments of jade and gold, these fierce-visaged chiefs passed proudly through the door, but in an anteroom to the council chamber they stripped off their ornaments. Then bareheaded and barefooted, with downcast eyes, they made their way to the throne, where sat the slim figure of Montezuma, simply dressed but for the gold crown and jade earrings of his exalted office. (See Plate 33a.)

The austerity of the council chamber was not borne out by Montezuma's other apartments, which contained all the appurtenances of a sybaritic potentate. The war chief's two wives and his many concubines occupied magnificent quarters. Kitchens and storehouses were spread over another great space, for not only were there some three hundred guests served at each meal but also a thousand guards and attendants. In contrast to the profusion within, outside the kitchen door squatted patiently a threadbare group of countrymen from whose carrying bags swayed the mottled heads of the trussed turkeys which they had brought as offerings for the royal larder.

Other rooms in Montezuma's palace contained the tribal treasure, composed of the tribute wrung from many towns. Gold, jade, rich feather mantles, baskets of produce, were heaped in abundance. Clerks were listing the goods in picture writing to see that each subject town had fulfilled its quota, or else were calculating the share that should be turned over to the various clan stewards. Another patio presented a more animated scene. Here acrobats were practising their feats, and poor warped dwarfs were composing grosser contortions to win a chiefly smile. In another set of buildings was housed the zoo, where serpents undulated sluggishly and where, from behind wooden bars, peered the greedy, yellow eyes of jaguars and ocelots. In a side room a human arm projecting from a basket of raw meat showed how the bodies of some sacrificial victims were utilized.

The highway to Tlaltelolco extended north from this great plaza, which even today is the centre of the city. This wide road, with a canal beside it, was filled with the same indecisive multitude that thronged the southern artery. The setting sun had brought people out on their rooftops. Some leaned over parapets to watch the crowd below, while idlers, squatting in a shaded bit of the street, took equal interest in the slow movements of the householders above them.

A path and a canal, debouching into the main avenue, led to a small square, in the centre of which loomed a pyramid. From the patio of an adjacent building shrill cries arose and the dull clash of wooden instruments. Within, a number of boys were receiving instruction in the manual of arms. Each equipped with a small buckler and a flat wooden club, they learned the art of cut and parry under the scornful eye of a warrior. They dealt and received hard blows, but the clubs were not toothed with wedges of obsidian, the volcanic glass that made hand-to-hand combat so vicious in war. Another group was practising with the *atl-atl*, or throwing stick. The marksman laid his spear along a narrow wooden trough with a hook at the farther end, the nearer end being grasped in the hand. By lengthening the arm in this way it was possible to give a great propulsive force to the spear.

On the other side of the plaza the boys in the religious-training school presented a less animated scene. Their little legs and faces lacerated by maguey spines, their bodies thin from fasts and penance and their eyes dulled by the monotony of self-denial, these children were chanting strophes from a ritualistic chant. Their preceptor, who led the singing, showed by his own scarred and emaciated body that the propitiation of the gods was a relentless and never-ending task. Priest, chief, warrior, or husband, every Aztec, from boyhood on, spent much of his life either in a kind of beseeching penance, to ensure his future, or in a state of grateful atonement for not having had a worse past. The Aztecs lived on intimate if uncomfortable terms with the supernatural powers.

Another aspect of this lack of individualism was to be seen in the *tecpan* or clan building. Here elders of the clan were arranging the affairs of the tribal unit, twenty of which made up the city-state of Tenochtitlan. One old man peered over picture maps as he adjusted a question of land tenure between two contesting families and made his final judgement on the basis of how much land each family could cultivate by its own efforts. Another elder distributed pottery vessels, given up as tribute by a town across the mountains, to some of the poorer members of the community. None of these people, litigants or applicants, bestowed more than occasional glances into the back courtyard, where an adulterer was being stoned to death by members of the affronted family. Urban existence contained too many interests and life was too cheap for them to view as an excitement the inevitable result of wrong-doing.

Each of the twenty tribal divisions regulated its own affairs. The great plaza where Montezuma had his palace and where all the gods were worshipped in many temples was for the use of all the clans together; and was the civic centre for the sixty thousand households of Tenochtitlan. Yet in spite of the importance of this centre of religion and government, the great plaza of Tlaltelolco near the northern edge of the islands was almost as striking. Once a Mexican tribe acknowledged the sway of another power it was supposed to furnish fighting men and tribute, but its government and economics were seldom modified.

Thus the recently conquered Tlaltelolco had a communal centre as majestic as that of Tenochtitlan. It seemed more dramatic to Spanish eyes because its great temple to the War God, Huitzilopochtli, was thrust into prominence by the wide spread of the market-place, while in Tenochtitlan the great buildings were so close together it was hard to gain an impression of their size.

The market-place of Tlaltelolco consisted of a large area of polished pavement, bordered by arcades which sheltered many of the merchants. At one edge a basin opened out from the canal beside the northern causeway, where boats bringing goods and produce could find an anchorage. Each kind of product was concentrated in a special place. Thus one section was completely devoted to vegetables, and compactly squatting women sat watching their goods, arranged before them in symmetrical heaps on woven mats. In another section cotton mantles were being sold, some spread to show the full design and others neatly folded. Elsewhere was a row of vendors of implements and tools, such as obsidian blades, carved and burnished pottery, spindle, whorls, deerhorn awls, bone bodkins, and a few copper axes and needles. A brilliant mass of colour characterized the booths of the feather salesmen. Some sold merely bunches of plumes, the lovely green of the quetzal or trogon, and the multi-coloured plumage of parrots. At the other stands feather cloaks, mats, and shields gave evidence of charming fancy in their design and patient toil in their execution. (See Plates 37, 38.)

Jewellers displayed jade ornaments and gold worked into precious rings of filigree or massive beaten gorgets. It was the jade, however, that caught the envious eye and was produced with furtive circumspection as a material of great price. Other merchants sold ornaments of shell, and the pinks, whites, and subtle mottled browns of sea-shells contrasted with the rich dark sheen of tortoise carapaces. At one booth a rich warrior earnestly bargained with the proprietor for an exquisite pair of earplugs, cunningly inlaid with a mosaic of turquoise and mother-of-pearl.

The smiling whispers and admiring glances of the crowd at the jeweller's abruptly changed in the slave quarters to appraising stares. Some of the chattels wore wooden collars, and their brutish faces had a hopeless expression. These had sunk to servitude long ago as a result of crime or of capture in war. Others were thin and emaciated but did not wear the collar of bondage. They had met with misfortune and were selling themselves for the first time to ensure food and shelter.

A low hum rose from the market-place; there was none of the strident shouting of the European fair. The bargaining for goods was carried on slowly, quietly, but, none the less, keenly. The Aztecs had no money, so that barter was the usual means of purchase. The cacao bean, however, had a standard value, and this, in equalizing exchanges, performed the nearest approach to the function of currency. Passing through the crowd were warriors who acted as police and, should a disagreement arise, haled disputants into a court where a clan elder settled the question in his capacity as judge.

Beyond the market was a double line of walls which divided the market from the temple precinct of Tlaltelolco. Rectangular buildings, with patios in their centres, housed the priests and the various schools and councils of the central organization of the community. Farther on were grouped the principal shrines. In their midst the great temple to the War God shouldered its bulk into the sky. There was a skull rack here, like the one in Tenochtitlan, and another heap was made of the bones of the victims. Near the great pyramid stood a circular temple, the door of which was built to resemble the mouth of a serpent, the place of worship of the god Quetzalcoatl. The sacrificial block in front was black with the smoke of incense and the blood of victims. A pile of stone knives and axes gave a sinister indication of what rites were practised there.

Pools fed by the pipes of an aqueduct leading from the mainland gave an impression of quiet peace. The reflections of the temples, distorted occasionally by the breeze, intensified the brooding mysticism of the sacred enclosure. In contrast to the austerity of the priests, young girls, their eyes virtuously downcast, slipped back and forth, carrying out the various errands of their training school within the enclosure. The great pyramid and the temple of the War God completely dominated the place. At regular intervals terraces broke the lines of the sloping sides and increased the impression of its size. A wide staircase of one hundred and fourteen narrow steps led up the western side, and so steep was this stair that not until one's head rose clear of the platform did the temple itself come into view.

The temple, in reality, comprised two shrines, built side by side, each having stone walls and soaring roofs of wood coated with plaster. Through the right-hand door one could clearly see the squat figure of Huitzilopochtli carved from the stone and covered with a paste in which were set jade, turquoise, gold, and seed pearls. A girdle of gold snakes, picked out in precious stones, adorned his waist, and around his neck hung a string of gold masks covered with turquoise mosaic. By his side stood the statue of an attendant deity, equipped with a short lance and a gold shield, richly decorated with the customary mosaic.

In the adjoining shrine stood an image of Tezcatlipoca, one of the most prominent Aztec gods. His eye sockets were inlaid with mirrors of obsidian, the black depths of which reflected the red gleams of the afternoon light. This statue, too, was adorned with gold and precious stones. High in the wooden roof of this temple perched a small figure of Xipe, the God of Seedtime. Braziers of incense discharged greasy coils of smoke which deepened the gloom of the temples, whose walls were already black with the blood of many victims. In dim corners stood heaps of ritualistic paraphernalia, conch-shell trumpets, knives, banners, and baskets of shapeless lumps of meat, surplus human hearts which, for some reason, had not yet been placed upon the braziers. The priests who glided through this murk seemed fitting satellites to the diabolic images to which they ministered. In front of the temples stood the great drum which was soon to throb across the lake as a nation suffered its death agony.

It was from this point that Montezuma showed Cortés his empire, and Bernal Díaz, who witnessed the scene, left us this unforgettable description:

Then Montezuma took Cortés by the hand and told him to look at his great city and all the other cities that were standing in the water and the many other towns and the land around the lake. . . . So we stood looking about us, for that huge and cursed temple stood so high that from it one could see over everything very well, and we saw the three causeways which led into Mexico . . . and we saw the [aqueduct of] fresh water that comes from Chapultepec, which supplies the city, and we saw the bridges on the three causeways which were built at certain distances apart . . . and we beheld on the lake a great multitude of canoes, some coming with supplies of food, others returning loaded with cargoes of merchandise, and we saw that from every house of that great city and of all the other cities that were built in the water it was impossible to pass from house to house except by drawbridges, which were made of wood, or in canoes; and we saw in those cities Cues [temples] and oratories like towers and fortresses and all gleaming white, and it was a wonderful thing to behold![3]

Chapter 15 The Death-throes of the Aztec Nation

A chapter in which are set forth the factors which brought about the success of the Spaniards and the downfall of the Aztecs

The romantic circumstances which attended the fall of the Aztec civilization have long captured the fancy of the European world. A whole nation submitting to a handful of desperate Spanish soldiers offers a dramatic situation, seldom paralleled in our annals. Yet given the unflinching generalship of a Cortés, the collapse of Aztec power was inevitable. The psychological conditions inherent in this type of Indian culture could not withstand European military technique any more than could the varied civilizations which became colonies of Europe in every continent on the face of the globe.[1]

There are times in the histories of all peoples when the national will seems to disintegrate before intangible factors individually insignificant. All students of military affairs are familiar with these sudden routs affecting the high courage of victors as well as the grim fortitude of those who previously have unflinchingly endured successive defeats. The Aztecs' war against the Spanish conquistadores is an elusive example of the paralysis of the national morale, followed by a defence carried on with that courage found in forsaken men, in this case abandoned by their very gods. We have seen, in the bitter year of 1940, the same pattern repeated when France collapsed and England found a new strength in despair.

An examination of the Mexican social structure in relation to the psychological state of the Aztec mind shows that the Spaniards arrived at a time very favourable for conquest. Comparison of the Aztec military technique with the European discipline and armament of the day reveals an exceptional

238

opportunity for the triumph of European tactics. To explain the familiar tale of the Conquest from the Indian point of view may throw into sharper relief this conflict between two systems of civilization.

Aztec war was highly ceremonial and fought in a spirit very different from the realistic calculation of European strife. The *technical* equipment of the Indians did not meet the requirements of a conflict waged in terms of European military *practice*. Moreover, Cortés arrived at the end of the summer, when the Mexicans were too busy harvesting the crops essential for their survival to think seriously of military affairs. A final factor dooming the Aztecs to inevitable defeat was the political structure of Indian Mexico, which provided no way of converting military success to the establishment of a powerfully consolidated state.

The Aztec theocracy did not lend itself to governing or absorbing conquered peoples, although in time a social mechanism might have been developed. While the Aztecs received tribute from over a wide territory, there were constant revolts and betrayals showing that the political organization of the region as a whole was far from efficient. In reality a multitude of independent city-states seethed with intrigue and war and were further disunited by differences in language, dialect, physical type, and geographic economy. An invader, with a strongly disciplined force small enough to live off the country and thus to stay in the field, could have an astonishing success, particularly if he had a taste for intrigue. Cortés, as events proved, was the ideal man for such a purpose, and he was further favoured by the psychological reaction of the Aztecs to his arrival.

The years before the Spanish Conquest had, to the Aztecs, been full of portents suggestive of future evil. There seems to have been in the air that same sense of paralysis that the French knew to their cost in 1939 and 1940. Montezuma, the war chief of the Aztecs and an amateur of witchcraft, had had an experience calculated completely to shake his nerve. He and Nezahualpilli, the chief of Texcoco, had fallen to arguing about the respective merits of their soothsayers, since the Texcocan held that strangers were going to rule the land of Anahuac. So convinced was Nezahualpilli of the correctness of his interpretation that he wagered his kingdom against three turkey

Fig. 26. The years before the Spanish Conquest had been full of evil omens for the Aztecs. To determine whether the dire predictions of Nezahualpilli, chief of Texcoco, were correct, Montezuma played and lost a ritualistic game of 'basketball' with him as depicted on left. *Codex Florentino.*

Fig. 27. Montezuma views the magical bird in the head of which was a mirror, showing first the heavens, then hosts of armed men, foretelling, according to tradition, the Spanish Conquest. *Codex Florentino.*

cocks, the result to be decided by a ritualistic ball game with Montezuma. The latter won the first two games, but Nezahualpilli took the last three in a row. The defeat must have been disheartening to Montezuma, not only because he had so much to fear from the future, but also because his own experts had been held so cheap. (See Figure 26.)

In close succession followed a series of phenomena, each bearing its message of woe to come. A column of fire was seen every midnight throughout the year; two temples were destroyed, one by a sudden fire, the other by lightning unaccompanied by thunder. A comet was seen by day, and sudden waves came up on the Lake of Texcoco. A sixth sign was a woman's voice crying, 'My children, we are lost'. Monsters appeared and were brought before the chief, only to disappear as soon as he had seen them. Most sinister of all was a bird brought in by some hunters. This bird had a mirror in its head, revealing the heavens, and when Montezuma peered at it a second time a host of armed men was disclosed. When the chief brought his soothsayers to witness this augury and to explain its significance, the bird flew away. Distorted as these occurrences seem to us, they must have had a most upsetting effect on the population of the Valley of Mexico.[2] (See Figures 27, 51a–b.)

Consequently the emotional condition of the people was peculiarly receptive to the rumours, drifting in from the southeast, which told of four-legged monsters with human bodies issuing from their backs. As these strange beings moved up the coast Montezuma's spies and ambassadors began to bring back more precise reports as to their nature, and even presents and messages for their chief. (See Figure 28.)

The strangers were human, for they were vulnerable, receiving wounds and dying from assaults upon them. They had new and strange weapons, noisy and lethal, for cannon, muskets, crossbows, and steel swords were unknown to the Aztecs. Also novel and dreadful adjuncts of war were the horses and the savage mastiffs of the Spaniards. In battle the strangers were invincible, operating in a manner completely foreign to Indian principles of war. The simple Indian methods of mass attack were of little avail against the manoeuvring of a well-drilled force, for the native tactics could only bring the merest fraction of their fighting force in direct contact with the enemy.

The Spaniards also resisted witchcraft on the occasion when Montezuma seriously applied it. However, sorcery, according to native standards, was at best a two-edged weapon, so that it is doubtful if this failure had any other than a confirmatory bearing on the Indian attitude of mind towards the super- natural quality of the Spaniards. The problem that beset Montezuma was not that the invaders were themselves gods, but that they were the symbols, the vicars on earth, as it were,

Fig. 28. The Spaniards land in 1519 at the site of Vera Cruz. Their ships and equipment are carefully shown. At the right, Marina, Cortés's interpreter, is exercising her diplomacy on a native. *Codex Florentino.*

of vast unearthly forces bent on establishing a new social order. As such the Spaniards required the most gingerly handling.[3] (See Figure 29.)

When the Spaniards were approaching the capital a politi- cal problem entered to complicate the spiritual one. The city- states, or pueblos, between the Valley of Mexico and the coast were independent communities and, even if tributary to the Valley powers, were often reluctantly so. Therefore, many of these peoples, like the Totonacs, welcomed the invaders as the spearhead for an open revolt. Others, like the completely independent and warlike Tlaxcalans, put the power of Cortés to a practical test in open battle and, when the Spaniards won, became the most loyal of Cortés's supporters. Cholula, a large town loosely allied to the Aztecs, met the Spaniards as friends, plotting to overcome them by treachery, a good Indian

Fig. 29. Aztec sorcerers, sent from the highland, offer bewitched food to Cortés and his staff, who disdain the viands. *Codex Florentino.*

political manoeuvre instigated, perhaps, by Montezuma. The Spaniards, suspecting such a move, counteracted its efficacy by a judiciously executed massacre, thus, if not gaining a friendly community, at least creating a non-combatant one. (See Figures 30–32.)

Montezuma and his more cautious counsellors watched this slow ascent from the coast with apprehensive interest. He has been condemned by many commentators as an appeaser, and has been made the scapegoat of this great débâcle of Indian civilization. Yet consider his position. While the leading man in his community, he was not a completely authoritarian monarch. For mass action he had to rely on the group decision of the clan leaders as well as on the very doubtful allegiance of the vassal states, whose immediate needs transcended any sacrifice of a far-reaching political nature. Montezuma had no method of enforcing a long-range diplomatic policy,

Fig. 30. Cortés and his army, on passing the great volcanoes south-east of Mexico City, ask the way. Note the smoke issuing from the crater of Popocatepetl. *Codex Florentino.*

such as is so characteristic of European and oriental political history. Nor must the extraordinary gifts of Cortés and his Indian mistress Marina be underrated. The pair played on Indian psychology as master pianists would execute a duet on the piano.

His hands tied by both practical and psychological considerations, Montezuma received Cortés and the Spaniards without having struck a positive blow. Then ensued a new chapter in the story. Cortés promptly seized Montezuma as a hostage, and the latter's power to influence his tribesmen disintegrated. A mass revulsion against the invaders slowly began to crystallize, but it was confined to the city itself, without

Fig. 31. Montezuma, upset by the magical premonitions of disaster and by the failure of his sorcerers, does not know whether to flee or hide in a cave. *Codex Florentino.*

extending to the neighbouring towns. People kept themselves within their houses; the market closed, yet no overt act was made. Cortés was allowed to leave for the coast to subjugate his new commander, Narvaez, without open hostilities on the part of the Aztecs. (See Figure 33-6.)

The storm broke during Cortés's absence. Some inhabitants of Tenochtitlan had assembled to celebrate the feast of the god Huitzilopochtli. Alvarado, a tough soldier, lacking all Cortés's gifts of intrigue, scented trouble in this gathering, the actual innocence of which he had no way of knowing. Following the Spanish technique at Cholula, he fell upon the celebrants and killed them all. The city rose like one man and drove the garrison to cover. Actuated by the single motive of revenge against the invaders, the Aztecs were ready to destroy the

Fig. 32. Cortés meets high dignitaries from Tlaxcala, the pueblo most loyal to the conquerors. Marina interprets while supplies of corn, tortillas, turkeys, etc., are accumulated. *Lienzo de Tlaxcala.*

Spanish garrison. However, the structural weakness of the Indian government became bitterly evident when the chiefs permitted Cortés and his reinforcements from the army of Narvaez to join the beleaguered troops of Alvarado. The ceremonial aspect of war in Indian Mexico did not envisage

Fig. 33. The Spanish forces reach Tenochtitlan, the modern Mexico City, and Montezuma and his nobles come to greet Cortés. *Codex Florentino.*

Fig. 35. A great aid to the Spanish military success was the use of cavalry. Here we see mounted crossbowmen, whose weapons were no less deadly than the firearms of the day. *Codex Florentino.*

Fig. 34. Marina's value to Cortés cannot be underestimated. Here she is ordering an Aztec to perform some duty. To judge from the speech scrolls, he complies with ill grace. *Codex Florentino.*

Fig. 36. Cortés seizes Montezuma as a hostage. The Aztec chief tries to calm his rebellious subjects who treat him with the contempt due a traitor. *Codex Florentino.*

247

the splitting of an adversary's army and the separate destruction of its weakened parts, a rudimentary law of European military tactics.

Yet once the Spaniards were united in the city they ceased to be a military problem and became the emotional focus of the

Fig. 37. Following a series of outrages committed by the invaders, the citizens rise in arms against the Spanish. The Spaniards and their Tlaxcalan allies are besieged in the palace of Axayacatl. In this scene a field piece is shown in action, while the horsemen are held in reserve for a sortie. *Lienzo de Tlaxcala*.

Indians' wrath and fear. They had to shut themselves up in the palace of Axayacatl to resist the force of this uprising in which the whole community participated. The Aztecs, having immobilized their enemies, visited their hate and rage in a manner unparalleled in the annals of Indian campaigns. Every citizen joined in hurling missiles at the besieged invaders, and masses of warriors blocked every sally the Spaniards made from their refuge. (See Figures 37, 38.)

yeqtlatı tetzavitl
yn mal ques.

Fig. 38. Here the Spanish are dislodging the Aztecs from a temple, where the Indians had gathered to enfilade them. *Lienzo de Tlaxcala.*

The Spaniards could not manoeuvre in the narrow footpaths along the canals, and the portable fortresses they constructed of wood, the first tanks used in the New World, were useless against enemies on housetops and in canoes.[4] (See Figure 39.) The Spaniards lost heavily, and the unfortunate Montezuma met his death either at the hands of his own people, whom he was trying to calm, or, as two excellent authorities have it, at those of the Spaniards.[5] After having passed a week shut up in the palace Cortés decided to withdraw from Tenochtitlan. Just before dawn his forces made their way through the hushed streets out along the causeway to Tacuba.

Fig. 39. Wooden tanks were built by Cortés to protect his men when Aztecs took up positions on the housetops out of reach of the sallies of Spanish cavalry. This spirited picture reveals the tanks separated by a canal into which a horse had fallen. The Aztecs on the roofs impede its rescue. *Lienzo de Tlaxcala.*

A woman getting water from a canal saw them and raised the alarm. The whole male population surged forth along the roofs and through the streets. Some seized canoes and attacked the flanks of the marching column. The Aztecs tore up the bridges, and many Spaniards, laden down with gold, sank ignominiously beneath the waters or, while trying to keep afloat, were clubbed to death by warriors in boats. Alvarado, ever the precipitous man of action, confronted by a wide gap in the causeway, plunged his lance into the lake bottom and in full armour vaulted over to the other side.[6]

Fig. 40. A handful of the Spaniards reach the mainland. The Aztecs, instead of following up their advantages, plunder the bodies of the killed and drowned. Be it remembered, however, the Spanish carried off the entire Aztec treasure. *Codex Florentino.*

The panic increased, and order was not restored until the Spaniards reached Tacuba. Cortés sat under a giant cypress and wept as he took toll of his losses. Three quarters of the Spanish army had been lost in this rout and in the preceding siege. (See Figure 41.)

The Spaniards found a temporary sanctuary on the hill of Los Remedios. Their adversaries, instead of following up their advantage, plundered the dead and tried to recover the booty stolen by the Spaniards from the Aztec treasury. They lost a precious opportunity to destroy the remnants of the Spanish army by not carrying their attack to its logical conclusion. (See Figure 40.)

However, the Indians did make some effort towards concerted action later. The Texcocans, formerly the principal

Fig. 41. Supplies run low and Cortés secretly tries to reach the mainland along a causeway. His retreat is discovered and the Aztecs, massing their forces in canoes, wreak havoc on the Spanish forces. Tearing up the bridges, the Aztecs further hindered the retreat and all but destroyed the invading army. *Lienzo de Tlaxcala.*

allies of the Aztecs, gathered their forces together and tried to intercept the Spaniards as they made their way cross country to the homeland of their allies, the Tlaxcalans. At Otumba battle was joined. The Indians in their battle formation could not overcome the mobility and tactical sense of the Spaniards. Wounded as every man was, and exhausted from lack of food and sleep, they kept their discipline; and a desperate charge by the cavalry reached the chiefs, who fell before the Spanish swords. Once their leaders were slain, the scant Indian discipline dissolved, and the Texcocans took flight. The Spaniards made their way to Tlaxcala to recuperate and to await reinforcements.

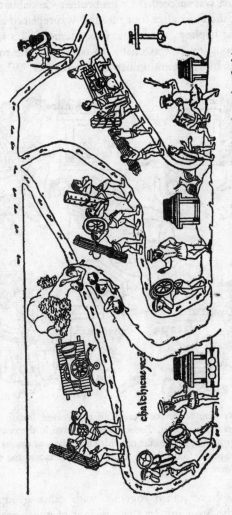

chalchicuey

Fig. 42. Due to the hesitancy of the Aztecs, Cortés was able to reach Tlaxcala and refit his army. Here we see military supplies being brought from the coast. In the left centre a minor disaster, involving the drowning of several Indian allies, is depicted. *Lienzo de Tlaxcala.*

Montezuma was succeeded by his brother Cuitlahuac, and he, dying of the fever after four months, was replaced as war chief by their nephew, the heroic Cuauhtemoc. This strong and courageous leader was unable to overcome the mutual distrust of the Indian communities for one another. When the

Fig. 43. Cortés's plan to retake Tenochtitlan involved isolating the island city from the mainland. Tenochtitlan is shown in the centre of the picture, surrounded by the lake on which float the war canoes of its defenders. The Spanish forces devote themselves to reducing the mainland towns. *Lienzo de Tlaxcala.*

Aztecs might have joined together with other groups to overwhelm the Spaniards by sheer weight of numbers, they did nothing.

In the meantime Cortés, having rested his army, began to

consolidate his position. He made two series of campaigns, one eastwards to the sea and the other in a south and westerly direction in the present state of Morelos. Utilizing Indian allies both as carriers and as a screen to conceal his more serious tactical movements, he subjugated town after town. In each

Fig. 44. Cortés built brigantines to defend his flanks while moving along the causeways into Tenochtitlan. In this picture a brigantine comes to the aid of Cortés and his allies, who are beset by Aztecs afoot and in canoes. *Lienzo de Tlaxcala.*

case the Indian war convention of a single decisive mêlée proved worthless against the versatility of the Spanish attack. Cortés soon pacified the eastern country sufficiently to try to regain Tenochtitlan. (See Figure 42.)

Indian perfidy, from our point of view today, but commonsense to the people of that era, virtually accomplished the downfall of Mexico. The Texcocans, closest allies of the Aztecs, and for that reason perhaps the most jealous of their success, resented the part Montezuma had taken in forcing the election of a war chief. When the Aztecs had had a strong chance of maintaining their supremacy after Cortés's retreat from Mexico the Texcocans valiantly took the field at Otumba. Now they switched to the Spanish side, seeing a chance of

Fig. 45. The Spanish flotilla puts to sea. These galleys, equipped with oars and a sail and armed with a cannon in the bow, could play havoc with the Aztec war canoes. *Codex Florentino.*

assuming a dominant position in Valley of Mexico affairs. Their defection gave the Spaniards a base on the Lake of Mexico and a means of mopping up whatever tribes remained unsubjugated in the previous campaign.

Having quieted the countryside, Cortés put into effect his plan of siege. He launched a fleet of small galleys armed with cannon which had been constructed in Tlaxcala and brought

Fig. 46. The Spanish military problem was to raze enough of the city to permit the use of cavalry. The drawing shows the gunboats taking part in an offensive with this end in view. *Codex Florentino.*

Fig. 47. Time and again the brigantines relieved situations like this where armed tribesmen in canoes sailed up to attack the Spanish rear. *Codex Florentino.*

piecemeal across the mountains, to be assembled on the lake. These ships were to sweep the lake clear of canoes and protect the Spanish flanks as they moved in across the three causeways to the island city, Tenochtitlan. Cortés divided his forces in three parts to move along these approaches and close in on the capital. (See Figures 43–45.)

The galleys soon cleared the lake of any hostile fleets of canoes, and the Spaniards began to invest the city. The Aztecs, fighting for their lives, stubbornly defended their position. Every night they sallied forth to destroy the bridges the Spaniards had made across the canals during the day. In fighting of this kind the Spaniards could not manipulate their troops, and neither side had any great advantage. The Aztecs, however, still persisted in trying to take prisoners to sacrifice to their War God instead of exterminating their enemies whenever the occasion offered. To offset this gain the thousands of Indian allies, who flocked to the Spanish side to participate in the expected victory, jammed the causeways and hampered rather than helped the besiegers. (See Figure 44.)

Cortés decided to change his manner of campaign, and his solution, while reasonable to us, must have been little short of miraculous to the Mexicans. He sent the Indian allies forward to tear down all the houses they could find and fill the canals with the debris. When counter-attacked, the allies retired, leaving room for the Spaniards on horse and foot to deal with the Aztecs. Each day the Spanish forces gained more room to manoeuvre and thus could count on recovering more ground on the morrow. The Aztecs, animated by a rare unity, fought desperately but without avail. (See Figures 46, 47.)

Towards the end of the siege an event occurred which indi-

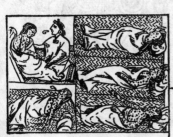

Fig. 48. Pestilence was a formidable ally on the Spanish side. Colds, smallpox, measles, and the like, were unknown to the Indians who, lacking any sort of immunity, died by the thousands. *Codex Florentino.*

Fig. 49. A factor in the downfall of the Aztecs was their custom of taking captives for sacrifice rather than to kill in direct battle. The heads of the sacrificed victims, both men and horses, were displayed in front of the temples. *Codex Florentino.*

259

cated to the now desperate Aztecs hope of eventual release in a common rising against the invaders. The people from the islands at the south of the lake, the Xochimilcas and their neighbours, filtered through the Spanish galleys by night and told the Aztecs that, as neighbours, they would make com-

Fig. 50. Cuauhtemoc, who conducted the defence of Tenochtitlan, is received with all the honours of war by Cortés and his consort, Marina. In the upper right Cortés may be seen greeting Cuauhtemoc's wife and family. The legend translated reads: 'With this event, the Mexicans were finished.' *Lienzo de Tlaxcala.*

mon cause against the whites. Overjoyed, Cuauhtemoc and his chiefs loaded them with ornaments, fine mantles, and cacao beans, precious for the favourite drink of the Aztecs, chocolate. When night closed in again on the beleaguered city the Aztecs were startled by a great commotion. The new allies were trying to drag off the Aztec women and children as slaves. It is pleasant to record that this knavery received its just reward, and the Xochimilcas were all either slaughtered or disposed of in sacrifice.[7]

Only when its members were too weak to resist and could no longer deal wounding blows did the garrison yield. Cuauhtemoc and his family took to the lake in a canoe, as did many others. He was picked up by one of the Spanish galleys and brought before Cortés, where his dignity and chiefly demeanour received the respectful attention of the Spanish general staff. The request for treasure brought the answer that there was none: it lay under the lake with the Spaniards who were slain the preceding winter in their disastrous flight from the city. Cuauhtemoc then underwent prison and torture, to be murdered years later on Cortés's march to Honduras. He is now revered in Mexico as a national hero. (See Figures 48–50.)

The downfall of the Aztecs cannot be explained in terms of European history, and the standard reasons give a false picture. Montezuma, singled out by European authors as a weak and vacillating monarch, was a theocratic leader devoid of the constitutional rights of a European sovereign. His empire is also a European creation, since it consisted, in reality, of communities sufficiently intimidated to pay tribute but in no wise bound to Aztec governmental conventions. Warriors the Aztecs were, but not soldiers in the European sense.[8] Given, as we have said, the requisite leadership and organization, any European expeditionary force could have taken Mexico. The tragically courageous resistance at Tenochtitlan was not a military defence so much as a heroic group action by individuals fighting for their lives.

Hunger and thirst, plagues and wounds, had literally so weakened the Aztecs that they could not resist. The horrors of the last stand made by these desperate people are too awful to describe. For long after, the memory of the tragedy lin-

Figs. 51A–B. The story of the Conquest of Mexico in native characters. In the cartouches are to be seen the symbols One Reed and Two Knife, the Aztec names for the years 1519 and 1520. Under One Reed is a Spaniard below whose horse's feet are the shield, club and arrows symbolic of war. At the right the bearded Cortés sits in the temple of

Tenochtitlan, represented by the cactus. An Indian with the glyph of
Montezuma offers a tribute of gold beads. Under Two Knife we find
Alvarado massacring the Indians at the great temple and at upper right
a comet in the sky. *Codex Vaticanus A.*

gered about the place, a sort of exhalation of spiritual un-
cleanliness like that of a haunted house or the scene of a crime.
All through the colonial era, and even up to now, the northern
district of Mexico has found favour neither as a residential
quarter nor as a business centre. Today there are railroad
yards and slums where the Aztec civilization bled to death.
The ghosts of its heroic defenders still haunt the place.

The history of the Aztecs after the Conquest
and suggestions for a tour through their domain

Aztec civilization died, but the Aztecs still live. Remove the pure-blooded Indian from Mexico, and you lose two fifths of the population; take out those with Indian blood in their veins, and a bare twentieth of the population will remain. The face of Mexico is an Indian face. Yet travel in Mexico and read its history, and you will see, as if in strata, the impress of the colonial period, the republic, the empire of Maximilian, the dictatorship of Díaz and the modern social thinking of the Revolution. The Indian civilization you do not see, except for its descendants, who are everywhere, who are the Mexican people. Though their outward aspect and their material and social culture are European, the stamp of the Aztec character is on their minds, just as the masonry of broken Aztec temples is built into the walls of their churches.

The original purpose of the Crown and the Church was to convert the Indian population into Spanish citizens with full civic rights. For two generations the authorities almost succeeded in their intent, but finally the individualism so emphasized in European culture broke through their legislative controls, and the white conquerors reduced the Indians to slavery. Now, after four hundred years, it seems that the present Republican government might achieve by means of their Indian education programme the humane purpose formulated under the colonial system.

After 1520, when the Conquest was established, the Spaniards began the process of converting a matured Indian culture into a European one. The conquerors were granted lands and in return were supposed to exploit the new territory for the economic advantage of Spain. The Church had in its custody the education of the Indians and their spiritual and corporal welfare. The different monastic orders undertook the control of the Indians in specified localities. Their first steps were to eradicate the local idolatry and to learn the language and customs of their new charges, the better to accomplish conversion.[1]

The friars, especially selected for the task, showed great understanding. They immediately replaced one theological structure with another. The Indians tore down their temples to build churches and monasteries in their place. The use of statues and paintings in Catholic ritual answered so well the requirements of Aztec worship that the friars had great trouble in preventing adoration of the images themselves.

The studies that the friars made of the Indian customs were admirable, with the Franciscans and Dominicans showing exceptional abilities.[2] The children of Indian leaders were educated in schools to spread the gospel. Under this Spanish control there was no recognition of the old communal land tenure, but the Aztec nobles and officials were frozen into possession of the lands that they occupied. The chiefs who had held the usage of the official lands found themselves the owners of extensive estates by which their descendants could profit. The Spaniards married into chiefly families according to their own cultural pattern to achieve wealth and status in the new colonial society. In some cases chiefs, like those of Tlaxcala, received coats of arms and patents of nobility from the king for their service in the Spanish cause. Out of 190 coats of arms presented for services during the Conquest of Spanish America, at least twenty were granted to Indians. In consequence there took place a modest renaissance of Indian culture. Indian authors like Ixtlilxochitl and Chimalpahin set forth, in Spanish or Nahuatl, the annals of their forebears as proof of their descent from great Indian nobles and of their right to Spanish honours as well.[3] (See Plate 42.)

The old culture died slowly. In the Indian towns the records were kept in both Spanish and the old Aztec pictographic system to avoid dispute. Dress maintained its old form, except that the friars insisted on trousering the Indians. The rich agriculture was a great boon to the conquerors, who modified it little except for the addition of fruit trees and wheat. Household utensils, like pottery, revealed an engaging fusion of Indian and Spanish ideas, and glazing delighted the Indians, who applied the flux to purely aboriginal forms. Some enchanting little sculptures in clay reveal the old gods and goddesses masquerading as saints in a very thin disguise.

The Indians were used to building temples, and it seemed to them perfectly fitting that they should labour long hours in great numbers to rear structures honouring the new gods. The conversion was so popular that the churches were too small to hold the worshippers, and several conventual temples, like Acolman, Actopan, and Tlalmanalco, had chapels which opened on a large court to accommodate converts who gathered literally in their tens of thousands. Indian craftsmen found steel tools a superb improvement on their stone hammers and chisels. After the original plateresque architecture shifted into baroque, they revelled in shaping the blocks into ornate shapes, for it was as easy as cutting cheese in comparison to the labour of their aboriginal days.[4]

This period of fusion lasted for almost a century. In the meantime the original Conquistadors and their descendants, together with later immigrants to the new colony, had encroached more and more on the natives. The development of the mining industries absorbed thousands of Indians, lured to work for a pittance under noisome conditions which brought sickness and even death. The exercise of the *encomienda*, an arrangement whereby a man had the right to a native's labour in return for his care and the assurance of his religious instruction, led to abuse of the privilege, and the luckless Indians were reduced to serfdom. European diseases, like smallpox, measles, and tuberculosis, wiped out great sections of the population, which had no hereditary resistance to such maladies. The Crown and the Church, through its Council of the Indies, sent questionnaires and enacted ameliorative legislation on the basis of the information received, but such laws were more honoured in the breach than in the observance. Many of the whites who went to New Spain wanted to get rich and enjoy an easy old age in the homeland. Others who had settled in the country enjoyed an almost feudal existence, no part of the profits and comforts of which they wished to yield, either for the betterment of the Indians or for the enrichment of the Crown. When the British destroyed the Armada in 1588 and weakened Spanish sea power, the communication between the mother country and the colonies became increasingly difficult. Control was loosened, and laws for the benefit of the Indians were ignored. They became, indeed, an inferior majority, labouring as peons without hope of legal or social justice.[5]

Most of the Indians lost their land and laboured on haciendas or in the mines. Some communities like Tlaxcala, having performed notable service to the Crown during the Conquest, kept their land although they had lost social status. Other groups, like the lake peoples of Xochimilco and Chalco, occupied territory which the Spaniards considered unsuitable for their own purposes. A fourth group lived relatively unmolested in primitive little villages tucked away in the mountains. These refugees had taken to the hills not only because of the white conquerors but also to avoid the rising Indian powers in the centuries before the Conquest. The several score languages and dialects spoken in Mexico are preserved in these tiny villages where inhabitants are only lightly veneered with Christianity.

What remains of Indian culture today is largely the blend of early indigenous practices with the teachings of the friars in the sixteenth century. Yet the physical type and the languages have resisted absorption for four centuries. In Mexico there is hardly a group which remains as completely Indian as some of the North American tribes, but they, after all, have for the most part been conquered and put on reservations only in the last three generations. The groups who had earlier contact with the whites were exterminated many years ago.[6]

The Mexican Indians have endured and have done the work of Mexico for four centuries. They have seen the whites struggle for the right to consume the fruits of their labour. They probably do not realize that the unmixed group of the ruling class gets smaller each generation, having in the last century dropped from thirteen per cent to seven per cent of the population. Individuals, like Juarez the Liberator, and Díaz, the greatest of Mexican dictators, shouldered their way from the anonymous Indian mass to lead the country and modernize its culture. The men of the Revolution had Indian blood in their veins, and one of them, former President Lazaro Cardenas, made superhuman efforts to drag the Indians out of bondage into participation in the active and political life of the country.

The crafts of Mexico are the product of Indian hands. Humble artisans have handed down from generation to generation the love of the old days, the traditions of form and pattern. This background, like that of the social make-up of the people, was illumined in the Mexican Renaissance, when during the Revolution, Mexican painters like Orozco, Rivera and Goitia, and foreigners like Charlot, became conscious of Mexico's native American background. It is beside the point that Mexico's art is technically derivative from Europe. Socially and emotionally it is one of the four truly national arts in the world today.[7]

The visitor to Mexico is strongly conscious of the Indian. Sometimes he is appalled by the apathy of the people who have been oppressed for so many years, whose nations and whose temples have been levelled to make the foundations of a new society. Yet in these days, when our American world has greater meaning for us, we can think more deeply of those earlier colonists from another continent who, like ourselves, built a new world.

Mexico, the most American of American nations, opens a thrilling perspective down the corridors of time. One can read widely and yet completely miss the sense of a still-living past which affects the visitor to this extraordinary country. To take a car and drive through the rich valleys, hemmed in by their mountain ramparts, is to absorb the full favour of our Indian past. A fortnight so spent will enable a visitor to survey much of the Aztec domain.[8]

The first day one should visit the Museum, just to realize the bulk and quantity of the infinitesimal part of Indian workmanship housed there. A block away, near the Cathedral, yawns an excavation which reveals a corner of the Great Temple's stair. The street behind the Cathedral, running east and west, produced myriads of ceremonial objects cast out from the temple by the outraged conquerors. The *Zocalo*, the great Plaza de la Constitucion, covers the main square of Tenochtitlan. Its twenty feet of foundation are made of the temples torn down for the greater glory of God, and heaven knows what incomparable masterpieces of Aztec art are buried there. The Presidential Palace on the west rests on the ancient halls of Montezuma. A few blocks north the murals of the Ministry of Public Education show the tragedy of the Indian and his liberation, painted in the full tide of Rivera's genius. (See Plate 49, bottom.)

After lunch in the neighbourhood the visitor may well drive west past the Palace of Bellas Artes, built just beyond the ancient shore of Tenochtitlan in the former lake bottom. The hill and park of Chapultepec merit a visit, for the cypresses, hoary with Spanish moss, date from Montezuma's time. Here the Tenochcas made their first settlement, the elder Montezuma built the aqueduct for his city and the younger had a relief carved in his honour. Crowning the hill stands the palace of the Austrian Maximilian, emperor of all the Mexicans during the American Civil War, and at this place a few years previously a handful of Mexican military-school cadets stood off a brigade of United States Regulars in their one unhappy conflict with our southern neighbour.

Turning south, one may visit the little palace of the chief of Mixcoac and go on through the Villa Obregon (San Angel) to see the remains of the Lower Pre-classic peoples buried under the lava of Copilco. Continuing south the highway rises to the top of the Pedregal lava and passes the University City. Just beyond one may turn off to visit Cuicuilco. Here the oval temple of the Pre-classic peoples emerges from the surrounding lava waste, a dismal and uncanny background appropriate to this earliest monument of Mexican religion. Then the visitor can return to Mexico via Tlalpam and Coyoacan, on a road built over the same causeway which Cortés followed into Tenochtitlan. (See Plate 18, bottom.)

The second day, equipped with lunch or self-control, the visitor might drive out to the Calle de Tacuba, which follows the old western causeway to ancient Tlacopan. Here Cortés made his dismal retreat, and two blocks are named for Alvarado's famous leap. The cypress beneath which Cortés wept is worth a glance, and the church in the main plaza of Azcapotzalco, capital of Teotihuacan and Tepanec chiefs, squats heavily on the remains of a once-lofty platform. The votive temple of Los Remedios on the hills behind was built where Cortés re-formed his shattered army and has a wonder-working statue of the Virgin, patroness of the Conquistadores.

Below the hill just to the east is Tlatilco, but there is nothing to see there today, and the visitor will be wise to proceed at once to Tlalnepantla, where the church is built from the ruins of temples, and go on from there to Tenayuca. Here the Mexican archaeologists have dissected, as with a surgeon's knife, the six temples that epitomize the history of that town from its Chichimec foundation until its conquest in 1520. On the hills to the east, at the foot of which runs a Spanish aqueduct, are strung the Pre-classic sites of El Arbolillo, Ticoman, and Zacatenco. (See Plates 1, 48.)

It would be worth while to visit, on returning, the Villa de Guadalupe, built in honour of the apparition of the Virgin to Juan Diego. Her portrait, miraculously painted, is preserved in the church; and in December the Indians come from miles around to honour their special patroness, just as before the Conquest they made pilgrimages to this very spot to do honour to Tonantzin, the Aztec Goddess of Motherhood. Returning by way of the ancient northern causeway, the visitor should turn right at Peralvillo and pass by the grubby railroad yards and slums which cover Tlaltelolco and its famous market-place and the site of the Aztec Cuauhtemoc's last stand against the Spaniards. Here recent excavations have uncovered the principal pyramid of Tenochtitlan's sister city, and have shown it to have been occupied at a much earlier date than had been supposed.

On the third day the tourist should visit Teotihuacan, re-traversing the northern causeway and passing through Guadalupe. The road skirts the bed of Lake Texcoco and crosses, on a causeway of Spanish construction, the straits between it and the now drained Xaltocan. The strategic site of Chiconauhtla at its northern terminus offers little to see, but a small museum to the left of the road farther on marks the spot where Tepexpan man was found. Beyond this it is well to turn right and visit the great Acolman Indian School or Convent, 'convento', as the Spaniards called any establish-ment where the friars educated the Indians. In the distance loom the pyramids of Teotihuacan; a short drive through In-dian villages brings the motorist to this site, the most impos-ing in Mexico. The ruins are a tribute to the cultural interests of the present government, which has expended much time and money in interpreting and uncovering the remains. There is a good museum where one can see the craftsmanship of the builders of this magnificent sacred city, which still retains much of the grandeur of its ancient days. (See Plates 21–4.)

There is a restaurant at Teotihuacan, and after lunch the visitor should go back as far as Tepexpan and take the road to Texcoco. On the way he should visit the remains of Nezahualcoyotl's palace, where magnificent cypresses border a garden, and in their shade one can evoke memories of the life of the poet king. Today Texcoco reflects none of its former grandeur. It is an old, sad town, dim and ruined. A few mounds at the eastern entrance are gloomy reminders of its ancient splendours. One passes Huexotla and its great wall as one returns to Mexico by the main road, and hard by at the agricultural school in the hacienda of Chapingo are some of the best of Rivera's frescoes, symbolizing the growth and fertility of the Mexican earth and translating Aztec ideas into modern painting.

An alternative procedure would be to give a fourth day to the Texcoco region. Leaving Mexico by the eastern road, pass south along the former shores of Lake Texcoco and turn east at Los Reyes on the main road to Texcoco. At Coatlinchan a tip will command the services of an Indian to take one to see the massive Teotihuacan monument to the Goddess of the Waters, which lies unfinished in a gulley, a long half-hour's walk from the town. Returning to the car, go to Chapingo and Huexotla, and at Texcoco turn off to see the rock-cut baths of Nezahualcoyotl, built into the hill behind Texcotcingo. The countryside is dotted with little towns, and the Indian and colonial periods are very close to the surface.

Still another day should be given to Tula, which lies to the east of the Laredo highway. On the way one should visit the sixteenth-century convent of Actopan, which is on the south-west of the road, just before the Valley of the Mesquital, formerly arid lands of the Otomi which have been irrigated and made to blossom as only the desert can blossom when its thirst is quenched. The ruins of Tula are small but interesting and its sculpture is dramatic. Compared to Teotihuacan, however, it has a shoddy look.

The fifth day could commence a profitable two-day tour to Cuernavaca. The motorist will have an unforgettable experience if he takes the back road via Xochimilco, Tulyahualco, and Chalco, where direct descendants of the ancient peoples occupy their old lakelands, fast shrinking today, and till them as did their ancestors. Still speaking Nahuatl, they pole their canoes through the network of canals surrounding their *chinampas,* or garden plots. Before leaving the lakes one should visit Tlapacoya, which lies less than three miles north of Chalco. Then, if there is time, avoiding the great highway, one may still follow the old road to Tlalmanalco and Amecameca, through Ozumba, and drop from there into a new world, the hot Valley of Morelos, home of the Tlalhuicas. The motorist goes past sugar haciendas burned during the revolution, through Yolotepec, seat of a Tlahuica tribe and home of the feared revolutionary leader Zapata, and ascends again to reach Cuernavaca for lunch.

Here the Conquest is starkly represented by the huge fortified church and Cortés's palace, now the seat of the state government, where Rivera has painted an exciting fresco of the conquest and subjugation of the once-powerful Tlahuicas. At the railroad station is a cluster of temples, one of which is extraordinarily well preserved and represents the dramatic values of Aztec architecture. Later one can drive in half an hour to the Nahuatl-speaking village of Tepoztlan, whose people blend the material and spiritual cultures of Indian Mexico, colonial Spain, and the modern republic. The great convent towers over the shattered sculptures from the ancient temples, but, high in the mountains and easily accessible to those sound in wind and limb, the temple of the Tepozteco stands battered but unsubdued. Returning to Cuernavaca, a few mounds on the right of the road at Tlaltenango are a furtive monument to the Pre-classic people whose remains at Gualupita were studied in a brickyard near the Hotel Selva. (See Plate 29, bottom.)

After passing the night in one of the many good hotels in this charming resort of Cuernavaca, one can drive down the Taxco road and turn at Alpuyeca to visit the hill city of Xochicalco. The main temple has a superb carved façade which would suggest a Maya origin were it not for the fire snakes, dates, and ritualistic symbolism of Mixteca-Puebla Culture. Below the hill on which the temple stands there is a ball court almost identical to those at Tula and another large pyramid with what appear to have been priestly dwellings. At a still lower level there remain many mounds yet to be excavated. The uncovered mounds and terraces undoubtedly contain sculptures and pottery that will illumine many dark places in Indian history.

Taxco can be fitted in for lunch and Mexico City reached by nightfall over a fine road across the mountains. The traveller will realize how the mountain chains scaled off one group of people from another, so that language, art, and culture could develop along special lines without outside influence. Coming down from the heights, the panorama of the southern Valley is laid out below one: the lakes, the valley floor, and, looming up in the centre, the Hill of the Star, where each fifty-two years the Aztecs received the promise of continued life.

On the seventh day the rugged traveller who can maintain this schedule might take a dramatic two-day trip to Puebla. Driving down the southern shore of Texcoco, 'where the sedge is withered from the lake and no birds sing', he crosses the mountain chain to the south-east, close under the snow-covered shoulders of the great volcanoes. As he emerges from the pine forests on the other side, the rich Valley of Puebla opens before him. At San Cristobal a mound crowning a big hill on the left was the chief offertory of a group of Pre-classic mounds at the base, but they are not worth the time available, so that the motorist pushes on to Texmelucan, where he turns left on the road to Tlaxcala. Here the Indian population is prosperous because Spain recognized the services of its most effective allies and did not let them be despoiled. The town itself is old and charming, little affected by change since the eighteenth century. The oldest church in Mexico, where the first Indian baptism took place, is on an eminence near the centre of the town. Across the river at Tizatlan there is a little temple whose painted altars, their colours still preserved, de-pict the great god Tezcatlipoca and some of the symbolism of the ancient religion. Near by a former open chapel, delight-fully naïve, is screened by an atrocious nineteenth-century church. There are also the dubious remains of an early six-teenth-century house, said to be the residence, after the Con-quest, of Xicotencatl, who led the armies of Tlaxcala. Near by can be seen the spot where Cortés built his brigantines to be transported, piecemeal, to the lakes of the Valley. (See Plate 57, top.)

Returning to Texmelucan for lunch, one regains the Puebla road and stops at the once-important city-state Huexotcingo. The earliest civilization is obliterated by a marvellous old Franciscan convent, where simple, honest construction reflects the virtues of these holy men who accomplished the conver-sion of the Indians. The measure of their success can be gauged by the huge court, or *atrio*, where the Indians congre-gated in thousands to hear Mass.

Back to the road, in less than an hour Cholula looms on the horizon. Hundreds of little churches, whose coloured tiles shimmer in the sun, bear witness to a dense population which once had a temple in each place where a church is now. One can see why people from this region made their way to the Valley to get living space. Even today every field is culti-vated. The people themselves are very Indian, and the strange sounds of Nahuatl often break in on the smooth syllables of Spanish. The big temple of Cholula is incredible. It seems like the counterpart of Babel, to which the friars compared it. On top the church rests proudly, and on a terrace below are the remains of rooms and the altar enclosing human burials, all carefully excavated by government archaeologists. Within the big mound run more than a mile of tunnels, which the archaeologists hollowed from the adobe bricks to follow the walls and stairs of the ceremonial precinct of earlier times. Deep inside, frescoed representations of the Butterfly God are awe-inspiring in the dim lantern light.

Passing on to Puebla itself, one finds a large provincial town, whose dull respectability is leavened by the burst of inventive creativeness reflected in the ornate church architecture. Examination of Puebla and its museum can be made during the morning of the next day, after which the return to Mexico City is accomplished leisurely.

Another variation is to drive past Puebla to Tepeaca, the old Segura de la Frontera of the Conquest, and thence through a desolate waste to Tehuacan. Here one may turn up over the hills to Orizaba and down into the moist, tropical regions of Cordoba, through populous Indian territory. Or one may take the long drive over the mountains to Oaxaca, a charming provincial capital, unchanged since colonial days. The lofty hill which dominates the city is completely transformed by the terraces, temples, and tombs which constitute the great Zapotec site of Monte Alban. Another valley, another culture, another language, make this region into one more Indian world. The ruins of Mitla are exquisite great buildings, and their intricate wall carvings attest the skill of their Mixtec architects. The regional museum in Oaxaca houses, besides collections drawn from Mitla and other parts of the state, the superb jewel collection found in Tomb 7 at Monte Alban. Indian life is near the surface at Oaxaca, and at the market one can hear not only the Zapotec and Mixtec of the rival groups who contested the hegemony of the valley, but the language of other mountain traders who bring their own obscure tongues to this modern babel. (See Plates 9, 10, 30.)

A trip easily accomplished from Mexico City leads over the mountains to Toluca, the capital of the state of Mexico, where an enlightened governor constructed a state museum, showing the varied handiwork of the Matlatzincas, the Indian group who held this valley. Beyond Toluca on the Nogales highway the ruins of Calixtlahuaca boast a round temple to the Wind among the structures reared in honour of their gods. The more venturesome motorist should drive down past Metepec to Tenancingo, and from there to Malinalco. These rock-cut temples are really thrilling, both because of the fine carving and for the strangely remote effect they produce on the visitor. In this mountain niche one can look far down the valley and back to the temples which, hewn from the rock, were cognate to their gods, envisaged in the manifold variety of nature.

If our visitor has not yet been overwhelmed by these skeletons of a once lively civilization, there are today good roads to Tajin, Zempoala, and even La Venta. He can fly or drive to Yucatan where the great white ceremonial centres of Chichen Itza, Uxmal, Labnah, thrust themselves from the enveloping bush. Half hidden in thatched villages, growing their corn in little clearings, the modern Mayas carry on their ancient life, but their religion has lost much, and a simple Catholicism tinged with magic provides a slender bond with the supernatural. A visit to Yucatan will enhance the conception of the variety of the Mexican world, where once men of many tongues and many tribes wrought out their destinies. (See Plates 7, 8.)

The civilization of the Indian may not offer a direct inspiration to us modern individualists, yet we have profited from their labour in our food plants and the wealth produced by our neighbour republics to the south. In this world, torn with hate and war, adrift without an anchor or a compass with which to chart our course, we may well consider their example. The Indians worked together for their common good, and no sacrifice was too great for their corporate well-being. Man's strength lay in the physical and spiritual welfare of the group, and the individual was honoured only in as much as he contributed to the common good. The Indian civilization may have been powerless to resist the culture of the Western world, but it did not consume itself, as we are doing, in the expression of military power.[9]

The American countries today share the ideal of the republic and individual freedom. We share also an older tradition left us by our Indian forebears, that of mutual service for the benefit of man. With our continents spread before us, we have boundless opportunity to create on earth a wider life for everyone, an American civilization where old and new contributions to human welfare may be fused and amalgamated for the benefit of all.[10]

Notes*

FOREWORD TO REVISED EDITION

1 The whole problem of dating merits a chapter to itself, but I shall content myself with referring the student to a few recent publications on the subject. Armillas, 1952;† Ekholm, 1958; Lathrap, Holden, and Coe, 1957, use mainly the archaeological approach. Jimenez Moreno, 1954, 1959, combines archaeology with his study of documents. Wauchope, 1947, attempts also to correlate archaeology with native annals and 1950, 1954, appraises the radiocarbon method in the light of archaeology as does Martinez del Rio, 1957. Crane and Griffin, 1958, 1959, and Libby, 1955, are standard references for radiocarbon dating and new results will continue to be published, as by Flint and Deevey, 1959. See also McNutt and Wheeler, 1959. Linné, 1956, has published an interesting and perhaps the most reliable date on Teotihuacan, but more are promised (Griffin, personal communication).

It had been hoped that the new method might settle for all time the differences of opinion about Maya correlations, but a glance at Andrews, 1959, and Satterthwaite, 1960, to mention only two recent papers, shows the scholars as far apart as ever. The 'Olmec' Stela C at Tres Zapotes, the Tuxtla statuette, etc., can give us only partial help if we cannot agree how to interpret them. For data on a new method of dating obsidian the student is referred to Friedman and Smith, 1960, and Evans and Meggers, 1960; and on the possibility of dating pottery by thermoluminescence, to Kennedy, 1960. There have also been experiments with the dating of bone by fluorine, Cook and Ezra-Cohn, 1959. Another seemingly very accurate method of dating rocks and structures like hearths and kilns is described by Cook and Belshé, 1959.

CHAPTER I

For recent general writings on early man in America see Martinez del Rio, 1953; Armillas, 1957; Howells, 1959; Willey, 1960 (which has a fine bibliography); and Wormington, 1957. A good popular account of

* The text of these notes, with the exception of those initialled G.C.V., and the bibliographical references after 1941 are the reviser's.

† See Bibliography for book titles.

South-western archaeology is to be found in Martin, 1959. For general reading on Mesoamerican archaeology Bernal, 1950, 1959a, 1959b. Caso, 1953; Piña Chan, 1960; Covarrubias, 1957; Lothrop, 1957; Peterson, 1959; Wolf, 1959, are the most recent. *Esplendor del México Antiguo*, 1959, is an anthology by outstanding authors on special aspects of prehistoric Mexico. It is especially recommended.

1 Howells, 1959; Nelson, 1933; MacCurdy, ed., 1937; Howard, 1935; Wormington, 1957; Willey, 1960; Aveleyra Arroyo de Anda, 1950; Martinez del Rio, 1953.

2 Wissler, 1938.

3 Howells, 1959; Hooton, 1933; Dixon, 1923; Hrdlička, 1923; Wormington, 1957.

4 Nelson, 1933; Roberts, 1940; Howells, 1940; Bird, 1938; De Terra, 1949; Aveleyra Arroyo de Anda, 1953; Wormington, 1957.

5 Wissler, 1938; Swanton, 1940; Kroeber, 1939.

6 Gladwin, 1937; Sayles, 1935. Willey, 1960, gives a short and excellent summary.

7 Kroeber, 1939; Millon, 1959; MacNeish, 1958, sheds important new light. See also Carter in Smith, 1953.

8 Mesoamerica, a term coined by Kirchhoff, 1952, comprises the higher cultures of Mexico and the Maya area in Northern Central America, which passed from village agriculture to a complex ceremonial civilization sometime after 1500 B.C. The digging stick, step pyramids, stucco floors, a year of eighteen months of twenty days, the sacred ball game, the worship of a rain god, and many other cultural traits are shared by the groups of this area. For a view of the relations between Mesoamerica and the Andean region, see Willey, 1955, 1957, 1960; Coe, 1960.

9 Sauer, 1936; Yanovski, 1936; Mangelsdorf and Reeves, 1938; Willey, 1960.

10 Bird, 1951; MacNeish, 1958; Mangelsdorf, 1958; Sears, 1953; Willey, 1960.

11 Wissler, 1938.

12 Linton, 1940; Ferdon, 1959.

13 At some earlier time, probably about 2500 B.C., pottery was being made in coastal Ecuador, in the Valdivia Phase, as well as in Panama. It may be that from this intermediate area the knowledge spread north to Mesoamerica and south to Peru. Willey, 1960; Estrada, 1962; Coe, 1960.

14 Griffin, ed., 1952.

15 At present it is not clear whether the ceremonial centre developed first in the lowlands of Tabasco or at Kaminaljuyú in the Guatemalan

highlands, where earthen mounds occur at the Arevalo phase in the earliest Pre-classic. Shook and Kidder, 1952. Further excavation may answer this question. See Millon, 1959; Sanders, 1956.

16 Spinden, 1928; Means, 1931; Vaillant, 1935.

17 Vaillant, 1940. Since this writing, evidence has accumulated to bolster the importance of trans-Pacific contacts. See Ekholm and others in Smith, 1953; Ekholm, 1955; Estrada, 1962.

18 In this edition the word Olmec will be enclosed by quotation marks when it refers to the creators of the La Venta culture or their influence on other peoples. The name Olmec, not so enclosed, will be reserved for the peoples so called in later tradition. See Jimenez Moreno, 1942, and also 1954–5.

19 Garcia Payon, 1949, 1955. For some picture of Vera Cruz and Tabasco cultures that have been studied since 1941 the student is referred to Berlin, 1960; Bernal, 1953; Drucker, 1943a, 1955; Ekholm, 1946; Proskouriakoff, 1960; Spratling, 1960; Medellin Zenil, 1960.

20 Gann and Thompson, 1931, 1940; Thompson, 1932; Morley, 1956; Caso, 1958b; Brainerd, 1954; Lizardi Ramos, 1959a.

21 Morley, 1915; Spinden, 1924; Teeple, 1931; Thompson, 1935; Andrews, 1940; Thompson, 1954; Satterthwaite, 1960; Lizardi Ramos, 1959b.

22 The student should read Brainerd, 1954, and Morley, 1956, for a general picture of the Maya area. Shook, 1958, and Andrews, 1959, as well as Kidder, 1945, 1946, give reports on Tikal, Dzibilchaltun, and Kaminaljuyú.

23 Vaillant, 1935; Gann, 1900; Tozzer, 1930; Bancroft, 1883; Butler, 1940; Dutton, 1955. Also see Acosta's writings and above all Tozzer, 1957.

24 Stirling, 1939, 1940; Weiant, 1943; Vaillant, 1931, 1932; Ricketson and Ricketson, 1937; Caso, 1932, 1935, 1936–7; Holmes, 1907; Drucker, 1943b, 1952; Drucker, Heizer, and Squier, 1959.

25 The Tuxtla Statuette (A.D. 329?) and Stela C (31 B.C.?) at Tres Zapotes. See Morley, 1956; also Drucker, 1943b.

26 At Chalcatzingo (Piña Chan, 1955), and Piedra Parada (Thompson, 1943).

27 This was the first time, but by no means the last, that influence from the Gulf Coast region reached Central Mexico. It is interesting to speculate with Anne Chapman, 1959, on a trading centre like Xicalango, and the part it must have played again and again in the spreading of new cults and new art styles.

28 See note 19 above; also Covarrubias, 1957.

²⁹ Batres, 1902; Caso, 1934–5, 1936–7; Dauterman, 1938; Bernal, 1958b.

³⁰ Bernal, 1958a.

³¹ Vaillant, 1938; Jimenez Moreno, 1959; Bernal, 1959.

TABLE I

³² I begin the Classic at 0, but it must be noted that some chronological tables start it at A.D. 300. In some parts of Mesoamerica the Classic begins later and persists longer than in others, so that an arbitrary date of any sort may be misleading.' See Jimenez Moreno, 1959; Lathrap, 1957. I have added to the original Table I three sequences that have been worked out since 1941; at Kaminaljuyú, Kidder, 1945, 1946; Shook, 1951; at Chiapa de Corzo, MacNeish, 1958; Dixon, 1959; and in the Huaxteca, Ekholm, 1944.

CHAPTER 2

There are no truly popular accounts of the Pre-classic Cultures. Since the original edition of this book appeared, however, the transitional site of Tlatilco has been excavated and described by Covarrubias, 1957; Piña Chan, 1958; and Porter, 1953. Cuicuilco has been further explored by Heizer and Bennyhoff, 1958. Barba de Piña Chan, 1956, has published a detailed report on the interesting pyramid of Tlapacoya; and Noguera has described El Tepalcate, 1943, and El Opeño, 1941. Chalcatzingo in Morelos has been found by Piña Chan, 1955b, to be contemporaneous with Gualupita, and he has published in detail the petroglyphs which tie this site in to the 'Olmec'. Miles (personal communication) tells me there are such petroglyphs all along the Pacific coast of Guatemala. For a general picture of this period one may read Piña Chan, 1955a, and the appropriate section of Piña Chan, 1960a, as well as the first three chapters of the admirable *Indian Art of Mexico and Central America*, by Miguel Covarrubias, 1957.

¹ Porter, 1953; Piña Chan, 1958.

² Vaillant, 1935.

³ Vaillant, 1935.

⁴ Vaillant, 1939.

⁵ Sejourné, 1957, has an interesting theory that these early figurines represented symbolically the young ears of corn.

⁶ Vaillant and Vaillant, 1934.

⁷ Weiant, 1943. Type A is very rare in Morelos, and, where it occurs, is probably by trade from the valley. Type D, on the other hand, which is common in Morelos, is extremely rare, and occurs probably only as trade in the climax area. It would seem then that Tlatilco, where Type

A and Type D and the 'Olmec' baby face all occur, is the bridge between Morelos and the Gulf coast.

8 Here we find another parallel between Tlatilco and Gualupita, in that more than half the burials at the former, and almost all at the latter site, had offerings, and in many cases these were figurines. Vaillant and Vaillant, 1934; Porter, 1956; Piña Chan, 1958.

9 Vaillant, 1935.

10 Vaillant, 1935.

11 See the recent publications of Millon.

12 Linné, 1934, pp. 162-7. This pottery is diagnostic for the earliest period at Teotihuacan.

13 Here may be further evidence of the Gulf coast origin of what we have called the Transitional influence.

14 Vaillant and Vaillant, 1934; Stirling, 1940. Also see Drucker, 1943b, 1952, 1959; Piña Chan, 1955b, 1958; Porter, 1953.

15 We know more about the early concepts of the 'Olmec' now, and I would hazard the guess that the Tiger God of the Gulf coast is older than the Fire God of the Valley. It is this jaguar-baby-deity, call him what you will, who appears in stone and pottery all through Morelos and Guerrero, in Michoacan, Puebla, and Oaxaca, who is conventionalized at Uaxactun in Guatemala, and turns up again even as far away as Honduras and Costa Rica. Perhaps his features become stylized as Tlaloc at Teotihuacan, from where he will go on to other areas as Tajin, Chaco and Cocijo. He, who appears so early, will not finally be defeated until the coming of the Nahua eagle. The frieze at Tetelco in Teotihuacan is his and later at Tula and Chichen Itza he is changed but still recognizable. The ball game must be his too, and some of the serpents of Mexico must have come with him, though others are definitely associated with the Fire God.

We do not know yet what god the early inhabitants of Kaminaljuyú worshipped in the days of the earliest ceremonial centre there. They played ball; perhaps they invented the game. More likely, however, the early culture in Guatemala developed independently up to a certain point and then spread out and touched the 'Olmec', perhaps at Xicalango. More excavations are needed before we can be sure who thought of anything first.

16 Cummings, 1933; Heizer and Bennyhoff, 1958.

17 Kidder, 1924, pp. 16-35, 1931; Vaillant, 1935, pp. 160-7.

18 Noguera, 1943; Barba de Piña Chan, 1956; see map, pp. 6-7.

TABLE 2

[19] The only basis for confining Tlatilco to the Transitional period, when contemporary sites in Morelos are seen as running into the Upper period, is the occurrence at Gualupita of Ticoman pottery and figurines, proving contemporaneity with that site, whereas Tlatilco, so much closer, has none. I have consulted everyone I could think of who might have an opinion on the proper dating of Tlatilco, and have had answers beginning as far back as 1500 and ending as late as 400 B.C. If we accept 800–400 B.C. for the great period of 'Olmec' art, it seems logical to assume that Tlatilco was influenced by some ancestral form of it, which passed on in part to the Morelos sites, where for some reason it continued longer. The 'Tzaccualli' phase of Teotihuacan seems closer to Cuicuilco-Ticoman than to Tlatilco or the Morelos sites. Yet Tlapacoya is believed by Piña Chan to be the monument that links Tlatilco with Morelos. If we think of the 'Olmec' influence as travelling the other way, from Xicalango to the valley and then southward into Morelos, it would be natural for this transitional culture to persist longer in Morelos and Puebla. It might explain its further evolution in Guerrero, where serpentine and jade heads in the 'Olmec' style are so plentiful until they are replaced by new ones, of the same fine workmanship but now in the Teotihuacan style. (See Plate 24.)

CHAPTER 3

The so-called Toltec Question has been partially resolved in the years following the publication of the original edition of this book. The capital of the historic Toltecs has been accepted as being Tula in Hidalgo, and Teotihuacan is believed to have been the urban centre of a people unknown to history, though not to legend; 'Giants', whose influence in Mesoamerica was perhaps even greater than that of the Toltecs. It is still possible, figuratively speaking, that Quetzalcoatl as a culture-bearer appeared and vanished twice; that he was the beneficent giver of civilization to the Teotihuacanos and later to the Maya, by the way of Tajin and later Xochicalco; that from Xochicalco he brought culture again to Tula and the Toltec, and from there carried to Chichen Itza, in what is known as the Mexican occupation, a culture complex including the skull rack, ball courts with rings, colossal statues, Chacmools, and the tiger frieze. For an interesting reconstruction, the student should read Jimenez Moreno, 1941, 1959.

For information on the recent excavations at Teotihuacan, he should see all Linné's titles and those of Millon and Armillas in the bibliography, as well as Tolstoy, 1958, and Mayer-Oakes, 1959.

¹ Linné, 1934; Gamio, ed., 1922; Charnay, 1888; Seler, 1915, and the more recent works cited above.

² Indeed Armillas believes that the whole city was destroyed by fire sometime between A.D. 600–650. It then ceased to be important and was inhabited by marauding peoples. Perhaps the first of these were the Otomi, followed later by the Toltecs. There is not, however, general agreement. Millon (personal communication) believes that further study may show a longer occupation by Teotihuacanos.

³ Noguera, 1935; Millon, 1959, 1960, 1961b.

⁴ With the possible exception of the incineration tomb of Tlamilolpa, Linné, 1956. More are promised.

⁵ From San Juan Ixcaquixtla, Leonard, 1953.

⁶ As early as the *Tzacualli* period, during which an obsidian figurine was offered at a structure within the great Pyramid of the Sun. Millon and Drewitt, 1961.

⁷ Linné, 1934. For the second time the jaguar comes into the Valley to fertilize the indigenous cultures, brought perhaps by Totonacs from Vera Cruz, whose traditions claim that they built Teotihuacan before Tajin. And indeed the relation with Upper Remojadas would bear this out. Spratling, 1960; Medellin Zenil, 1953. See Figure 2.

⁸ Chavero, 1903.

⁹ Caso, 1942a; Villagra Caleti, 1952, 1954, 1957. Further study of these paintings in conjunction with the designs on pottery is being made.

¹⁰ Caso, 1958–9, thinks that the Teotihuacanos knew the calendar and used points and bars to express dates.

¹¹ See all Linné's titles. At this time influences from Teotihuacan were felt in the most distant parts of Mesoamerica. These influences to the south-east into the Maya area permit the correlations of Tlamilolpa-Xolalpan (or Period III) with the early half of the Maya classic, and provide for it the approximate dates of A.D. 300–600. At Tikal, with Stela 31 (date 445?), there was Teotihuacan III pottery found. For radiocarbon dating, see Satterthwaite, 1960.

¹² Sejourné, 1959, excavating a palace at Zacuala, in Teotihuacan found evidence of both sacrifice and penitence.

¹³ At Tikal Stela 31, bearing a date which may be 9.0.10.0.0., was found associated with Teotihuacan pots. The figure on the stela carries a shield with a mask reminiscent of the god Tlaloc. A fragment of another, Stela 32, shows the head of a human figure very similar to this mask, with Tlaloc-like eyes and nosebead and various other details almost identical. (Satterthwaite, personal correspondence.)

¹⁴ Cholula has a long and important history and was a centre of influence from the Upper Pre-classic times until the coming of

the Spaniards. Noguera, 1956; Jimenez Moreno, 1959; Nicholson, 1961.

15 Sears, 1951, confirms the author's theory, saying that the Classic period is shown by his studies to have been drier than the preceding or succeeding periods. He believes that the lack of water may have seriously hampered the Teotihuacanos in their last days at the site.

16 Morris, Charlot, and Morris, 1928.

17 So named for the site at which this author first identified it. It is now known to be one of the Toltec wares.

18 The Aztec occupation of Teotihuacan would seem to have been at the earlier period, known as Aztec II–III. There are very few Tenochtitlan sherds. Millon, 1960.

19 Seler, 1915; Tozzer, 1921, a complete study of a building; Vaillant, 1938.

20 A Teotihuacan pot was recovered from Casas Grandes, Chihuahua. Kidder, 1946.

21 Jimenez Moreno, 1959.

TABLE 3

22 The modern nomenclature for Teotihuacan periods, first suggested by Armillas and approved by Kidder, has been adopted in this edition. It would now seem that Teotihuacan was, from earliest times, a large city, influenced by various trends from outside to be sure, but from the first the planned centre of a high civilization which developed *in situ* with no break in its traditions. At its greatest period it may have occupied as large an area as six square miles. Further excavation will probably discover its exact boundaries and make it possible for archaeologists to break down the three phases into sub-phases.

23 The relative dating of these may be worked out in the near future, according to Millon, who adds (personal correspondence) that it may be found on further excavation that the great city continued to be occupied until the end of the Classic period.

24 Mayer-Oakes, 1959, 1960, believes this phase contemporary with the ceremonial site. Tolstoy, 1958. Nicholson has not yet published the final conclusions on Portezuelo.

CHAPTER 4

This chapter incorporates part of the original Chapter 3, which had dealt with the Toltecs as the builders of Teotihuacan, and part of Chapter 4 which had dealt with them as Dynastic Toltecs, with some clarification based on recent opinion. The best recent publications on the Toltecs are those of Caso, 1941, and Jimenez Moreno, 1941, 1954–5, for the traditional sources, and Acosta, 1942, 1943, 1945, 1957; Armillas, 1950; and Dutton, 1955, for the archaeology.

¹ Brinton, 1890, pp. 83–100.

² Ixtlilxochitl, 1891; Bancroft, 1883, Vol. 5. This historian is a veritable mine of information, but he worked from written records without the archaeological check accessible to modern students. Krickeberg, 1937, contains an excellent summary of current and past interpretation of history; Beyer, in Gamio, 1922; Vaillant, 1938, an effort to tie in historical with archaeological information in the Valley of Mexico; Nicholson, 1955, a criticism of that effort.

³ Caso, 1937, 1941, 1958–9.

⁴ Sahagún, 1938, Vol. 1, Book 1, p. 8; Vol. 2, Book 8, Chapter 5; Vol. 3, Book 10, Chapter 29, paragraphs 1, 12. *Anales de Cuauhtitlan*, 1885. Ixtlilxochitl, 1891.

⁵ Ixtlilxochitl, 1891.

⁶ As we have seen, Cholula was founded in the Tzacualli period of Teotihuacan, but its great period came later.

⁷ Quetzalcoatl, or feathered serpent, refers sometimes to the god whose day is Ce Acatl or to the priests who serve him, sometimes, apparently, to a mythical bringer of culture, and sometimes to a historic person, Topiltzin, a priest of the god, who was born on this holy day. Huemac, whom the author here identifies with him, is the name of an early priest, the leader of the migrations described in the *Historia Tolteca Chichimeca*, and also that of the last king of Tula who died at Chapultepec. Bernal, 1959. Jimenez Moreno, 1956. Kukulcan, too, may have come twice to the Maya area, once when tradition says he left Tula (in the tenth century) and again after its final destruction in 1224–44 according to Roys, 1960.

⁸ At the time of the first edition of the present book, this account was believed to refer to the peoples of Teotihuacan, and indeed it may; but the dates given seem too late for this to be the case, and too early for Tula. There is not agreement as to whom it does refer. It should be noted that here Huemac is the first leader and Topiltzin, the ninth king. Also that Huitzilopochtli is today considered an Aztec god.

⁹ *Anales de Cuauhtitlan*, 1885. See Jimenez Moreno, 1954–5.

¹⁰ Whom we shall find later as a god of the north in the Aztec pantheon, a god of the wandering Chichimec. Caso, 1954; Nicholson, 1959. (Caso, however, tells me there is no connexion.)

¹¹ See Table 5, Tozzer, 1957. Acosta, 1957b, gives the dates of 850–1174 for the occupation of Tula. He sees no evidence there of the worship of Tezcatlipoca.

¹² *Historia Tolteca Chichimeca*, 1937, 1942, 1947.

13 Not to be confused with the thin orange which was so widely traded in Classic times. Smith, 1958, has divided fine orange into five types and traced its distribution in time from Puuc to very late Classic, as well as in space from Chichen Itza to Tabasco. See also Berlin, 1960.

14 Vaillant, 1935; Butler, 1940; Shepard, 1948; Wauchope, 1947.

15 Coyotlatelco, as this author and Tozzer and Noguera use the term, is narrower than that used by more recent writers like Tolstoy, Mayer-Oakes, and Nicholson. When there has been more work such as Tolstoy's surveys of the Valley and when Brainerd's results at Cerro Portezuelo have been published, the whole matter will be clearer.

16 Interesting evidence for Xochicalco having been a meeting-point for the Classic cultures of Mesoamerica, and a place where they continued after the abandonment of Teotihuacan, is found in Piña Chan, 1960a. Here Noguera, Saenz, and Sanchez found a remarkable cache in a room tacked on to the base of the south-east side of the principal edifice: two yokes (of the type associated with the 'Totonacs'), a plaque combining Nahua and Zapotec glyphs, and a pottery head (also 'Totonac'). Under the floor was a secondary burial which had as offerings: Pacific shells, points and knives of obsidian, two stone figurines of the Teotihuacan style and a jadeite pectoral suggesting Maya workmanship. (See also Plate 25.)

17 Curiously enough, Acosta found no evidence at Tula of the worship of Xipe.

18 Chacmool figures occur in Michoacan, in Tlaxcala, at Zempoala and as far south as El Salvador. Covarrubias, 1957. For possible significance see also Palacios, 1940. The identity of Toltec Chichen with Tula can only be explained by large-scale migration or conquest.

19 Later identified as the god of Monsters and the twin of Quetzalcoatl. A persistent tradition says Xolotl found Tula in ruins, so perhaps the destruction was due to civil war. See Bernal, 1959, for one version.

CHAPTER 5

This era is just emerging from darkness and confusion. The author, in the original edition, by suggesting identification of ceremonial dumps with fifty-two-year cycles, attempted to clarify the annals. Contemporary opinion does not altogether accept his views. Nicholson, 1955.

In calling the interim between the fall of Tula and the rise of Tenochtitlan the Toltec-Chichimec period, it is essential to remember that the annals often use the term Toltec loosely, to describe the civilized inhabitants of any large city (Tollan), and use Chichimec, also loosely, to describe marauders. In this chapter, Toltec refers specifically to the culture of Tula, and to its carriers, some of whom, under Nauhyotl, settled at Culhuacan after the fall of Tula. Chichimec refers specifically to the probably Pame Otomi-speaking people who came into the Valley from the Mezquital near Tula, under the great leader Xolotl, who established themselves first at Tenayuca, later at Texcoco, and finally at Culhuacan, where they replaced the Toltec lineage there with one of their own. The Culhua, who were a very important force in the Valley and surrounding country (Barlow, 1949), were thus probably a mixture, both of peoples and civilizations, who politically and culturally made possible the later Aztec Empire.

[1] Joyce, 1914, gives a straightforward interpretation. *Anales de Cuauhtitlan*, 1885. *Relación de Genealogía and Origen de los Mexicanos* are abridgements of the *Anales de Cuauhtitlan*. Lehmann, 1938, is a careful, analytical translation of the Annals of Cuauhtitlan. Orozco y Berra, 1878, is a useful critique. Kirchhoff, 1940, is important for interpretation of annals. Vaillant, 1938, gives a résumé of the basis of this chapter as originally written. Barlow, 1949, and Jimenez Moreno, 1954-5, 1956, give some new interpretations. For a contemporary study of the pottery of this and the subsequent period, see Tolstoy, 1958.

[2] Ixtlilxochitl, 1892. *Mapa Quinatzin, Mapa Tlotzin, Codex Xolotl* are important picture manuscripts for this period.

[3] *Codex Ramirez, Historia de los Mexicanos*, in Radin, 1920. *Codex Boturini, Codex of 1576*, picture manuscripts.

[4] Bancroft, Vol. 5, 1883, Chaps. V–VII cites early authorities. Orozco y Berra, 1880, cites early authorities and picture writings. Radin, 1920, an invaluable series of translations of early Mexican records.

[5] Vaillant, 1938; Tolstoy, 1958.

[6] O'Neill, 1956-7. Jimenez Moreno, 1954-5, thinks that Culhuacan black-on-orange is the pottery of the historic Olmecs who ruled Cholula from 792 until its conquest by Toltecs in 1292. He thinks also that it stopped being made in Culhuacan in 1200 but not until 1270 in Chalco. At both places it is succeeded by Tenayuca black-on-orange, which he considers to have been the pottery made by the Toltecs left behind at Tula. Acosta, writing in the same volume, 1954-5, says Tenayuca black-on-orange is the pottery of those who destroyed Tula. Since the Chichimecs of Xolotl came from near Tula, they may, as we suggest, have brought it with them; and it may in some cases be contemporary with Culhuacan black-on-orange, and in others be diagnostic for the conquest by Chichimecs, which took place in different parts of the Valley at different times. See also Griffin and Espejo, 1947, 1950; Franco, 1949.

[7] Vaillant, 1938; Tolstoy, 1958.

[8] Marquina, Reygadas Vertiz and Noguera in Tenayuca, 1935.

9 Historic Olmecs, according to Jimenez Moreno, 1959.

10 Noguera, 1937. This would seem to indicate Toltec conquest. Jimenez Moreno, 1954–5; 1959.

11 Preuss and Mengin, 1937; Lehmann, 1937; Muñoz Camargo, 1892; Sahagún, 1938, Vol. 3, Book 10, Chapter xxix; Bancroft, Vol. 5, Chapters xi–xiii.

12 Ekholm, 1939, 1940; Griffin, 1952. For contemporary view of Mixteca-Puebla Concept see Nicholson, 1961.

13 The original edition had a group of tables identifying certain migratory groups with specific wares and certain historical rulers and cyclical dumps with archaeological findings. These are today so controversial, and present authorities are still in such disagreement on dates, that it seemed best to eliminate them in the revision. The interested student is referred to Vaillant, 1938.

CHAPTER 6

The picture is much clearer for Aztec times. As the author says in the original edition, the archaeology is better known, and the historical records are in more accord. Therefore this chapter has been left almost exactly as written, with the history of the Aztec proper beginning with Table 6 (Table IX in the original edition) after the rise of the Tenochca. This corresponds to the author's archaeological period of Aztec III–IV, which is equivalent to Tolstoy's time after B (*Surface Survey*, 1958) and the distribution through the valley of Texcoco (or Tenochtitlan) black-on-orange pottery, followed by Tlaltelolco black-on-orange, the ware which was being made at the time of the Conquest. A good popular account of this period is found in Bernal, 1959a. The student should read Jimenez Moreno, 1954–5, and Tolstoy, 1958.

1 EXHAUSTIVE ACCOUNTS OF AZTEC HISTORY: Bancroft, 1883, Vol. 5; Orozco y Berra, 1880.

POPULAR ENGLISH DIGESTS: Thompson, 1933; Joyce, 1914. Radin, 1922, gives translations and reproductions of important native sources, as well as a superb critical analysis. Peterson, 1959; Wolf, 1959.

OTHER SOURCES: Torquemada, 1723; Clavigero, 1783.

PICTURE WRITINGS: the *Codices of 1560, 1590, Boturini, Mendoza, Siguenza, Telleriano-Remensis, Vaticanus A, Tepechpan.*

DIGESTS OF PICTURE WRITINGS IN SPANISH AND NAHUATL: *Anales de Cuauhtitlan*, 1885; Chimalpahin, 1889; *Codex Ramirez*, 1878; Tezozomoc's *Cronica*, 1878; *Histoire Méxicaine*, 1891; *Historia de los Mexicanos*, 1886; Ixtlilxochitl, 1892; Duran, 1867, 1880.

Tenayuca, 1935, is the great work of the Department of Monuments of the Mexican Ministry of Public Education, which blends archaeology and history in a masterly exposition of the Aztec past.

² *Codex Boturini.*

³ *Historia de los Mexicanos.*

⁴ *Anales de Cuauhtitlan*, 1885, p. 49, Year 8 Rabbit. Palacios, *Fundación de México* 1925, résumé of historical evidence for founding of Mexico. *Codex of 1590* shows Acamapichtli being crowned by the chief of Tlaltelolco in the presence of the Tenochca clan council; cf. Vaillant, *Correlation*, 1938, p. 563.

⁵ Sahagún, 1938, Vol. 3, Book 10, Chap. xxix pp. 137-8; also 1956.

⁶ Bancroft, 1883, Vol. 5, quotes early authorities on pp. 414-15.

⁷ Bancroft, 1883, Vol. 5, p. 434; Tezozomoc, Chapter liv; Duran, I, 1867, Chapter xxxii.

⁸ Tezozomoc, 1878; Chapters xli-xlii.

⁹ Tezozomoc, 1872; Chapter li; Duran, L, 1867, Chapter xxxvi.

¹⁰ Ixtlilxochitl, 1892.

¹¹ Bancroft, 1883, p. 449, quotes Torquemada, Clavigero, and Ixtlilxochitl.

¹² Saville, 1929.

¹³ Bancroft, 1883, pp. 439-40, quotes Ixtlilxochitl, Duran, Torquemada, and *Codex Telleriano-Remensis.*

¹⁴ Bancroft, 1883, p. 471, quotes Tezozomoc, Torquemada, and Duran.

¹⁵ Bancroft, 1883, p. 507, quotes Ixtlilxochitl.

¹⁶ Díaz del Castillo, 1908-16. Cortés, 1908.

¹⁷ See O'Neill, 1959.

TABLE 6

¹⁸ Table 6 is the same as Table ix in the first edition. The dates given vary little from those cited by contemporary writers, who, however, do not accept the author's assumption of cyclic dumps. See Figure 22, p. 123.

CHAPTER 7

The customs of the Aztecs were a source of great interest to the conquerors and their palliative companions, the friars. The system of controlling the conquered depended on knowledge of the native methods of life. Consequently there is a full literature based on contemporary reports sent back to Spain by her civil and ecclesiastical administrators in the new colony. (G.C.V.)

There has been some criticism of the following chapters as leaning too heavily on Bandelier. Ekholm and Nicholson (personal communications), and Paddock, 1956. The student is referred for contemporary views of Aztec civilization to Romerovargas, 1959; Alba, 1948; Kirchhoff, 1954-5; Caso, 1953a; Monzon, 1949; Leon-Portilla, 1956, 1959.

For new editions of sources Leon-Portilla, 1957; Carrera Stampa, 1959.

At the present time there are two conflicting points of view concerning how Aztec society should be regarded, as democratic and tribal or as heavily stratified and sharply divided into social classes. It is of course both, depending on whether one looks at the early theoretical base, or at the newly-formed empire that the Spaniards found. Since present studies have found both exogamous and endogamous clan structure in modern Mexico (Nutini, 1961) it is quite possible also that both existed when Cortés came. The present fad is for class structure and castes, just as once it was for idealization of our Indian heritage. That there were nobles with special privileges and the usufruct of land does not alter the communal tradition that underlay Mexican society and that made the 'ejido' seem so natural a concept to the modern Indian. It will in my opinion be a long time before a truer picture of pre-Columbian Mexico is painted than emerges from the Chapters that follow. Note that the very first paragraph recognizes both views.

[1] EXCELLENT POPULAR ACCOUNTS: Thompson, 1933; Biart, 1883; Joyce, 1914; Prescott, 1922; Soustelle, 1959; Burland, 1947; Peterson, 1959.

EXHAUSTIVE ENGLISH STUDIES: Bandelier, 1880; Bancroft, 1883, Vols. 2 and 5. Note that Bandelier is frowned on in 1961.

MEXICAN STUDY: Orozco y Berra, 1880.

BEST CONTEMPORARY ACCOUNTS: Sahagún, 1938, 1956, 1957, 1959; Pomar, 1891; Zurita, 1891; Motolinia, 1914; Torquemada, 1723, 1943; Clavigero, 1787.

PICTURE WRITINGS: *Codex Mendoza, Codex Florentino* (illustrations for Sahagún's *Historia General*).

The transition from the tribal council to the domination of the chiefs is shown by the presence of individual members in the early times and their disappearance after the foundation of the lineage; *cf.* Vaillant, 1938, pp. 563-4. Bandelier, 1880, pp. 576-88. *Mapa de Siguenza, Codex of 1590. Histoire Mexicaine. Codex Mendoza,* and *Codex Telleriano-Remensis.*

[2] *Codex Mendoza.* Sahagún, 1938, Vol. 2, Book 6. See Dibble and Anderson, Translation, 1957 and 1959.

[3] Bandelier, 1880, cites early authorities. Romerovargas, 1959.

[4] Bandelier, 1880; Bancroft, 1883, Vol. 2. See also Kirchhoff, 1954–5, who describes five kinds of land tenure; Monzon, 1949.

[5] *Codex Mendoza*.

[6] Bandelier, 1880; *cf.* Waterman, 1917, for a critique of Bandelier; Romerovargas, 1959.

[7] Sahagún, 1938, Vol. 1, Book 3, Appendix; Vol. 2, Books 6, 9; Vol. 3, Book 10; 1959; Acosta Saignes, 1945; Chapman, 1959.

[8] Bancroft, 1883, Vol. 2; Bandelier, 1880; Caso, 1953b; Romerovargas, 1959.

[9] *Ceballos Novelo*, 1935; Kohler, *Derecho de los Aztecas*, 1924; Alba, 1948. Moreno, 1931; Romerovargas, 1959.

[10] Kirchhoff, 1954–5; Espejo and Monzon, 1945.

CHAPTER 8

This aspect of life is fully covered in the contemporary literature of the Conquest. (G.C.V.) The student should note recent titles.

[1] POPULAR AUTHORS: Thompson, 1931; Joyce, 1914; Biart, 1883.
EXHAUSTIVE ENGLISH STUDIES: Bandelier, 1878; Bancroft, 1883.

EXHAUSTIVE MEXICAN STUDY: Orozco y Berra, 1880.

CONTEMPORARY ACCOUNTS: Sahagún, 1938; Torquemada, 1723; Clavigero, 1787.

PICTURE WRITINGS: *Codex Florentino* (illustrations for Sahagún's *Historia General*). *Codex Mendoza*, Tribute Roll of Montezuma.

[2] Bandelier, 1878; Kirchhoff, 1954–5, for a broader view.

[3] *Mapa Tlotzin*. Cortés, 1908, p. 221, referring to Valley of Puebla, 'Such is the multitude of people who live in these parts that there is not a palm of land which is not cultivated . . . [in] many places they suffer for want of bread.' See also Sanders, 1956; Mayer-Oakes, 1960; Millon, 1959.

[4] Nuttall, 1925.

[5] Bandelier, 1878; Kirchhoff, 1954–5; Romerovargas, 1959.

[6] Tribute Roll of Montezuma, *Codex Mendoza*, Tribute Roll; Yanez Ruiz, 1959.

[7] Articles on Shell and Commerce in Hodge, 1907; Lumholtz, 1902, plumbate ware in Tepic; Lothrop, 1937, gold in Yucatan.

[8] Díaz del Castillo, 1908–16, Chapter XCII; McBryde, 1933.

[9] Blom, 1932.

[10] The recent discovery and development of jade areas in the western United States had led to limited jade-carving in late years.

[11] Nuttall, 1901; Díaz del Castillo, 1908–16, Chapter CXXVIII.

[12] Saville, 1920; Sahagún, 1938, Vol. 5, pp. 193–219.

[13] Sahagún, 1938, Vol. 3, Book 11; Emmart, 1940; Sauer, 1936; Hernandez, 1790; Spinden, 1928.

[14] Alcocer, 1938; Wicke, 1959.

[15] Bancroft, 1883, Vol. 2, pp. 160–74, 553–74, cites authorities.

[16] Vaillant, 1938.

[17] Anonymous Conqueror, 1917, narrative.

[18] Motolinia, 1914, Book I, Chapter XII. Bandelier's translation in Art of War 1877, p. 104. How similar this is to the great city of Teotihuacan, as modern excavations reveal it.

[19] Bernal Díaz, 1908–16, Chapter XCII, p. 72.

[20] Bancroft, 1883, Vol. 2, pp. 553–74, cites authorities on temple architecture; Tenayuca, 1935; Marquina, 1928, 1951.

[21] *Codex Mendoza, Codex Florentino*; Seler, 1904; Peñafiel, 1903.

CHAPTER 9

There are abundant data on crafts and craftsmanship to be drawn from the contemporary authorities and from museum collections. Examples of the textile art, however, are conspicuously lacking, since few fabrics have survived natural disintegration or have survived from collections made by the Conquistadors. Pictures in the manuscripts do give the impression, none the less, that this art was on a par with the others. (G.C.V.)

[1] POPULAR ENGLISH DIGESTS are found in Thompson, 1935; Joyce, 1922, 1927; Spinden, 1928; Vaillant, 1935.

SERIOUS SPECIAL STUDIES: Saville, 1920, 1922, 1925.

[2] Saville, 1900; Holmes, 1919; Nuttall, 1904.

[3] Holmes, 1914–19.

[4] Mason, 1927.

[5] Saville, 1900; Holmes, 1919.

[6] Sahagún, 1938; Peñafiel, 1903; *Codex Mendoza, Codex Magliabecchiano*, Tribute Roll of Montezuma. The manufacture of paper is described by Lenz, 1959.

[7] Nuttall, 1888; Seler, 1904; Sahagún, 1938; *Codex Florentino*.

[8] Saville, 1922.

[9] Holmes, 1895; Saville, 1909.

[10] Saville, 1925.

[11] Saville, 1920; Sahagún, 1938, Vol. 5, Orfebrería.

[12] Caso, 1932.

[13] Lothrop, 1937.

[14] Noguera, 1930, 1935; Boas, 1911–12; Brenner, 1931; Vaillant, 1937, 1938, Figs. 3 and 4. Griffin and Espejo, 1947, 1950; Tolstoy, 1958.

[15] Foster, 1960, suggests the Olmecs did.

[16] Boas, 1911–12, Pls. 1–10.

[17] Boas, 1911–12, Pls. 11–24.

[18] Boas, 1911–12, Pls. 25–31.

[19] Noguera, 1935, Pl. 58, 1934.

[20] Vaillant, 1937; Noguera, 1935.

[21] Vaillant, 1938, Figs. 2 and 5-x.

[22] Noguera, 1928, 1927.

CHAPTER 10

When this book was written, the study of Mesoamerican art was in its infancy. Twenty years later, due in part to the enthusiasm of this author, it is fully realized what a great contribution in this field was made by the American Indian. Whereas in 1941 Douglas and d'Harnoncourt, 1941, and Vaillant, 1939, were among the few publications on North American Indian art, there are many today among which Dockstader, 1961, is outstanding. For Mesoamerica the author recommended Caso, 1938; Cahill, 1933; Castro Leal, 1940; Holmes, 1914–19; Marquina, 1928; Spinden, 1913; Totten, 1928; and his own short papers. There are today so many splendidly illustrated volumes on Mesoamerican art that it is hard to know where to begin in listing them.

Lothrop, 1957; Collier, 1959; Covarrubias, 1957; Keleman, 1943; Marquina, 1951; Bernal, 1950; Toscano, 1944, 1946; Linné, 1961; the many studies of design made by Proskouriakoff, and of the paintings by Villagra Caleti, are only a few of the works on Mesoamerican art available today.

[1] Marquina, 1928, 1935; Holmes, 1895–7; Vaillant, 1935; Marquina, 1951.

[2] Cummings, 1933.

[3] Which may well be as early as Cuicuilco, Millon, 1960.

[4] For some idea of what the temple looked like, we have the frescoes at Tetitla, Villagra Caleti, 1954.

[5] Noguera, 1937.

[6] Today we can also see the remains of the temple of Tlaltelolco, its sister city.

[7] Tenayuca, 1935; Saville, 1896; Seler, 1904; Larsen, 1938; Marquina, 1928; Pollock, 1936; Garcia Payon, 1958c.

[8] Pollock, 1936.

[9] Gallop, 1938; Larsen, 1938; Garcia Payon, 1958c.

[10] Vaillant, 1935. This is less true in 1961 than when it was written. Pre-Columbian art is now fashionable.

[11] Vaillant, 1935.

[12] Spinden, 1928.

13 Caso, 1927.

14 Saville, 1929.

15 Caso, 1932. Compare the Mixtec Codices *Cospi, Vaticanus B, Borgia,* with the Aztec Codices *Telleriano-Remensis* and *Borbonicus.* Covarrubias, 1957. For recent excavations, see Bernal, 1958a.

16 Saville, 1920, 1922, 1925; Lothrop, 1957.

17 Villagra Caleti, 1949, 1952, 1954, 1956-7.

18 Caso, 1927; Vaillant, 1935.

19 PRE-CONQUEST MANUSCRIPTS: *Codex Borbonicus, Codex Boturini,* Tonalamatl Aubin.

POST-CONQUEST MANUSCRIPTS: *Codex Telleriano-Remensis, Codex Vaticanus A, Codex of 1576, Codex of 1590, Manuscrit Méxicaine.*

POST-CONQUEST DRAWINGS TO SPANISH ORDER: *Codex Mendoza, Codex Florentino,* Lienzo de Tlaxcala.

20 Castañeda, 1933.

21 *Codex Borbonicus.*

22 Orozco y Berra, 1880; Spinden, 1928; for oratory, Sahagún, 1938, Vol. II, Book 6; Brinton, 1887.

CHAPTER II

Aztec religion is a fascinating and confusing subject. Ritualism ran wild, and the early Spanish observers, trained in rigorous Christian theology, found the subject interesting but baffling. Sahagún is far and away the best contemporary source. He checked his data in three different localities and spent many years in the process. The late Eduard Seler was the great modern authority, bringing a philosophical background to aid a meticulous interest in ritual. Spence, the best English writer, was his disciple, as was the infinitely learned Hermann Beyer. Alfonso Caso, the distinguished Mexican scholar, has combined brilliantly the meticulousness of the German school with the long-continued Mexican tradition, passed on by many sympathetic and learned minds. Among modern American students J. Eric Thompson is outstanding. (G.C.V.)

1 POPULAR ENGLISH ACCOUNTS: Thompson, 1933; Spinden, 1928; Caso, 1937, 1958a.

MORE DETAILED STUDIES: Bancroft, 1883, Vol. III; Spence, 1923, standard text; Sahagún, Books 1-4, 1932, 1957. A comprehensive work is promised by Burland.

FOREIGN LANGUAGE: Beuchat, 1912; Caso, 1927, 1954; Paso y Troncoso, 1898; Seler, 1902-23; commentaries on Codices Borgia, 1904-9; Fejervary-Mayer, 1901-2; *Vaticanus B,* 1902; and Tonalamatl Aubin, 1900-1; Nicholson, 1959; Leon-Portilla, 1956.

[2] Caso, 1927; Spence, 1923. Official version of Calendar Stone.

[3] At Teotihuacan, Azcapotzalco, Tula, Culhuacan.

[4] Xiuhtecuhtli, Lord of the Year, the Grass, and the Turquoise also known as Huehueteotl, the Old God, is perhaps the earliest of the Mexican gods of the central plateau, although the tiger deity of the 'Olmecs' may have been his contemporary. He was portrayed at Ticoman and at Teotihuacan and also in Vera Cruz at Cerro de las Mesas, in Zapotec urns in Oaxaca, and later again at Tenayuca was worshipped by the Chichimecs.

[5] Spence, 1923; Caso, 1958a, gives only the Mixtec version (see p. 165) and places the divine creative pair at the centre.

[6] Chac to the Maya, Cocijo to the Zapotec, Tajin to the Totonac. His paradise is represented at Tepantitla, in Teotihuacan.

[7] Spence, 1923; Sahagún, 1957.

[8] Spence, 1923.

[9] For definitions of gods: Caso, 1927, 1958a; Spence, 1923; Seler, 1901, 1902, 1903.

[10] Bandelier, 1884; Caso, 1954, 1958a.

[11] Caso, 1958–9, believes the Teotihuacanos knew the calendar. Teotihuacan warriors were at Tikal (Shook, 1958), as evidenced by a Stela (31) accompanied by a tripod vessel showing armed men. (Satterthwaite, personal communication.) Noguera, 1951, finds Maya influence at Xochicalco from where tradition brings Topiltzin to Tula. Finally Toltec influence, more probably conquest, is undeniable at Chichen Itza. Quetzalcoatl as a culture-bearer did a lot of travelling!

[12] FOR FURTHER DEFINITIONS: Caso, 1928, 1938, 1954; Spence, 1923; Seler, 1901, 1902; Nicholson, 1959; Hvidtfeldt, 1958, for a stimulating view of the Aztec place in comparative religion.

CHAPTER 12

The religious organization of the Aztecs is relatively clear. The ritual and the identification of deities is much more perplexing, as a certain amount of interpretation is involved. The working of the calendar has puzzled many a distinguished scholar, but its main principles are known. So elaborate a system of worship must have led to considerable local variation, so the student need not too greatly despair over the lack of agreement among authorities. The methods of pictographic writing are well known. (G.C.V.) For a critical review see Caso, 1942b. Compare the tables with those in Lizardi Ramos, 1959a.

[1] POPULAR ACCOUNTS: Thompson, 1933; Joyce, 1922; Spinden, 1928; Caso, 1958a; Soustelle, 1959; Saenz, 1959.

MORE DETAILED STUDIES: *for the priesthood*, Bandelier, 1880; *for ritual*, Spence, 1923; Seler, 1900–9; Bancroft, 1883, Vols. 1, 3; Del Paso y Troncoso, 1898; Beuchat, 1911; Robelo, 1905. *For calendar*, Caso, 1939, 1958b, 1959; De Jonghe, 1906; Orozco y Berra, 1880; Palacios, 1925; Seler, in Bulletin 28, 1904, 1902–23; Spence, 1923; Spinden, 1933, 1940; Lizardi Ramos, 1959a. *For writing*, Aubin, *Mémoires sur la Peinture*, 1885; Orozco y Berra, *Historia Antigua*, 1880; Peñafiel, *Nombres Geográficos*, 1885; *Nomenclatura Geográfica*, 1895.

CONTEMPORARY: Sahagún, 1938, 1957; *Codex Florentino*; Torquemada, 1923, 1943.

² Bandelier, 1880, cites early authorities.

³ Thompson, 1933; Beuchat, 1911; De Jonghe, 1906; Spence, 1923; Spinden, 1933, 1940; Caso, 1940; Morley, 1915; Thompson, 1960; Lizardi Ramos, 1959b; Orozco y Berra, 1880; Seler, in Bulletin 28, 1904, 1900–9.

This system was common to all the advanced cultures of Mesoamerica, probably originated in 'Olmec' pre-classic times and reached its highest development in the Maya area. It was adopted by the Tenochca after they came into contact with the more civilized inhabitants of the Valley of Mexico.

⁴ Seler, 1900–9.

⁵ AZTEC RECORDS: Tonalamatl Aubin, *Codex Borbonicus*, *Codex Florentino*, *Codex Telleriano-Remensis*, *Vaticanus A*.

MIXTECA-PUEBLA RECORDS: *Vaticanus B*, Borgia, Bologna (Cospi).

⁶ Caso, 1940; Duran, 1880; Sahagún, 1938; *Codex Borbonicus*; Beuchat, Manuel, 1911; Caso, 1954, 1958b, calls *izcalli* the first month. For a discussion of the controversy see Lizardi Ramos, 1959a.

⁷ De Jonghe, 1906; *Codex Mariano Jimenez*; Sahagún, 1938; Fewkes, p. 285, 1893.

It is also quite possible that no intercalation was made and that the calendar did tend to go out of kilter. (Ekholm, personal communication.)

⁸ Seler, *Venus Period*, 1904.

⁹ Bancroft, *Native Races*, 1883, Vol. 3, pp. 393–6, cites authorities.

¹⁰ Duran, *Historia*, II, 1880, pp. 155–60.

¹¹ Linton, Pawnee Sacrifice, 1926; Wissler and Spinden, *Pawnee Sacrifice*, 1916.

¹² Bancroft, *Native Races*, 1883, Vol. 3, pp. 387–8.

¹³ Sahagún, *Historia General*, 1938; Codex Florentino.

¹⁴ Bancroft, *Native Races*, 1883, Vol. 3, pp. 422–5; Blom, *The Maya Ball Game*, 1932; Duran, *Historia de las Indias*, II, 1880, Vol. 2, Chapter CI; Oviedo, *Historia General*, 1851, Vol. 1, p. 165.

This game goes back to Pre-classic times.

¹⁵ Caso, 1927, 1958. Evidence that this game was played at Teotihuacan appeared in 1960 during excavations of the plaza in front of the Pyramid of the Moon (personal observation).

¹⁶ Clavigero, 1787, Book 7, Section 46; Larsen, Volador, 1937.

¹⁷ Bancroft, 1883, Vols. 2 and 3; Nuttall, 1904.

¹⁸ *Codex Borbonicus* for monthly ceremonies.

Telleriano-Remensis and copy *Vaticanus A* record this sacrifice in year 8 Reed (1487).

Bancroft, 1883, Vol. 2, pp. 585–6, cites authors.

¹⁹ Orozco y Berra, 1880; Spinden, 1928; Peñafiel, 1897, 1885; *Codex Mendoza*; Tribute Roll of Montezuma.

²⁰ *Memorial de Tepetlaostoc.*

²¹ Chimalpahin, 1889; Introduction, pp. vii–viii.

²² TEXCOCAN STYLE: *Mapa Tlotzin, Mapa Quinatzin, Codex Xototl, Mapa de Siguenza.*

TENOCHCAN STYLE: *Codices Boturini,* 1576, 1590, *Telleriano-Remensis, Vaticanus A, Histoire Méxicaine, Mapa de Tepechpan*

²³ Sahagún, 1938, Vol. 3, Book 10, Chapter XXIX, pp. 137–8, paragraph 12.

²⁴ *Codex Mendoza,* Tribute Roll of Montezuma.

²⁵ *Codex Chalchihuitzin Vasquez,* in Vaillant, 1939a; Boban, *Documents,* 1891; *Tlaquiltenango Manuscript,* in American Museum of Natural History.

²⁶ Tozzer, 1912; Boban, 1891.

CHAPTER 13

The post-Conquest native historians approached Aztec history from an annalistic point of view. Only occasionally did economic and political ideas enter in. Bancroft's and Orozco y Berra's recapitulations of the early history give fullest materials for a detailed scrutiny of Aztec foreign affairs and war. Bandelier's technical study of their method of warfare is the best general outline of Aztecan procedure in this field. (G.C.V.)

For recent views on Aztec war-making, Soustelle, 1955, and Peterson, 1959, give good popular accounts. Palerm, 1956, Orellana, 1959, and Armillas, 1948a, shed light on special aspects.

¹ Bancroft, 1883; Orozco y Berra, 1880; Bandelier, 1877.

OLDER AUTHORITIES: Duran, 1867, 1880. Ixtlilxochitl, 1891; Historia, 1892; Tezozomoc, 1878; Torquemada, 1723; Clavigero, 1787.

² Mapa Tlotzin. Barlow, 1949.

³ Ixtlilxochitl, 1892.

⁴ Commentary of Hamy in *Codex Telleriano-Remensis.* Aragon, 1931.

5 Chapman, 1959; Berlin, 1960; Acosta Saignez, 1945.

6 Bancroft, *Native Races*, Vol. 5, cites versions of various authorities.

7 Bandelier, *Art of War*, 1877.

8 Díaz del Castillo, *True History*, 1908, Vol. 1, Chapter IX, p. 43; Chapter XX, p. 74; Chapter XXIII, p. 85. Toltec figurines show warriors wearing such armour.

9 *Codex Mendoza*.

10 Bandelier, *Art of War*, 1877.

11 Bandelier, *Art of War*, 1877. See, however, Armillas, 1948a; Palerm, 1956; Orellana, 1959.

12 Vaillant, *Correlation*, 1938, footnote 81. *Codex Mendoza*.

13 Bancroft, *Native Races*, 1883, Vol. 2, pp. 603–23.

CHAPTER 14

This chapter was adapted from *Natural History*, Vol. 33, No. 1, pp. 17–30, January–February 1933. It is based on contemporary accounts of Tenochtitlan and on various later archaeological studies on the topography of Tenochtitlan, the ancient Mexico City. (G.C.V.) It has not been revised.

1 CONTEMPORARY ACCOUNTS: Cortés, 1908; Díaz del Castillo, 1908–16; Anonymous Conqueror, 1917; Mendieta, 1870; Motolinia, 1914; Sahagún, 1938, Vol. 4, Book 12; *Codex Florentino*.

LATER STUDIES: Prescott, 1922; Maudslay, 1912; Peñafiel, 1910; Alcocer, 1935; maps reproduced in Maudslay's edition of Bernal Díaz del Castillo, 1908–16, Vol. 3: Plan on Maguey Paper, Map of 1524, Map of Alonso de Santa Cruz, 1560.

2 Díaz del Castillo, 1908–16, Vol. 2, Chapter LXXXVIII.

3 Díaz del Castillo, 1908–16, Vol. 2, Chapter XCII.

CHAPTER 15

Prescott has unforgettably told the story of the Conquest of Mexico. This chapter seeks to stress the Indian side of the Conquest, as told by Sahagún, Duran, and others and as illustrated in the *Codex Florentino* and the Lienzo de Tlaxcala. The latter was prepared as a memorial to show the services Tlaxcalan warriors rendered the cause of Spain. This chapter is adapted from *Natural History*, Vol. 39, No. 3, pp. 185–95, March 1937. (G.C.V.) It has not been revised.

1 Prescott, 1922; Orozco y Berra, 1880; Cortés, 1908; Díaz del Castillo, 1908–16; Anonymous Conqueror, 1917; Duran, 1867, 1880; Ixtlilxochitl, 1829; Sahagún, 1938, Vol. 4, Book 12; *Codex Florentino*; Lienzo de Tlaxcala.

2 Sahagún, 1938, Vol. 4, Book 12, Chapter I; *Codex Florentino*.

[3] Sahagún, 1938, Vol. 4, Book 12, Chapter VIII.

[4] Lienzo de Tlaxcala, Pl. 17.

[5] Sahagún, 1938, Vol. 4, Book 12, Chapter XXIII; Duran, 1880, Chapter LXXVI, p. 50.

[6] Díaz del Castillo, 1908–16, Vol. 2, Chapter CXXVIII, p. 247, says no!! Bancroft, Vol. 1, p. 480, says yes!! on authority.

[7] Sahagún, 1938, Vol. 4, Book 12, Chapter XXXIII.

[8] Soustelle, 1959, emphasizes how different Mexican notions of conquest were from the European.

CHAPTER 16

In the original edition the author recommended the following books to the visitor to Mexico:

Henry Bamford Parkes, *History of Mexico*, Houghton Mifflin Co., Boston, 1938. A history devoted chiefly to colonial and republican Mexico.

Herbert Joseph Spinden, *Ancient Civilization of Mexico and Middle America*, American Museum of Natural History, Handbook Series, No. 3, New York, 1928. A masterpiece of exposition, short and simple, incredibly packed with knowledge, a *sine qua non* for the understanding of Indian civilization.

Charles Flandrau, *Viva Mexico*, D. Appleton & Company, New York, 1908. An enchanting series of impressions of Mexico under Díaz.

Bernal Díaz del Castillo, *The True History of the Conquest of New Spain*, Hakluyt Society, Series 2, Vols. 23–5, 30, 40, London, 1908–16. *The Conquest of New Spain*, Penguin Books Ltd, 1963. This old warrior, a soldier under Cortés, gives the most personal account of the Conquest.

William Hickling Prescott, *The Conquest of Mexico*, Henry Holt and Co., New York, 1922, and Everyman Library, London. Not only a brilliant account of the Conquest as seen through Spanish eyes, but one of the masterpieces of American literature.

J. Eric Thompson, *Mexico before Cortés*, Scribners, New York, 1933. An intimately alive picture of the Aztec civilization.

George C. Vaillant, *Artists and Craftsmen in Ancient Central America*, American Museum of Natural History Guide Leaflet Series 88 and 103, 1935. A survey of Middle American art, fully illustrated, for a very low price.

Anita Brenner, *Idols behind Altars*, Payson and Clarke, Ltd, New York, 1929. A superb picture of the Mexican artistic renaissance of 1918 and the essential continuity of Indian life.

C. S. Braden, *Religious Aspects of the Conquest of Mexico*, Duke

University Press, Durham, N. C., 1930. The theory of the evangeliza-
tion of the Mexican Indian, showing the humanitarian theories behind
the consolidation of the Spanish Conquest.

Madame Calderon de la Barca, *Life in Mexico*, E. P. Dutton and Co.,
New York, 1931. The Scottish wife of the Spanish ambassador to
Mexico in 1828 writes a most entertaining account of contemporary
habits and customs. A classic.

Stuart Chase, *Mexico, A Study of Two Americas*, Macmillan Co., New
York, 1931. A succinct, slightly *simpliste* account of contemporary
Mexico with special emphasis on the virtues of unmechanized life.
(G.C.V.)

In recent years the great archaeological discoveries and the opening
up of new roads have not been matched by new popular classics,
except for Miguel Covarrubias, *Mexico South*, 1946, and *Indian Art of
Mexico and Central America*, 1957, both published by Knopf. John A.
Crow, *Mexico Today*, Harper & Brothers, New York, 1957, is also
satisfactory.

The Instituto Nacional de Antropologia e Historia has published excellent guides to all the archaeological sites; and Davis et al., 1959, give
the latest information on highways.

¹ Braden, 1930; Ricard, 1933.

² The amount of writing by the different monastic orders is interesting as a reflection of direct interest in Indian affairs: Franciscan, 68;
Jesuit, 19; Dominican, 18; Augustinian, 3; parish priests, 18; civilians,
6; *cf.* Clavigero, *History*, 1787, and Ricard, *Conquête Spirituelle*: Spanish
friars, 61; Indians and Mestizos, 61; Spanish civilians, 6; foreign friars, 7.

³ Indian authors and approximate dates of composition: Tezozomoc,
before 1561; *Anales de Cuauhtitlan*, 1570; Duran, 1581; Ixtlilxochitl,
1600; Chimalpahin, 1613.

Post-Conquest picture writings and closing dates: *Codex Telleriano-
Remensis* and *Vaticanus A*, 1563; *Codex of 1576*, 1607; *Codex of 1590*,
1590. *Histoire Méxicaine*, 1521.

⁴ —, *Tres Siglos de Arquitectura Colonial*, 1933, p. 27; Garcia Granados
y MacGregor, 1934.

⁵ Nuttall, 1926; *Del Paso y Troncoso*, 1905-6.

⁶ Redfield, 1930; Parsons, 1936.

⁷ Brenner, *Idols behind Altars*, 1929. Chase, *Mexico*, 1931. See above.

⁸ The perfect guide for Mexico has yet to be written. The only one
that is accurate archaeologically is Frances Toor, *New Guide to Mexico*,
Crown Publishers, Inc., New York, 1960.

⁹ Written twenty years ago, this description of our situation is still
true. There is much talk today of status and class among the early

Mexicans and the author's view is called an idealization. It was written by a man who had not only studied the remains and traditions of the prehistoric Indian, but knew and loved his descendants in a way that we know only those whom we do love. This plea for more understanding and less competition between individuals and nations will have meaning when the contemporary jargon of socio-economic class structure has been forgotten. I have proudly let it stand.

[10] How pleased the author would have been by the Alianza Para el Progreso!

Bibliography

ACOSTA, JORGE

   1942. 'La Ciudad de Quetzalcoatl' (*Cuadernos Americanos*, Vol. 1,
      No. 2, pp. 121–31, Mexico).

   1943. 'Los Colosos de Tula' (*Cuadernos Americanos*, Vol. 2, No. 6,
      pp. 138–46, Mexico).

   1945. 'La Cuarta y Quinta Temporada de Excavaciones en Tula,
      Hidalgo' (*Revista Mexicana de Estudios Antropológicos*, Vol. 7, Nos.
      1–3, pp. 23–65).

   1957a. 'Resumen de los Informes de la 9 y 10 Temporada en Tula,
      Hidalgo' (*Anales del Instituto Nacional de Antropología e Historia*,
      Vol. 9, No. 38, pp. 119–69).

   1957b. 'Interpretación de Algunos de los Datos Obtenidos en Tula
      Relativos a la Época Tolteca' (*Revista Mexicana de Estudios Antro-
      pológicos*, Vol. 14, Pt. 2, pp. 75–110, Mexico).

ACOSTA SAIGNES, MIGUEL

   1945. 'Los Pochteca' (*Acta Antropológica*, Vol. 1, No. 1, Mexico).

ALBA, CARLOS H.

   1948. 'Estudio comparado entre el Derecho Azteca y el Derecho
      positivo Mexicano' (*Edición del Instituto Indigenista Interamericano*,
      Mexico).

ALCOCER, I.

   1935. 'Apuntes sobre la Antigua México-Tenochtitlan' (*Instituto Pan-
      americano de Geografía e Historia*, Tacubaya).

   1938. 'Comidas de los Mexicanos' (in Sahagún, *Historia General*, Vol.
      3, pp. 365–74).

DE ALVA IXTLILXOCHITL, F.

   See Ixtlilxochitl, F. de Alva.

ANALES DE CUAUHTITLAN (CODEX CHIMALPOPOCA)

   1885. *Anales del Museo Nacional de México*, Tomo 3, Appendix,
      Mexico.

   See also Lehmann, *Die Geschichte von Colhuacan und Mexico*, 1938.

ANALES DE TLATELOLCO

   1948. 'Unos Anales Historicos de la Nación Mexicana y Codice de
      Tlatelolco' (*Fuentes para la Historia de México*. Colección publicada
      bajo la dirección de Salvador Toscano, No. 2, Mexico).

ANDREWS, E. WYLLYS

1940. 'Chronology and Astronomy in the Maya Area' (in *The Maya and Their Neighbors*, pp. 150–61, New York).

1959. 'Dzibilchaltun: Lost City of the Maya' (*National Geographic Magazine*, Vol. 115, No. 1, pp. 90–109, Washington).

ANONYMOUS CONQUEROR

1917. *Narrative of Some Things of New Spain and the Great City of Temestitan, Mexico*, (translated into English by Marshall H. Saville, *Documents and Narratives Concerning the Discovery and Conquest of Latin America*, No. 1, The Cortés Society, New York).

ANONYMOUS

1957. *Art of the Aztec Empire* (University of Kansas, Museum of Art, Lawrence).

ANTIGUEDADES MEXICANAS

1892. 'Antiguedades Mexicanas' (publicadas por la Junta Colombino de México en *El Cuarto Centenario de Descubrimiento de America*. Mexico).

ARAGON, JAVIER O.

1931. 'Expansión Territorial del Imperio Mexicano' (*Anales del Museo Nacional de Arqueología, Historia y Etnografía*, 4a Época, Tomo 7, pp. 5–64, Mexico).

ARMILLAS, PEDRO

1944. 'Exploraciones Recientes en Teotihuacan' (*Cuadernos Americanos*, Vol. 3, No. 4, pp. 121–36, Mexico).

1945. 'Los Dioses de Teotihuacan' (*Anales del Instituto de Etnología Americana*, Tomo 6, pp. 35–59, Mexico).

1948a. 'Fortalezas Mexicanas' (*Cuadernos Americanos*, Vol. 7, No. 5, pp. 143–63, Mexico).

1948b. 'A Sequence of Cultural Development in Meso-America' (In 'A Reappraisal of Peruvian Archaeology', *American Antiquity*, Vol. 13, No. 4, Pt 2, pp. 105–11).

1950. 'Teotihuacan Tula y los Toltecas' (*Runa*, Vol. 3, Pt 1, pp. 37–70, Buenos Aires).

1952. 'Cronología de la Cultura Teotihuacana' (*Tlatoani, Boletín de la Sociedad de Alumnos de la Escuela Nacional de Arqueología e de Historia*, Mexico).

1957. 'Cronología y Periodificación de la Historia de la America Precolombina' (*Suplemento de Tlatoani*, 1, Mexico).

1958. 'Program of the History of American Indians' (Pan American Union, *Social Science Monographs*, No. 2, Washington).

AUBIN, J. M. A.

1885. Mémoires sur la peinture didactique' (*Mission Scientifique au*

Mexique et dans l'Amérique Centrale: Recherches historiques et archéologiques. Première Partie–Histoire. Paris).

1893. *Histoire de la nation mexicaine* (Réproduction du Codex de 1576, Paris). *See also* Codex of 1576.

AVELEYRA ARROYO DE ANDA, LUIS

1950. *Prehistoria de México.* Mexico.

1956. 'The Second Mammoth and Associated Artifacts at Santa Isabel, Iztapan, Mexico' (*American Antiquity*, Vol. 22, pp. 12–28, Salt Lake City).

AVELEYRA ARROYO DE ANDA, LUIS; AND MALDONADO KOERDELL, MANUEL; AND MARTINEZ DEL RIO, PABLO

1956. 'Cueva de la Candelaria' (Instituto Nacional de Antropología e Historia, *Memorias*, Vol. 1, No. 5, Mexico).

BANCROFT, HUBERT HOWE

1883a. *The Conquest of Mexico* (3 vols., New York).

1883b. *The Native Races* (5 vols., San Francisco).

BANDELIER, ADOLPH F.

1877. 'On the Art of War and Mode of Warfare of the Ancient Mexicans' (*Tenth Annual Report of the Peabody Museum of American Archaeology and Ethnology*, Vol. 2, pp. 95–161, Cambridge).

1878. 'On the Distribution and Tenure of Lands, and the Customs with Respect to Inheritance, among the Ancient Mexicans' (*Eleventh Annual Report of the Peabody Museum of American Archaeology and Ethnology*, Vol. 2, pp. 385–448, Cambridge).

1880. 'On the Social Organization and Mode of Government of the Ancient Mexicans' (*Twelfth Annual Report of the Peabody Museum of American Archaeology and Ethnology*, Vol. 2, pp. 557–699, Cambridge).

1884. 'Report of an Archaeological Tour in Mexico in 1881' (*Papers, Archaeological Institute of America*, American Series, Vol. 2, Boston).

BARBA DE PIÑA CHAN, BEATRIZ

1956. 'Tlapacoya, un sitio Preclásico de Transición' (*Acta Antropológica*, Época 2, Vol. 1, No. 1, p. 183, Mexico).

BARLOW, ROBERT H.

1949. 'The Extent of the Empire of the Culhua Mexica' (*Ibero-Americana*, 28. University of California, Berkeley).

BATRES, LEOPOLDO

1902a. *Explorations in Escalerillas Street, Mexico City.* Mexico.

1902b. *Exploraciones de Monte Albán, México.* Mexico.

1904. *Exploraciones en Huexotla, Texcoco, y El Gavilán, México.* Mexico.

BEALS, RALPH L.
   1932. 'The Comparative Ethnology of Northern Mexico before 1750' (*Ibero-Americana*, 2, University of California, Berkeley).

BENNETT, WENDELL C., AND ZINGG, R. M.
   1935. *The Tarahumara*. Chicago.

BERLIN, HEINRICH
   1947. See Historia Tolteca-Chichimeca.
   1960. 'Late Pottery Horizons of Tabasco, Mexico' (*American Anthropology and History*, Carnegie Institution of Publication 606, No. 59, Washington, D.C.).

BERNAL, IGNACIO
   1950. 'Compendio de Arte Mesoamericano' (*Enciclopedia Mexicana de Arte*, 7, Ediciones Mexicanas, S. A., Mexico).
   1953. *Mesoamerica: Periodo Indigena* (Instituto Panamericano de Geografía e Historia, Mexico, D. F.).
   1958a. 'Archeology of the Mixteca' (*Boletín de Estudios Oaxaqueños*, No. 7, Oaxaca).
   1958b. 'Monte Alban and the Zapotecs' (*Boletín de Estudios Oaxaqueños*, No. 1, Oaxaca).
   1959a. *Tenochtitlan en una Isla* (Instituto Nacional de Antropología e Historia, Mexico).
   1959b. 'Evolución y Alcance de Las Culturas Mesoamericanas' (*Esplendor del México Antiguo*, Vol. 1, pp. 97–124).

BERNAL, IGNACIO Y DAVALOS, ED.
   1953. *Huastecos, Totonacos, y sus Vecinos* (Sociedad Mexicana de Antropología, Mexico).

BERNAL, IGNACIO, AND SOUSTELLE, JACQUES
   1958. *Mexico: Pre-Hispanic Paintings* (United Nations Economic and Social Council, World Art Series, No. 10, Paris).

BEUCHAT, HENRI
   1912. *Manuel d'archéologie américaine*. Paris.

BEYER HERMANN
   1921. 'Sobre Antiguedades del Pedregal de San Angel' (*Memorias de la Sociedad Científica 'Antonio Alzate'*, Tomo 37, pp. 1–16, Mexico).

BIART, LUCIEN
   1913. *The Aztecs* (translated by J. L. Garner, Chicago).

BIBLIOTECA MEXICANA
   1878. *Crónica Mexicana escrita por D. Hernando Alvarado Tezozomoc ... anotada por el Sr. Lic. D. Manuel Orozco y Berra, y precedida del Códice Ramirez, Manuscrito del Siglo XVI intitulado: Relación del Origen de los Indios que habitan esta Nueva España según sus Historias, y de un Examen de Ambas Obras al cual va anexo un estudio de Crono-*

logía Mexicana por el mismo Sr. Orozco y Berra (Biblioteca Mexicana, José M. Vigil, editor, Mexico).

BIRD, JUNIUS

1938. 'Antiquity and Migrations of the Early Inhabitants of Patagonia' (*Geographical Review*, Vol. 28, pp. 250–75, New York).

1951. 'South American Radiocarbon Dates' (in *Radiocarbon Dating*, Memoirs, Society American Archaeology. *American Antiquity*, Vol. 17, No. 7, Pt. 2).

BLOM, FRANS

1932a. 'Commerce, Trade and Monetary Units of the Maya' (*Middle American Research Series*, pub. no. 4, pp. 531–56, Tulane University, New Orleans).

1932b. 'The Maya Ball-Game *Pok-ta-pok* (called *tlachtli* by the Aztecs)' (*Middle American Research Series*, pub. no. 4, pp. 485–530, Tulane University, New Orleans).

BOAS, FRANZ

1911–12. *Album de Colecciones Arqueológicas* (Publicaciones de la Escuela Internacional de Arqueología y Etnología Americanas, Mexico). *See* Gamio, Texta, 1921.

BOBAN, EUGENE

1891. *Documents pour servir à l'histoire du Mexique* (Catalogue raisonné de la collection de M. E. Eugène Goupil; 2 vols. of text and atlas, Paris).

BORHEGYI, STEPHAN

1959. 'Underwater Archaeology in Guatemala' (*33rd International Congress of Americanists*, Tomo 2, pp. 229–40. San José, C.R.).

BRADEN, C. S.

1930. *Religious Aspects of the Conquest of Mexico* (Duke University Press, Durham).

BRAINERD, GEORGE W.

1954. *The Maya Civilization* (Southwest Museum, Los Angeles).

1958. 'The Archaeological Ceramics of Yucatan' (University of California, *Anthropological Records*, Vol. 19, Berkeley and Los Angeles).

BRAND, DONALD

1932. *See* Sauer and Brand.

BRENNER, ANITA

1929. *Idols behind Altars*. New York.

1931. 'The Influence of Technique on the Decorative Style in the Domestic Pottery of Culhuacan' (*Columbia University Contributions to Anthropology*, Vol. 13, New York).

1932. *Your Mexican Holiday*. New York and London.

BRINTON, DANIEL G.

1887. *Ancient Nahuatl Poetry*. Philadelphia.

1890a. *Rig Veda Americanus*. Philadelphia.

1890b. *Essays of an Americanist*. Philadelphia.

BULLETIN 28

1904. 'Mexican and Central American Antiquities', 'Calendar Systems and History' (Papers by Seler and others, *Bureau of American Ethnology, Bulletin 28*, Washington).

BURLAND, C. A.

1947. *Art and Life in Ancient Mexico* (Bruno Cassirer, Oxford).

1952. 'In the House of Flowers. Xochicalco and its Sculptures' (*Ethnos*, Vol. 17, pp. 119–29, Stockholm).

BUTLER, MARY

1940. 'A Pottery Sequence from the Alta Verapaz, Guatemala' (in *The Maya and Their Neighbors*, pp. 250–67, New York).

CAHILL, HOLGER

1933. *American Sources of Modern Art* (The Museum of Modern Art, New York).

CALDERON DE LA BARCA, MADAME

1931. *Life in Mexico*. New York.

CARRERA STAMPA, MANUEL

1959. 'Fuentes para el Estudio de la Historia Indigena' (*Esplendor del México Antiguo*, Vol. 2, pp. 1109–19).

CASO, ALFONSO

1924–7. 'Un Antiguo Juego Mexicano: El Patolli' (*El México Antiguo*, Vol. 2, pp. 203–11, Mexico).

1927a. 'Las Ruinas de Tizatlan, Tlaxcala' (*Revista Mexicana de Estudios Historicos*, Vol. 1, pp. 139–72, Mexico).

1927b. *El Teocalli de la Guerra Sagrada*. Mexico.

1928. *Las Estelas Zapotecas*. Mexico.

1932a. 'Monte Albán, Richest Archaeological Find in America' (The *National Geographic Magazine*, Vol. 62, pp. 487–512, Washington).

1932b. 'Reading the Riddle of Ancient Jewels' (*Natural History*, Vol. 32, pp. 464–80, New York).

1932c. *Las Exploraciones en Monte Albán, Temporada 1931–32* (Instituto Panamericano de Geografía e Historia, pub. no. 7, Mexico).

1935. *Las Exploraciones en Monte Albán, Temporada 1934–35* (Instituto Panamericano de Geografía e Historia, pub. no. 19, Mexico).

1937a. *The Region of the Aztecs*. Mexico.

1937b. '¿Tenian los Teotihuacanos Conocimiento del Tonalpohualli?' (*El México Antiguo*, Vol. 4, Nos. 3–4, pp. 131–43, Mexico).

Bibliography

1938a. *Exploraciones en Oaxaca. Quinta y Sexta Temporadas 1936–37* (Instituto Panamericano de Geografía e Historia, pub. no. 34, Tacubaya).

1938b. *Thirteen Masterpieces of Mexican Archaeology.* Mexico.

1939. 'La Correlación de los Años Azteca y Cristiano' (*Revista Mexicana de Estudios Antropológicos*, Vol. 3, No. 1, pp. 11–45, Mexico).

1941. 'El Complejo Arqueológico de Tula y las Grandes Culturas Indigenas de Mexico' (*Revista Mexicana de Estudios Antropológicos*, Vol. 5).

1942a. 'El Paraiso Terrenal en Teotihuacan' (*Cuadernos Americanos*, Vol. 6, Mexico).

1942b. 'Aztecas de México' (*Cuadernos Americanos*, Vol. 1, pp. 155–60, Mexico).

1953a. 'New World Culture History: Middle America' (In A. L. Kroeber, *Anthropology Today: An Encyclopedic Inventory*, pp. 226–37, Chicago).

1954. *El Pueblo del Sol* (Fondo de Cultura Económica, Mexico).

1958a. *The Aztecs: People of the Sun* (translated by Lowell Dunham. University of Oklahoma Press).

1958b. 'El Calendario Mexicano' (*Memorias de la Academia Mexicana de la Historia*, Vol. 17, No. 1, pp. 41–96, Mexico).

1958–9. 'Glifos Teotihuacanos' (*Revista Mexicana de Etnología e Antropología*, Vol. 15, pp. 51–71).

1959. 'Nuevos Datos para la Correlación de los Años Aztecas y Cristianos' (*Estudios de Cultura Nahuatl*, Vol. 1, pp. 9–25, Mexico).

CASO, ALFONSO, WITH RUBIN DE LA BORBOLLA, D. F.

1936. *Exploraciones en Mitla, Temporada 1934–35* (Instituto Panamericano de Geografía e Historia, pub. no. 21, Mexico).

CASTAÑEDA, D., AND MENDOZA, V. T.

1933. 'Los Pequeños Percutores de las Civilizaciones Precortesianas' (*Anales del Museo Nacional de Arqueología, Historia y Etnografía*, 4a Época, Tomo 8, pp. 449–576, Mexico).

CASTRO LEAD, ANTONIO, AND OTHERS

1940. *Twenty Centuries of Mexican Art.* Mexico.

CATHERWOOD, FREDERICK

1844. *Views of Ancient Monuments in Central America, Chiapas and Yucatan.* London.

CEBALLOS NOVELO, R. J.

1935. *Las Instituciones Aztecas.* Mexico.

CHAPMAN, ANNE

1959. *Puertos de Intercambio en Mesoamerica Prehispanica* (Instituto Nacional de Antropología e Historia, Mexico).

311

CHARLOT, JEAN
  1931. *See* Morris, Charlot, and Morris.
CHARNAY, DÉSIRÉ
  1887. *The Ancient Cities of the New World* (translated by J. G. and
    H. S. Conant. New York).
CHARNAY, DÉSIRÉ, AND VIOLLET-LE-DUC, E. E.
  1863. *Cités et Ruines Américaines* (1 vol. text and atlas of plates, Paris).
CHASE, STUART
  1931. *Mexico, A Study of Two Americas.* New York.
CHAVERO, A.
  1887. *Historia Antigua y de la Conquista* (Vol. 1 of *V. Riva Palacio,
    México a través de los Siglos,* Mexico and Barcelona).
  1904. 'El Monolito de Coatlinchan' (*Anales del Museo Nacional de
    México,* 2a Epoca, Tomo 1, pp. 281–305, Mexico).
CHIMALPAHIN
  1889. *Anales de Chimalpahin Quauhtlehuanitzin, Sixième et Septième
    Relations, publiées et traduite par Rémi Siméon* (Bibliothèque Lin-
    guistique Américaine, tome 12, Paris).
CHURCHWARD, JAMES
  1926. *Lost Continent of Mu.* London.
CLAVIGERO, FRANÇESCO SAVERIO
  1787. *The History of Mexico* (translated by Charles Cullen, 2 vols.,
    London).

CODICES
    See also Lienzo, Mapa, Tonalamatl and Tribute Roll of Monte-
    zuma.
CODEX OF 1576
    A Post-Columbian Codex in the Goupil Collection (National Library,
    Paris).
    See Aubin, *Histoire,* 1893.
CODEX MEXICANUS OF 1590
    See Boban, *Documents,* 1891, Pls. 23, 24.
CODEX BOLOGNA
    See Codex Cospi.
CODEX BORBONICUS
  1899. *A Pre-Columbian Codex Preserved in the Library of the Chamber
    of Deputies,* Paris.
    See Paso y Troncoso, *Codice Pictorico,* 1898, and Vaillant, ed.,
    Sacred Almanac, 1940.
CODEX BORGIA
  1898. *A Pre-Columbian Codex Preserved in the Ethnographical Museum*

of the Vatican, Rome (published by le Duc de Loubat, Rome).

See also Kingsborough, *Antiquities of Mexico*, 1830, Vol. 3, Pt 1, pp. 1–76; and Seler, *Commentary*, 1904–8.

CODEX BOTURINI (TIRA DEL MUSEO)

See Garcia Cubas, *Atlas*, 1858; Radin, *Sources*, 1920, pp. 11–12, 33–5, Pls. 1 and 2; Orozco y Berra, *Histoira Antigua*, 1880, Vol. 3, Chap. 4; Kingsborough, *Antiquities of Mexico*, 1830, Vol. 1, Pt. 3, pp. 1–23.

CODEX CHALCHIHUITZIN VASQUEZ

See Vaillant, *Twilight*, 1939.

CODEX CHIMALPOPOCA

See Anales de Cuauhtitlan.

CODEX COSPI (BOLOGNA)

1898. *A Pre-Columbian Codex in the Library of the University of Bologna* (published by le Duc de Loubat, Rome).

Kingsborough, *Antiquities of Mexico*, 1830, Vol. 2, Pt 3, pp. 1–24.

CODEX FEJERVARY-MAYER

1901. *An Old Mexican Picture Manuscript in the Liverpool Free Public Museum* (published by le Duc de Loubat, Paris).

See Seler, *Commentary*, 1902.

CODEX FLORENTINO

1905. Illustrations for Sahagún's *Historia de las Cosas de Nueva España* (published by Francisco del Paso y Troncoso, Vol. 5, Madrid).

See Sahagún.

CODEX KINGSBOROUGH

1912. See Memorial de los Indios de Tepetlaostoc.

CODEX MAGLIABECCHIANO, XIII-3

1904. *Manuscrit Mexicain Post-Colombien de la Bibliothèque Nationale de Florence* (reproduit au frais du Duc de Loubat. Rome).

See Nuttall, *The Book of Life*, 1903.

CODEX MARIANO JIMENEZ

n. d. *Codice Mariano Jimenez* (edited by Nicolas Léon, Mexico).

CODEX MENDOCINO

See Codex Mendoza.

CODEX MENDOZA (MENDOCINO)

1938. *Codex Mendoza* (edited and translated by James Cooper Clark, 3 vols., London).

See also Museo Nacional de Arqueología, *Historia y Etnografía*, Mexico, 1925; Kingsborough, *Antiquities of Mexico*, 1830, Vol. 1, London.

CODEX NUTTALL (CODEX ZOUCHE)
    1902. *Ancient Mexican Codex belonging to Lord Zouche of Haryworth*. Introduction by Zelia Nuttall (Peabody Museum of American Archaeology and Ethnology, Cambridge).

CODEX RAMIREZ
    See Historia de los Mexicanos por sus Pinturas.

CODEX TELLERIANO-REMENSIS
    1899. *A Post-Columbian Codex published by le Duc de Loubat* (Commentary by E. T. Hamy, Paris).

CODEX VATICANUS 3738 (VATICANUS A) (Rios) (Copy of *Codex Telleriano-Remensis*).
    1900. *A Post-Columbian Codex Preserved in the Library of the Vatican, Rome* (published by le Duc de Loubat, Rome).
        See Kingsborough, *Antiquities of Mexico*, 1830, Vol. 2, Pt 1, pp. 1–149.

CODEX VATICANUS 3773 (VATICANUS B)
    1896. *A Pre-Columbian Codex Preserved in the Library of the Vatican, Rome* (published by le Duc de Loubat, Rome).
        See also Kingsborough, *Antiquities of Mexico*, 1830, Vol. 3, Pt 4, pp. 1–96; Seler, *Commentary*, 1903.

CODEX VIENNA
    See Codex Vindobonensis.

CODEX VINDOBONENSIS (VIENNA)
    1929. *Codex Vindobonensis Mexic.* I. Facsimile. Text by Walter Lehmann and Ottokar Smital. Vienna.
        See Kingsborough, *Antiquities of Mexico*, 1830, Vol. 2, Pt 4, pp. 1–66.

CODEX XOLOTL
    See Boban, *Documents*, 1891, Pls. 1–10; Radin, *Sources*, 1920, pp. 17–18, 41–5.

CODEX ZOUCHE
    See Codex Nuttall.

COE, MICHAEL D.
    1957. 'Pre-Classic Cultures in Mesoamerica' (Harvard Middle American Seminar, 1955–6. Kroeber Anthropological Society. *Papers*. No. 17, pp. 7–37, Berkeley).
    1960. 'Archaeological Linkages with North and South America at La Victoria, Guatemala' (*American Anthropologist*, n.s., Vol. 62, No. 3, pp. 363–93. Menasha).
    1959 *La Victoria: An Early site on the Pacific Coast of Guatemala*

(Doctoral dissertation, Dept. of Anthropology, Harvard University, Cambridge).

COLLIER, DONALD

1959. *Indian Art of the Americas* (Chicago Natural History Museum, Chicago).

COOKE, ROBERT M. AND BELSHÉ, JOHN C.

1959. 'Dating by Archaeomagnetism' (*Archaeology*, Vol. 12, No. 3, pp. 158–62, New York).

COOK, S. F. AND EZRA-COHN, H. C.

1959. 'An Evaluation of the Fluorine Dating Method' (*Southwestern Journal of Anthropology*, Vol. 15, No. 3, pp. 276–90, Albuquerque).

COVARRUBIAS, MIGUEL

1946. *Mexico South. The Isthmus of Tehuantepec*. New York.

1957. *Indian Art of Mexico and Central America*. New York.

CORTÉS, HERNANDO

1908. *Letters of Cortés* (translated and edited by F. A. MacNutt, 2 vols., New York and London).

CRANE, H. R., AND GRIFFIN, J. B.

1958. 'University of Michigan Radiocarbon Dates, II' (*Science*, Vol. 127, pp. 1098–105; Lancaster, Pa.).

1959. 'University of Michigan Radiocarbon Dates, IV' (*American Journal of Science, Radiocarbon Supplement*, Vol. 1, pp. 173–98, New Haven).

CUMMINGS, BYRON C.

1923a. 'Ruins of Cuicuilco May Revolutionize Our History of Ancient America' (The *National Geographic Magazine*, Vol. 44, pp. 203–20, Washington).

1923b. 'Cuicuilco, The oldest Temple Discovered in North America' (*Art and Archaeology*, Vol. 16, nos. 1–2, pp. 51–8, Washington).

1926. 'Cuicuilco and the Archaic Culture of Mexico' (The *Scientific Monthly*, Vol. 34, no. 8, pp. 289–304, Lancaster).

1933. 'Cuicuilco and the Archaic Culture of Mexico' (*University of Arizona Bulletin*, Vol. 4, no. 8, *Social Science Bulletin*, No. 4, pp. 1–56, Tucson).

DAUTERMAN, C. C.

1938. 'The Pottery Yard Stick at Monte Alban' (The *Scientific Monthly*, Vol. 46, pp. 157–65, Lancaster).

DAVIS, CLARK A.; PADDOCK, JOHN; SPORES, RONALD; AND WHITECOTTON, JOSEPH

1959. 'Anthropologists Guide to Mexican Highways' (*Boletín de Estudios Oaxaquenos*, No. 14, Mitla).

DE TERRA, HELMUT; ROMERO, JAVIER; AND STEWART, T. D.
  1949. *Tepexpan Man* (Viking Fund Publications in Anthropology, No. 11, New York).

DÍAZ DEL CASTILLO, BERNAL
  1908–16. *The True History of the Conquest of New Spain* (translated by A. P. Maudslay, Hakluyt Society, 5 vols., London).
  1963. *The Conquest of New Spain* (translated by J. M. Cohen, Penguin Books, Harmondsworth).

DIBBLE, CHARLES E., AND ANDERSON, ARTHUR J. O. (eds. and translators)
  1957. *Florentine Codex: General History of the Things of New Spain* (Fray Bernardino de Sahagún), Book 4, *The Soothsayers*, and Book 5, *The Omens* (Santa Fe School of American Research, *Memoirs*, No. 14, Pts. 5–6, University of Utah, Salt Lake City).
  1959. *Florentine Codex: General History of the Things of New Spain* (Fray Bernardino de Sahagún), Book 9, *The Merchants* (Santa Fe School of American Research, *Memoirs*, No. 14, Pt 10, University of Utah, Salt Lake City).

DIXON, KEITH A.
  1959. *Ceramics from Two Preclassic Periods at Chiapa de Corzo, Chiapas, Mexico* (Papers New World Archaeological Foundation, No. 5, Publication No. 4, Orinda, California).

DIXON, R. B.
  1923. *The Radical History of Man.* New York.

DOCKSTADER, FREDERICK J.
  1961. *Indian Art in America.* Greenwich, Connecticut.

DONNELLY, I.
  1882. *Atlantis, the Antedeluvian World.* New York.

DOUGLAS, FREDERIC C., AND D'HARNONCOURT, RENÉ.
  1941. *Indian Art of the United States* (The Museum of Modern Art, New York).

DRUCKER, PHILIP
  1943a. *Ceramic Stratigraphy at Cerro de las Mesas, Veracruz, Mexico* (Bureau of American Ethnology, Bulletin 141, Washington).
  1943b. *Ceramic Sequences at Tres Zapotes, Veracruz, Mexico* (Bureau of American Ethnology, Bulletin 140, Washington).
  1952. *La Venta, Tabasco. A Study of Olmec Ceramics and Art* (Bureau of American Ethnology, Bulletin 153, Washington).
  1955. *Cerro de las Mesas. An Offering of Jade and other Materials* (Bureau of American Ethnology, Bulletin 157, Washington).

Bibliography

DRUCKER, PHILIP; HEIZER, R. F.; AND SQUIER, R. J.

1959. *Excavations at La Venta, Tabasco, 1955* (Bureau of American Ethnology, Bulletin 170, Washington).

DUPAIX, GUILLELMO

1834. *Antiquités Mexicaines* (2 vols. and atlas, Paris).

DURAN, D.

1867–80. *Historia de las Indias de Nueva-España (XVI Century)* (2 vols. and atlas, Mexico).

DURAN, FRAY DIEGO DE

1951. *Historia de las Indias de Nueva España* (Editorial Nacional, S. A., Mexico).

DUTTON, BERTHA

1955. 'Tula of the Toltecs' (*El Palacio*, Vol. 62, Nos. 7–8, pp. 195–246, Santa Fe).

EKHOLM, GORDON F.

1939. Results of an Archaeological Survey of Sonora and Northern Sinaloa (*Revista Mexicana de Estudios Antropológicos*, Vol. 3, no. 1, pp. 7–10, Mexico).

1940a. 'The Archaeology of Northern and Western Mexico' (in *The Maya and Their Neighbors*, pp. 320–30, New York).

1940b. 'Prehistoric "Lacquer" from Sinaloa' (*Revista Mexicana de Estudios Antropológicos*, Vol. 4, nos. 1–2, pp. 10–15, Mexico).

1944. 'Excavations at Tampico and Panuco in the Huasteca, Mexico' (*Anthropological Papers*, American Museum of Natural History, Vol. 38, Pt 5, New York).

1946. 'Probable Use of Mexican Stone Yokes' (*American Anthropologist*, n.s., Vol. 48, pp. 593–606, Menasha).

1955. 'The New Orientation Toward Problems of Asiatic-American Relationships' (in 75th Anniversary Volume, *Anthropological Society of Washington*, pp. 95–109).

1958. 'Regional Sequences in Mesoamerica and Their Relationships' (*Middle American Anthropology*, Social Science Monograph, No. 5, pp. 15–27, Pan American Union, Washington).

EMMART, EMILY W.

1940. *The Badianus Manuscript. An Aztec Herbal of 1552.* Baltimore.

1934. *Escultura Mexicana Antigua.* Mexico.

1936. *Essays in Anthropology presented to Alfred Louis Kroeber.* Berkeley. (*See* Lowie.)

1940. *Essays in Historical Anthropology of North America* (published in honour of John R. Swanton, Smithsonian Miscellaneous Collections, Vol. 100, Washington).

317

ESPEJO, ANTONIETA, AND MONZŎN, ARTURO
  1945. 'Algunas Notas Sobre la Organisación Social de los Tlatelolca'
  (in *Tlatelolco a través de los Tiempos*, No. 6, Mexico).
ESPLENDOR DE MEXICO ANTIGUO
  1959. (*Centro de Investigaciones Antropológicas de México*, 2 Vols.,
  Mexico).
ESTRADA, EMILIO; MEGGERS, BETTY; AND EVANS, CLIFFORD
  1962. 'Possible Trans-Pacific Contact on the Coast of Ecuador'
  (*Science*, Vol. 135, No. 3501, pp. 371–2, 2 Feb., 1962).
EVANS, CLIFFORD, AND MEGGERS, BETTY
  1960. 'New Dating Method Using Obsidian, Part II, Method'
  (*American Antiquity*, Vol. 25, No. 4, Salt Lake City).
EVANS, CLIFFORD; MEGGERS, BETTY; AND ESTRADA, EMILIO
  1959. *Cultura Valdivia* (Museo Victor Emilio Estrada Publicación
  No. 6, Guayaquil).
FERDON, E. N., JR.
  1959. 'Agriculture Potential and the Development of Cultures'
  (*Southwestern Journal of Anthropology*, Vol. 15, No. 1, pp. 1–19,
  Albuquerque).
FERNÁNDEZ, JUSTINO
  1959. 'El Arte' (*Esplendor del México Antiguo*, Vol. 1, pp. 305–22,
  Mexico).
FEWKES, J. WALTER
  1893. 'A Central American Ceremony Which Suggests the Snake
  Dance of the Tusayan Villagers' (*American Anthropologist*, o.s.,
  Vol. 6, pp. 285–306, Washington).
FLANDRAU, C. M.
  1908. *Viva Mexico*. New York.
FLINT, RICHARD F., AND DEEVEY, EDWARD, JR., EDITORS
  1959. (*American Journal of Science, Radiocarbon Supplement* Vol. 1,
  New Haven.)
FOSTER, GEORGE M.
  1960. 'Archaeological Implications of the Modern Pottery of Acatlán,
  Puebla, Mexico' (*American Antiquity*, Vol. 26, No. 2, pp. 205–14,
  Salt Lake City).
FRANCO, C. JOSÉ LUIS
  1949. 'Algunos Problemas relativos a la Cerámica Azteca' (*El
  Mexico Antiguo*, Vol. 7, pp. 162–208, Mexico).
FRIEDMAN, IRVING, AND SMITH, ROBERT L.
  1960. 'A New Dating Method Using Obsidian. Part I, Method'
  (*American Antiquity*, Vol. 25, No. 4, Salt Lake City).

GALLOP, R.
　1938. 'Ancient Monuments of Mexico' (The *Geographical Magazine*, Vol. 7, pp. 321–38, London).

GAMIO, MANUEL
　1910. 'Los Monumentos Arqueológicos de las Inmediaciones de Chalchihuites' (*Anales del Museo Nacional de Arqueología, Historia y Etnología*, 3a Época, Tomo 2, pp. 469–92, Mexico).
　1920. 'Las Excavaciones del Pedregal de San Angel y la Cultura Arcaica del Valle de México' (*American Anthropologist*, n.s., Vol. 22, pp. 127–43, Lancaster).
　1921. *Album de Colecciones Arqueológicas, Texto* (Publicaciones, Escuela Internacional de Arqueología y Etnología Americanas, México).
　　See Boas, 1911–12.
　1924. 'The Sequence of Cultures in Mexico' (*American Anthropologist*, n.s., Vol. 26, pp. 307–22, Menasha).

GAMIO, MANUEL, AND OTHERS
　1922. *La Población del Valle de Teotihuacan* (Secretaría de Agricultura y Fomento, Dirección de Antropología, 3 vols., Mexico).

GANN, THOMAS
　1900. 'Mounds in Northern Honduras' (*19th Annual Report, Bureau of American Ethnology*, Pt 2, pp. 655–92, Washington).

GANN, THOMAS, AND THOMPSON, J. ERIC
　1931. *The History of the Maya*. New York.

GARCIA CUBAS, A.
　1858. *Atlas Geográfico y Estadístico de los Estados Unidos de México*. Mexico.

GARCIA GRANADOS, R., AND MACGREGOR, L.
　1934. *Huejotzingo. La Ciudad y el Convento Franciscano*. Mexico.

GARCIA ICAZBALCETA, J.
　1886–92. *Nueva Colección de Documentos para la Historia de México* (5 vols., Mexico).

GARCÍA PAYÓN, JOSÉ
　1941. 'La Ceramica del Valle de Toluca' (*Revista Mexicana de Estudios Antropológicos*, T.V., Nos. 2–3, pp. 209–38, Mexico).
　1947. *Los Monumentos Arqueológicos de Malinalco* (Contribución a la V Feria del Libro del Gobierno del Estado de México, Mexico).
　1949. 'Arqueología del Tajín' (*Universidad de Veracruz*, Vol. I, pp. 581–95. Jalapa).
　1955. *Exploraciones en El Tajín Temporadas 1953 y 1954* (Instituto Nacional de Antropología e Historia, Mexico).
　1958a. 'Síntesis de las Excavaciones en Malinalco' (*Revista Mexicana*

 de Estudios Antropológicos. 1956/1957. Vol. 14, Pt 2, pp. 161–5, Mexico, 1958).

 1958b. 'Síntesis de las Investigaciones Estratigráficas Practicadas en Tecaxic-Calixtlahuaca' (*Revista Mexicana de Estudios Antropológicos. 1956/1957.* Vol. 14, Pt 2, pp. 157–60, Mexico, 1958).

 1958c. *Malinalco, Guia Oficial* (Instituto Nacional de Arqueología).

GLADWIN, HAROLD S.

 1937. *Excavations at Snaketown: Comparisons and Theories* (Medallion Papers, Gila Pueblo, No. 26, Globe).

GLADWIN, HAROLD S.; GLADWIN, NORA; HAURY, EMIL; AND SAYLES, E. B.

 1937. *Excavations at Snaketown: Material Culture* (Medallion Papers, Gila Pueblo, No. 25, Globe).

GORDON, G. B., EDITOR

 1925. *Examples of Maya Pottery in the Museum and Other Collections* (The University Museum, University of Pennsylvania, Philadelphia).

 See Mason, *Maya Pottery*, 1928.

GRIFFIN, JAMES B., EDITOR

 1952. *Archaeology of Eastern United States* (University of Chicago Press, Chicago).

GRIFFIN, JAMES B., AND Y ESPEJO, ANTONIETA

 1947. 'La Alfarería correspondiente al Último Período de Occupación Nahua del Valle de México: I' (*Memorias de la Academia Mexicana de la Historia*, Vol. 6, No. 2, Mexico).

 1950. 'La Alfarería del Último Período de Occupación Nahua del Valle de México' (*Memorias de la Academia Mexicana de la Historia*, Vol. 9, No. 1, Mexico).

D'HARNONCOURT, RENÉ

 1941. *See* Douglas and d'Harnoncourt.

HAURY, EMIL W.

 1937. *See* Gladwin, Gladwin, Haury, and Sayles.

HEGER, FRANZ

 1908. 'Der Altamerikanische Federschmuck in den Sammlungen der anthropologisch-ethnographischen Abteilung des k. k. naturhistorischen Hofmuseums in Wien' (*Festschrift herausgegeben anlässlich d. Tagung d. XVI Internationalen Amerikanisten-Kongresses in Wien*, September 1908, vom Organisationskomitee, Wien).

HERNANDEZ, F.

 1790. De Historia Novae Hispaniae Plantarum. Madrid.

HISTOIRE DU MECHIQUE

 See de Jonghe, ed., *Histoire*, 1905.

HISTOIRE MEXICAINE
    See Boban, *Documents*, 1891, Pls. 59–64.
HISTORIA de los MEXICANOS por sus PINTURAS (CODEX RAMIREZ)
    1886. 'Anales del Museo Nacional' (1a Época, Tomo 2, pp. 83–106, Mexico).
        See also Phillips, Notes, 1883; Radin, Sources, 1920, pp. 57–66; Garcia Icazbalceta Nueva Colección, 1886–92, Vol. 3; Biblioteca Mexicana, 1878, Codex Ramirez.
HISTORIA TOLTECA-CHICHIMECA. *See* Preuss and Mengin.
HEIZER, R. F., AND BENNYHOFF, J. A.
    1958. 'Archaeological Investigation of Cuicuilco, Valley of Mexico, 1957' (*Science*, Vol. 127, No. 3292, pp. 332–3, Lancaster).
HODGE, F. W.
    1907. *Handbook of the American Indian* (Bureau of American Ethnology, Bulletin 30, 2 vols., Washington).
HOLMES, WILLIAM H.
    1895–7. 'Archaeological Studies among the Ancient Cities of Mexico' (Field Columbian Museum, *Anthropological Series*, Vol. 1, no. 1, Chicago).
    1907. 'On a Nephrite Statuette from San Andres Tuxtla, Vera Cruz, Mexico' (*American Anthropologist*, n.s., Vol. 9, pp. 691–701, Lancaster).
    1914–19. 'Masterpieces of Aboriginal American Art' (*Art and Archaeology*, Vol. 1, pp. 1–12, 91–102, 242–55; Vol. 3, pp. 70–85; Vol. 4, pp. 267–78; Vol. 5, pp. 38–49; Vol. 8, pp. 348–60, Washington).
    1919. *Handbook of Aboriginal American Antiquities. Pt. 1. Introductory.* The Lithic Industries (Bulletin 60, Bureau of American Ethnology, Washington).
HOOTON, ERNEST A.
    1933. 'Racial Types in America and Their Relations to Old World Types' (in Jenness, ed., *American Aborigines*, pp. 131–63).
HOLDEN, JANE
    1957. (Harvard Middle American Archaeological Seminar, 1955–6, *Kroeber Anthropological Society Papers*, No. 17, Berkeley.)
HOWARD, EDGAR B.
    1935. 'Evidence of Early Man in North America' (*Museum Journal*, University Museum, University of Pennsylvania, Vol. 24, nos. 2–3, pp. 61–175, Philadelphia).
HOWELLS, WILLIAM W.
    1940. 'Origins of American Indian Race Types' (in *The Maya and Their Neighbors*, pp. 3–9, New York).

1959. *Mankind in the Making*. Garden City, New York.

HRDLIČKA, ALÉS

1903. 'The Region of the Ancient "Chichimecs", with Notes on the Tepecanos and the Ruin of La Quemada, Mexico' (*American Anthropologist*, n.s., Vol. 5, pp. 385–440, Lancaster).

1923. 'Origin and Antiquity of the American Indian' (*Annual Report of the Smithsonian Institution for 1923*, pp. 481–94, Washington).

HUMBOLDT, A.

1810. *Vues des Cordillères et Monuments des Peuples Indigènes de l'Amérique*. Paris.

HVIDTFELDT, ARILD

1958. *Teotl and Ixiptlatli: Some Central Conceptions in Ancient Mexican Religion, with a General Introduction on Culture and Mythology* (Munksgaàrd, Copenhagen).

HYDE, G.

1922. *See* Mena and Hyde.

IXTLILXOCHITL, FERNANDO DE ALVA

1829. *Horribles Crueldades de los Conquistadores de México*. Mexico.

1891–2. *Obras Históricas* (XVI Century); *Relaciones*, Vol. 1; *Historia Chichimeca*, Vol. 2. Mexico.

JENNESS, D., EDITOR

1933. *The American Aborigines. Their Origin and Antiquity*. Toronto.

JIMÉNEZ MORENO, WIGBERTO

1941. 'Tula y los Toltecas según las Fuentes Historicas' (*Revista Mexicana de Estudios Antropológicos*, Vol. 5, Nos. 2–3, pp. 79–83).

1942. 'El Enigma de los Olmecas' (*Cuadernos Americanos*, Año 1, Vol. 5, pp. 113–45, Mexico).

1954–5. 'Síntesis de la Historia Precolonial del Valle de México' (*Revista Mexicana de Estudios Antropológicos*, Vol. 14, Pt 1, pp. 219–36, México).

1956. *Historia Antigua de México* (Apuntes Mimeografiados de la Sociedad de Alumnos del Instituto Nacional de Antropología e Historia, Mexico).

1959. 'Síntesis de la Historia Pretolteca de Mesoamérica' (*Esplendor del México Antiguo*, Vol. 2, pp. 1019–1108).

JOHNSON, FREDERICK

1940. *See* Mason and Johnson.

DE JONGHE, E.

1906. 'Le Calendrier Mexicain' (*Journal de la Société des Américanistes de Paris*, n.s., Vol. 3, pp. 197–227, Paris).

DE JONGHE, E., EDITOR

1905. 'Histoire du Méchique, Manuscrit Français inédit du XVIᵉ

Siècle' (*Journal de la Société des Americanistes de Paris*, n.s., Tome 2, pp. 1–41, Paris).

JOYCE, THOMAS A.

1914, 1920. *Mexican Archaeology*. London.

1916. *Central American and West Indian Archaeology*. London.

1927. *Maya and Mexican Art*. London.

KELEMAN, PÁL

1943. *Medieval American Art* (2 Vols., New York).

KENNEDY, GEORGE

1960. *Dating by Thermoluminescence*. MS.

KIDDER, A. V.

1924. *An Introduction to the Study of Southwestern Archaeology with a Preliminary Account of the Excavations at Pecos* (Papers of the Phillips Academy, Andover, Southwestern Expedition, No. 1, New Haven).

1931. *The Pottery of Pecos*, Vol. 1, The Dull-Paint Wares (Papers of the Phillips Academy, Andover, Southwestern Expedition, No. 5, New Haven).

1945. 'Excavations at Kaminaljuyú, Guatemala' (*American Antiquity*, Vol. 11, No. 2, pp. 65–75, Menasha).

KIDDER, A. V.; JENNINGS, J. D.; AND SHOOK, E. M.

1946. *Excavations at Kaminaljuyú* (Carnegie Institution of Washington, Publication 561, Washington).

KINGSBOROUGH, EDWARD KING, LORD

1830–48. *Antiquities of Mexico* (9 Vols., London).

KIRCHHOFF, PAUL

1940. 'Los pueblos de la Historia Tolteca-Chichimeca: sus Migraciones y Parentesco' (*Revista Mexicana de Estudios Antropológicos*, Vol. 4, Nos. 1–2, pp. 95–104, Mexico).

1947. 'Prologue' (*See* Historia Tolteca Chichimeca, 1947).

1952. 'Mesoamerica' (in Sol Tax ed., *Heritage of Conquest*, Glencoe).

1954–5. 'Land Tenure in Ancient Mexico' (*Revista Mexicana de Estudios Antropológicos*, Vol. 14, Pt 1, pp. 251–61).

1958. 'La Ruta de los Tolteca Chichimeca entre Tula y Cholula' (*Miscellanea Paul Rivet, Octogenario Dicata*, Universidad Nacional Autonoma de Mexico, Instituto de Historia, Publicaciones, Primera Serie, No. 5, Vol. 1, pp. 485–94, Mexico).

1959. 'The Principals of Clanship' (*Readings in Anthropology*, Vol. 2, Morton Fried, editor, New York).

KOHLER, J.

1924. *El Derecho de los Aztecas* (Spanish Translation, Edición de la Revista Juridica de la Escuela Libre de Derecho, México).

KRICKEBERG, W.

1918–22, 1925. 'Die Totonaken' (*Baessler Archiv*, Vol. 7, pp. 1–55; Vol. 9, pp. 1–75, Berlin. Spanish Translation, Mexico, 1933).

1937. 'Berichte uber neue Forschungen zur Geschichte der alten Kulturen Mittel-Amerikas' (*Die Welt als Geschichte*, 3 Jahrgang, pp. 194–230, Stuttgart).

KROEBER, ALFRED L.

1925. 'Archaic Culture Horizons in the Valley of Mexico' (University of California, *Publications in American Archaeology and Ethnology*, Vol. 17, pp. 373–408, Berkeley).

1939. Cultural and Natural Areas of Native North America (University of California, *Publications in American Archaeology and Ethnology*, Vol. 38, Berkeley).

LARSEN, H.

1937. 'Notes on the Volador and Its Associated Ceremonies and Superstitions' (*Ethnos*, Vol. 2, no. 4, pp. 179–92, Stockholm).

1938. 'The Monolithic Rock Temple of Malinalco, Mexico' (*Ethnos*, Vol. 3, nos. 2–3, pp. 59–63, Stockholm).

LATHRAP, DONALD W.

1957. 'The Classic Stage in Mesoamerica' (Harvard Middle American Seminar, *1955–56 Kroeber Anthropological Society Papers*, No. 17, pp. 38–74, Berkeley).

LEHMANN, WALTER

1909. 'Methods and Results in Mexican Research' (Translated by Seymour de Ricci from *Archiv für Anthropologie*, Vol. 6, pp. 113–68, Paris).

1920. *Zentral-Amerika* (2 vols., Berlin).

1933. *Aus den Pyramidenstädten in Alt-Mexiko*. Berlin.

1938. *Die Geschichte der Königreiche von Colhuacan und Mexico* (Quellenwerke zur Alten Geschichte Amerikas, Ibero-Amerikanischen Institut, Berlin). *See also* Anales de Cuauhtitlan.

LEHMANN, W., AND DOERING, H.

1924. *Kunstgeschichte des Alten Peru*. Berlin.

LEÓN, NICOLÁS

1904. 'Los Tarascos, Pt 1. México' (Reprinted from *Boletin del Museo Nacional de México*, 2a Época, Vol. 1, August, 1903 through June, 1904, Mexico).

1903, 1906. 'Los Tarascos, Pts 2 and 3' (*Anales del Museo Nacional de México*, 2a Época, Vol. 1, pp. 392–502, 592, México; and Vol. 3, pp. 298–479, Mexico).

See also Codex Mariano Jimenez.

Bibliography

LEON Y GAMA, ANTONIO
1832. *Descripción historica y cronológica de las Dos Piedras que se hallaron en al año 1790 en la Plaza Principal de México*. Mexico.

LE PLONGEON, AUGUSTUS
1896. *Queen Moo and the Egyptian Sphinx*. New York.

LENZ, HANS
1959. 'La Elaboración del Papel Indígena' (*Esplendor del México Antiguo*, Vol. 1, pp. 355–60, Mexico).

LEONARD, CARMEN COOK DE
1953. 'Los Popolocas de Puebla' (in *Revista Mexicana de Estudios Antropológicos*. Vol. 13, pp. 423–45, Mexico).

1959*a*. 'Prologo' (*Esplendor del México Antiguo*, Vol. 1, pp. 18–20).

1959*b*. 'Ciencia y Misticismo' (*Esplendor del México Antiguo*, Vol. 1, pp. 127–40, Mexico).

LÉON-PORTILLA, MIGUEL
1956. *La Filosofía Náhuatl, Estudiada en sus Fuentes* (Instituto Indigenista Interamericano, Mexico).

1959. 'La Filosofía' (*Esplendor del México Antiguo*, Vol. 1, pp. 149–60, Mexico).

LÉON-PORTILLA, MIGUEL, AND MATEOS HIGUERA, SALVADOR
1957. 'Catálogo de los Codices Indígenas del México Antiguo' (*Suplemento del Boletin Bibliografico de la Secretaria de Hacienda*, Año 3, No. 111, Mexico).

LIBBY, WILLARD F.
1955. *Radiocarbon Dating* (University of Chicago Press, Chicago).

LIENZO DE TLAXCALA
1892. 'Lienzo de Tlaxcala' (in *Antiguedades Mexicanas*, Junta Colombino, Pls. 66–175, Mexico).

LINNÉ, S.
1934. *Archaeological Researches at Teotihuacan, Mexico* (The Ethnographical Museum of Sweden, New Series, pub. no. 1, Stockholm).

1937. 'The Expedition to Mexico, 1934–35' (*Ethnos*, Vol. 1, no. 2, pp. 39–48, Stockholm).

1938. 'A Mazapan Grave at Teotihuacan Mexico' (*Ethnos*, Vol. 3, no. 6, pp. 167–78, Stockholm).

1939. *Zapotecan Antiquities and the Paulsen Collection in the Ethnographical Museum of Sweden* (Publications, Ethnographical Museum of Sweden, n.s., Vol. 4, Stockholm).

1942. *Mexican Highland Cultures* (Ethnographical Museum of Sweden, n.s., Publication No. 7, Stockholm).

1956. 'Radiocarbon Dates in Teotihuacán' (*Ethnos*, Vol. 21, Nos. 3-4, pp. 180-93, Stockholm).

1961. In *The Art of Ancient America*, by H. D. Disselhoff and S. Linné (Crown Publishers, Inc., New York).

LINTON, RALPH

1924. 'The Significance of Certain Traits in North American Maize Culture' (*American Anthropologist*, n.s., Vol. 26, pp. 345-9, Menasha).

1926. 'The Origin of the Skidi Pawnee Sacrifice to the Morning Star' (*American Anthropologist*, n.s., Vol. 28, pp. 457-66, Menasha).

1940. 'Crops, Soils and Culture in America' (in *The Maya and Their Neighbors*, pp. 32-40, New York).

1942. 'Land Tenure in Aboriginal America' (in *The Changing Indian*, editor: Oliver La Farge, Norman, Oklahoma).

LIZARDI RAMOS, CÉSAR

1959a. 'El Calendario Maya-Mexicano' (*Esplendor del México Antiguo*, Mexico, D. F., Vol. 1, pp. 221-42).

1959b. 'Los Jeroglíficos Mayas y su Descifración' (*Esplendor del México Antiguo*, Mexico, Vol. 1, pp. 243-62).

LOTHROP, SAMUEL K.

1924. *Tulum* (Carnegie Institution of Washington, pub. no. 335, Washington).

1927. 'Pottery Types and Their Sequence in El Salvador' (*Indian Notes and Monographs Museum of the American Indian*, Heye Foundation, Vol. 1, no. 4, pp. 165-220, New York).

1933. *Atitlan. An Archaeological Study of Ancient Remains on the Borders of Lake Atitlan, Guatemala* (Carnegie Institution of Washington, pub. no. 444, Washington).

1936. *Zacualpa. A Study of Ancient Quiché Artifacts* (Carnegie Institution of Washington, pub. no. 472, Washington).

1937. *Coclé. An Archaeological Study of Central Panama* (Pt. 1, Memoirs, Peabody Museum of American Archaeology and Ethnology, Harvard University, Vol. 7, Cambridge).

1960. 'A Ceremonial Pottery Mask from Peru' (*Archaeology*, Vol. 13, No. 2, pp. 91-6, New York).

LOTHROP, S. K.; FOSHAG, W. F.; AND MAHLER, JOY

1957. *Pre-Columbian Art* (New York).

1958. *Pre-Columbian Art* (Phaidon Press, London).

LOWIE, ROBERT L., EDITOR

1936. *Essays in Anthropology presented to Alfred Louis Kroeber*. Berkeley.

LUMHOLTZ, C.

1902. *Unknown Mexico* (2 vols., New York).

MACCURDY, G. G., EDITOR
1937. *Early Man*. Philadelphia and New York.

MACNEISH, RICHARD
1954. 'An Early Archaeological Site near Panuco, Veracruz' (*American Philosophical Society, Transactions*, n.s., Vol. 44, Pt 5, Philadelphia).
1958. 'Preliminary Archaeological Investigations in the Sierra de Tamaulipas, Mexico' (*American Philosophical Society, Transactions*, n.s., Vol. 48, Pt 6, Philadelphia).

MANGELSDORF, P. C.
1958. 'Ancestor of Corn' (*Science*, n.s., Vol. 128, No. 3335, pp. 1313–20, Lancaster, Pa.).

MANGELSDORF, P. C., AND REEVES, R. G.
1938. 'The Origin of Maize' (*Proceedings of the National Academy of Sciences*, Vol. 24, pp. 303–12, Lancaster).
1939. *Origin of Indian Corn and Its Relatives* (Texas Agricultural Experiment Station, Bulletin 574, College Station, Texas).

MAPA QUINATZIN
1885. *See* Aubin, *Mémoires*.

MAPA DE SIGUENZA
See Radin, Sources, 1920, pp. 12–13; Kingsborough, *Antiquities of Mexico*, 1830, Vol. 4; Orozco y Berra, *Historia Antigua*, 1880, Vol. 3, pp. 131–53; Garcia Cubas, *Atlas*, 1858.

MAPA DE TEPECHPAN
1887. *See Anales del Museo Nacional* (Tomo 3, 1a Época, Entrega 2, p. 368, Mexico).

MAPA TLOTZIN
1885. *See* Aubin, *Mémoires*.

MARETT, R. H. K.
1934. *Archaeological Tours from Mexico City*. London and Mexico.

MARQUINA, IGNACIO
1928. *Estudio Arquitectónico Comparativo de los Monumentos Arqueológicos de México* (Secretaría de Educación Pública, Mexico).
1951. 'Arquitectura Prehispánica' (*Memorias del Instituto Nacional de Antropología e Historia*, I, Mexico).

MARTIN, PAUL
1959. *Digging into History* (Chicago Natural History Museum, Popular Series, Anthropology 38).

MARTIN, PAUL S.; QUIMBY, GEORGE I.; AND COLLIER, DONALD
1947. *Indians Before Columbus* (Chicago).

MARTINEZ DEL RIO, PABLO
1953. *Los Origenes Americanos*, 3rd edition (Mexico).

1957. *Tula, Guia Oficial* (Instituto Nacional de Antropología e Historia, Mexico).

MASON, J. ALDEN

1927. 'Mirrors of Ancient America' (*The Museum Journal*, Museum of the University of Pennsylvania, Vol. 18, no. 2, pp. 201–9, Philadelphia).

1935. 'The Place of Texas in Pre-Columbian Relationships between the United States and Mexico' (*Bulletin of the Texas Archaeological and Palaeontological Society*, Vol. 7, pp. 29–46, Abilene).

1937a. 'Further Remarks on the Pre-Columbian Relationships between the United States and Mexico' (*Bulletin of the Texas Archaeological and Palaeontological Society*, Vol. 9, pp. 120–9, Abilene).

1937b. 'Late Archaeological Sites in Durango, Mexico, from Chalchihuites to Zape' (Twenty-fifth Anniversary Studies, *Philadelphia Anthropological Society*, Vol. 1, pp. 127–46, Philadelphia).

MASON, J. ALDEN, EDITOR

1928. *Examples of Maya Pottery in the Museum and Other Collections* (The University Museum, University of Pennsylvania, Philadelphia).

MASON, J. A., AND JOHNSON, F.

1940. 'The Native Languages of Middle America and the Linguistic Map of Central America' (in *The Maya and Their Neighbors*, pp. 52–114, New York).

MAUDSLAY, A. P.

1889–1902. *Archaeology* (Biologia Centrali Americana, 4 vols. plates. 1 vol. text, London).

1912. *A Note on the Position and Extent of the Great Temple Enclosure of Tenochtitlan.* London.

1940. *The Maya and Their Neighbors.* (dedicated to Alfred M. Tozzer, New York).

MAYER-OAKES, WILLIAM J.

1959. 'A Stratigraphic Excavation at El Risco, Mexico' (*Proceedings American Philosophical Society*, Vol. 103, pp. 332–73, Philadelphia).

1960. 'A Developmental Concept of Pre-Spanish Urbanization in the Valley of Mexico' (Middle American Research Institute, Tulane University, *Publication 18*, pp. 165–76, New Orleans).

MCBRIDE, G. MCC.

1923. *The Land Systems of Mexico* (Research Series, American Geographical Society, No. 12, New York).

MCBRYDE, WEBSTER

1933. 'Sololá, a Guatemalan Town and Cakchiquel Market-Center.

A Preliminary Report' (*Middle American Research Series*, pub. no. 5, pp. 43–152, Tulane University, New Orleans).

McNUTT, CHARLES, AND WHEELER, RICHARD P.

1959. 'Bibliography of Primary Sources for Radiocarbon Dates' (*American Antiquity*, Vol. 24, No. 3, pp. 323–4).

MEANS, PHILIP AINSWORTH

1931. *Ancient Civilizations of the Andes*. New York and London.

MEDELLIN ZENÍL, ALFONSO

1953. 'Secuencia Cronológico Cultural en el Centro de Veracruz' (in *Revista Mexicana de Estudios Antropológicos*, Vol. 13, pp. 371–8, Mexico).

1960. *Ceramicas del Totonicapan* (Universidad Veracruzana, Jalapa, Vera Cruz).

MEMORIAL DE LOS INDIOS DE TEPETLAOSTOC

1912. (Codex Kingsborough.) (Editor, F. Paso y Troncoso, Madrid.)

MENA, R., AND HYDE, G.

1922. 'Antigüedad del Hombre en el Valle de México. Nueva' Orientación Arqueológica e Histórica' (*Conferencias dadas en el Museo Nacional de Arqueología, Historia y Etnología, la noche del 27 diciembre de 1921*. Mexico).

DE MENDIETA, FRAY GERONIMO

1870. *Historia Eclesiástica Indiana* (XVI Century). Mexico.

MENDOZA, V. T.

1933. *See* Castañeda and Mendoza.

MENGIN, E.

1937, 1938. *See* Preuss and Mengin.

1939. 'Unos Anales Históricos de la Nacion Mexicana; Pt 1' (*Baessler Archiv*, Vol. 22, Berlin).

MERWIN, R. E., AND VAILLANT, G. C.

1932. *The Ruins of Holmul, Guatemala* (Memoirs, Peabody Museum of American Archaeology and Ethnology, Harvard University, Vol. 3, no. 2, Cambridge).

1933. *Monumentos Arqueologicos de México* (Departamento de Monumentos, Secretaría de Educación Publica, Mexico).

MESA REDONDA VIa

1954–5. Part I, Vol. 14, *Revista Mexicana de Estudios Antropológicos*.

1956–7. Part II, Vol. 14, *Revista Mexicana de Estudios Antropológicos*.

MILES, S. W.

1957. 'Maya Settlement Patterns: A Problem for Ethnology and Archaeology' (*Southwestern Journal of Anthropology*, Vol. 13, No. 3, pp. 239–48, Albuquerque).

MILLON, RENÉ F.

1957. 'New Data on Teotihuacan I, in Teotihuacan' (*Boletín de Centro de Investigaciones Antropológicas de México*, No. 4, pp. 12–18, Mexico).

1959. 'La Agricultura como Inicio de la Civilización' (*Esplendor del México Antiguo*, Mexico, D. F., Vol. 2, pp. 997–1018).

1960. 'The Beginnings of Teotihuacán' (*American Antiquity*, Vol. 26, No. 1, pp. 1–10, Kenosha).

1961. 'The Northwestern Boundary of Teotihuacán: A Major Urban Zone' (in *Homenaje al Dr Pablo Martine del Rio*, Ignacio Bernal and Luis Aveleyra de Anda, eds., Sociedad Mexicana de Antropología, Mexico).

MILLON, RENÉ F., AND DREWITT, BRUCE

1961. 'Early Structures within the Pyramid of the Sun at Teotihuacan' (*American Antiquity*, Vol. 26, No. 3, New York).

MONZÓN, ARTURO

1949. *El Calpulli en la Organización Social de los Tenochca* (Instituto de Historia, Universidad Nacional Autónoma de México).

MORENO, M.

1931. *La Organización Política y Social de los Aztecas* (Universidad Nacional de México Autónoma, Sección Editorial, Mexico).

MORLEY, SYLVANUS G.

1915. *An Introduction to the Study of Maya Hieroglyphs* (Bureau of American Ethnology, Bulletin 57, Washington).

1920. *The Inscriptions at Copan* (Carnegie Institution of Washington, pub. no. 219, Washington).

1956. *The Ancient Maya*, 3rd edition (revised by G. W. Brainerd, University Press, Stanford).

MORRIS, ANN A.

1931. *See* Morris, Charlot, and Morris.

MORRIS, EARL H., CHARLOT, JEAN, AND MORRIS, ANN A.

1931. *The Temple of the Warriors at Chichen Itza, Yucatan* (Carnegie Institution of Washington, pub. no. 406, Washington).

MOTOLINÍA (DE BENAVENTE, T.)

1914. *Historia de los Indios de la Nueva España* (XVI Century). Bardelona.

MUÑOZ CAMARGO, D.

1892. *Historia de Tlaxcala* (XVI Century). Mexico.

MURDOCK, G. P.

1934. *Our Primitive Contemporaries*. New York.

Bibliography

NELSON, N. C.
  1933. 'The Antiquity of Man in America in the Light of Archaeology (in Jenness, ed., *The American Aborigines*, pp. 87–130).

NICHOLSON, HENRY B.
  1955. 'Native Historical Traditions of Nuclear America' (*American Anthropologist*, n.s., Vol. 57, No. 3, Pt 1, pp. 594–613).
  1959. 'Los Principales Dioses Mesoamericanos' (*Esplendor del México Antiguo*, Vol. 1, pp. 161–78).
  1961. 'The Use of the Term "Mixtec" in Mesoamerican Archaeology' (*American Antiquity*, Vol. 26, No. 3, pp. 431–3).

NOGUERA, EDUARDO
  1927. *Ruinas de Tizatlan, Tlaxcala* (Publicaciones de la Secretaría de Educación Pública, Mexico).
  1928. 'El Ladrillo como Material de Construcción entre los Pueblos Nahuas' (*Revista Mexicana de Estudios Históricos*, Tomo 2, pp. 64–8, Mexico).
  1930a. 'Decorative Aspects of Certain Types of Mexican Pottery' (*Proceedings*, XXIII International Congress of Americanists, New York, 1928, pp. 85–92, New York).
  1930b. 'Algunas Características de la Cerámica de México' (*Journal de la Société des Américanistes de Paris*, n.s., Vol. 22, pp. 249–310, Paris).
  1934. 'Estudio de la Cerámica Encontrada donde estaba el Templo Mayor de México' (*Anales del Museo Nacional de Arqueología, Historia y Etnografía*, 5a Época, Tomo 1, pp. 267–81, Mexico).
  1935. 'Antecedentes y Relaciones de la Cultura Teotihuacana' (*El México Antiguo*, Vol. 3, nos. 5–8, pp. 1–81, Mexico).
  1937a. *El Altar de Los Cráneos Esculpidos de Cholula*. Mexico.
  1937b. *Conclusiones Principales Obtenidas por el Estudio de la Cerámica Arqueológica en Cholula* (Mimeograph, Mexico).
  1942. 'Excavaciones en "En Opeño", Michoacán' (*Actas del XXVII Congreso Internacional de Americanistas*, 1939, Mexico).
  1943. 'Excavaciones en El Tepalcate, Chimalhuacan, México' (*American Antiquity*, Vol. 9, No. 1, pp. 33–43, Mexico).
  1947. 'Cerámicas de Xochicalco' (*El México Antiguo*, Vol. 6, nos. 9–12, pp. 273–98. Mexico).
  1951. 'Exploraciones en Xochicalco' (in *The Civilization of Ancient America*, ed: Sol Tax. Vol. 1, pp. 37–42. Chicago).
  1954. *La Cerámica Arqueológica de Cholula* (E. Guarama, Mexico).
  1956. 'Un Edificio Préclasico en Cholula. Estudios Antropológicos Publicados en homenaje al Dr Manuel Gamio' (*Sociedad Mexicana*

331

de Antropología, Universidad Nacional Autónoma, pp. 213–24, Mexico, D. F.).

1959. 'Cerámica y Estratigrafía (*Esplendor del México Antiguo*, Vol. 1, pp. 411–38).

NOGUERA, EDUARDO, AND PIÑA CHÁN, ROMÁN

1957. 'Estratigrafía de Teopanzolco' (*Revista Mexicana de Estudios Antropológicos*, Vol. 14, Pt 2, pp. 139–56, Mexico).

NORDENSKIÖLD, ERLAND

1930. *L'Archéologie du Bassin de l'Amazone* (Ars Americana, I, Paris).

NUTINI, HUGO G.

1961. 'Clan Organization in a Nahuatl Speaking Village of the State of Tlaxcala, Mexico' (*American Anthropologist*, n.s., Vol. 63, No. 1, pp. 62–78, Menasha).

NUTTALL, ZELIA

1888. *Standard or Head-Dress?* (Papers, Peabody Museum of American Archaeology and Ethnology, Harvard University, Vol. 1, no. 1, Cambridge).

1901. 'Chalchihuitl in Ancient Mexico' (*American Anthropologist*, n.s., Vol. 3, pp. 227–37, New York).

1903. *The Book of Life of the Ancient Mexicans.* Pt 1, Introduction and Facsimile. Berkeley.

1904. *A Penitential Rite of the Ancient Mexicans* (Papers, Peabody Museum of American Archaeology and Ethnology, Harvard University, Vol. 1, no. 7, Cambridge).

1910. 'The Island of Sacrificios' (*American Anthropologist*, n.s., Vol. 12, pp. 257–95, Lancaster).

1925. 'Gardens of Ancient Mexico' (The Smithsonian Institution, *Annual Report*, 1923, pp. 453–64, Washington).

1926. *Official Reports (on Mexican towns) sent by Castañeda to Philip II in 1580, translated and edited* (Papers, Peabody Museum of American Archaeology and Ethnology, Harvard University, Vol. 11, no. 2, Cambridge).

1926. 'The Aztecs and Their Predecessors in the Valley of Mexico' (*Proceedings, American Philosophical Society*, Vol. 65, pp. 242–55, Philadelphia).

O'NEILL, GEORGE

1956–7. 'Preliminary Report on Stratigraphic Excavations in the Southern Valley of Mexico; Chalco-Xico' (Vol. 14, Pt 2, pp. 45–51, *Revista Mexicana de Estudios Antropológicos*, Mexico).

ORELLANA T., RAFAEL

1959. 'La Guerra' (*Esplendor del México Antiguo*, Vol. 2, pp. 837–60).

ORIGEN DE LOS MEXICANOS
    1886–92. *See* Garcia Icazbalceta, *Nueva Colección*, Vol. 3, pp. 281–308.

OROZCO Y BERRA, MANUEL
    1864. *Geografía de las Lenguas y Carta Etnográfica de México*. Mexico.
    1878. 'Ojeada de Cronología Mexicana' (in *Biblioteca Mexicana*, pp. 151–222).
    1880. *Historia Antigua y de la Conquista de México* (4 vols. and atlas, Mexico).
    1887. 'El Tonalamatl' (*Anales del Museo Nacional*, 1a Época, Vol. 4, pp. 30–44, Mexico).

PADDOCK, JOHN
    1956. 'Notes on G. C. Vaillant's, *The Aztecs of Mexico*' (*Antropología*, pp. 409–31, Mexico City College, Mexico).

PALACIOS, ENRIQUE JUAN
    1925. 'La Fundación de México-Tenochtitlan' (*Anales del Museo Nacional de Arqueología, Historia y Etnografía*, 5a Época, Tomo 1, No. 3, pp. 230–54, Mexico).

PALACIOS, E. J.
    1940. 'El Simbolismo del Chac-mool: su Interpretación' (*Revista Mexicana de Estudios Antropológicos*, Vol. 4, pp. 43–56, Mexico).

PALERM, ANGEL
    1955. 'La Secuencia de la Evolución Cultural de Mesoamérica' (*Ciencias Sociales-Union Panamericana*, Vol. 6, No. 36, pp. 343–70, Washington).
    1956. 'Notas Sobre las Construcciones Militares y la Guerra en Mesoamérica' (*Anales del Instituto Nacional de Antropología*, Vol. 8, pp. 123–34, Mexico).

PARKES, HENRY B.
    1938. *A History of Mexico*. Boston

PARSONS, ELSIE C.
    1936. *Mitla, Town of Souls*. Chicago.

DEL PASO Y TRONCOSO, F.
    1898. *Descripción Historia y Exposición del Codice Pictórico de los Antiguas Nauas que se conserva en la Biblioteca de la Camara de Diputados de Paris*. (Commentary on Codex Borbonicus, Florence.)

DEL PASO Y TRONCOSO, F., EDITOR
    1905. *See* Codex Florentino.
    1912. *See* Memorial de los Indios de Tepetlaostoc.

PAYÓN, J. GARCÍA
    1936. *Zona Arqueológica de Tecaxic-Calixtlahuaca*, Pt 1 (Departamento de Monumentos, Mexico).

PEÑAFIEL, ANTONIO

1885. *Nombres Geográficos de México* (Secretaría de Fomento, Mexico).

1890. *Monumentos del Arte Mexicano Antiguo* (1 vol., text; 2 vols., plates; Berlin).

1897. *Nomenclatura Geográfica de México* (1 vol. and atlas, Mexico).

1903. *Indumentaria Antigua* (Secretaria de Fomento, Mexico).

1910. *Destrucción del Templo Mayor de México Antiguo*. Mexico.

PETERSON, FREDERICK

1959. *Ancient Mexico*. New York.

Ancient Mexico (Allen and Unwin, London).

PHILLIPS, H.

1883. 'Notes upon the Codex Ramirez, with a translation of the same' (*Proceedings, American Philosophical Society*, Vol. 21, pp. 616–51, Philadelphia).

PIÑA CHÁN, ROMÁN

1955a. *Las Culturas Preclásicas de la Cuenca de México* (Fondo de Cultura Económica, Mexico).

1955b. *Chalcatzingo, Morelos* (Instituto Nacional de Antropológia e Historia, Mexico).

1958. 'Tlatilco' (*Serie Investigaciones*, Nos. 1–2, *Instituto Nacional de Antropológia e Historia*, Mexico).

1960a. 'Mesoamerica' (*Memorias*, No. 6, *Instituto Nacional de Antropológia e Historia*, Mexico).

1960b. *Descubierta Arqueológica en Xochicalco, Morelos* (Boletín Instituto Nacional de Antropológia e Historia, 20).

POLLOCK, H. E. D.

1936. *Round Structures of Aboriginal Middle America* (Carnegie Institution of Washington, pub. no. 471, Washington).

POMAR, JUAN BAUTISTA

1891. 'Relación de Tezcoco' (Garcia Icazbalceta, *Nueva Colección de Documentos para la Historia de México*, Vol. 3, pp. 1–69, Mexico).

PORTER, MURIEL NOÉ

1953. *Tlatilco and the Preclassic Cultures of the New World* (Viking Fund Publications in Anthropology, No. 19, New York).

1956. 'Excavations at Chupícuaro, Guanajuato, Mexico' (*Transactions of the American Philosophical Society*, n.s., Vol. 46, Philadelphia).

PRESCOTT, WILLIAM H.

1843. *The Conquest of Mexico* (3 vols., New York).

1922. *The Conquest of Mexico* (edited by T. A. Joyce and illustrated by Keith Henderson, 2 vols., New York).

1886. *History of the Conquest of Mexico* (edited by Kirk: Allen and Unwin, London).

History of the Conquest of Mexico (Everyman Library, London).

PREUSS, K. T., AND MENGIN, E.

1937. 'Die Mexikanische Bilderhandschrift Historia Tolteca-Chichimeca. Pt 1' (*Baessler Archiv*, Vol. 9, Berlin).

1938. 'Die Mexikanische Bilderhandschrift Historia Tolteca-Chichimeca. Pt 2' (*Baessler Archiv*, Vol. 21, Berlin).

1942. *Liber in lingua Nahuatl manuscriptus picturisque ornatus . . . cum praefatione in lingua Britannica, Gallica, Germanica et Hispana . . .* edited by Ernst Mengin (Corpus Codicum Americanorum Medii Aevi, Vol. 1. Einar Munksgaàrd, Copenhagen).

1947. With *Anales de Quauhtinchan*. Edited by Heinrich Berlin in collaboration with Sylvia Rendon, with prologue by Paul Kirchhoff (*Fuentes para la Historia de México*, Vol. 1, *Colección publicada bajo la Dirección de Salvador Toscano*, Mexico).

PROSKOURIAKOFF, TATIANA

1950. *A Study of Classic Maya Sculpture* (Publication 593, Carnegie Institution of Washington).

1958. 'Studies on Middle American Art' (*Middle American Anthropology, Social Science Monograph*, No. 5, pp. 29–35, Pan American Union, Washington).

1960. *Varieties of Classification of Veracruz Sculpture* (Publication 606, Carnegie Institution of Washington).

RADIN, PAUL

1920. 'The Sources and Authenticity of the History of the Ancient Mexicans' (*University of California Publications in American Archaeology and Ethnology*, Vol. 17, no. 1, Berkeley).

REDFIELD, ROBERT

1930. *Tepoztlan*. Chicago.

RELACIÓN DE GENEALOGIA Y LINAGE DE LOS SEÑORES QUE HAN SEÑOREADO ESTE TIERRA DE LA NUEVA ESPAÑA

See Garcia Icazbalceta, *Nueva Colección*, 1886–92, Vol. 3, pp. 263–81.

RICARD, R.

1933. *La 'Conquête Sprituelle' de Mexico* (Université de Paris, Travaux et Mémoires de L'Institut d'Ethnologie, Vol. 20, Paris).

RIVA PALACIO, VICENTE, EDITOR

1887–9. *México a Través de los Siglos* (5 vols., Mexico and Barcelona).

ROBELO, CECILIO A.

1911. *Diccionario de la Mitología Nahuatl*. Mexico.

ROBERTS, FRANK H. H., JR.

1935. 'A Survey of Southwestern Archaeology' (*American Anthropologist*, n.s., Vol. 37, pp. 1–35, Menasha).

1940. 'Developments in the Problem of the North American Paleo-Indian' (in *Essays in Historical Anthropology in North America*, pp. 51–116, Washington).

ROMEROVARGAS YTURBIDE, IGNACIO

1959. 'Las Instituciones' (in *Esplendor del México Antiguo*, Tomo 2, pp. 729–77, Mexico).

ROYS, RALPH L.

1960. *Maya Katun Prophecies of the Books* (Publication 606, No. 57, Carnegie Institution of Washington).

RUBIN DE BORBOLLA, D.

1936. *See* Caso with Rubin de Borbolla.

RUPPERT, KARL; THOMPSON, ERIC S.; AND PROSKOURIAKOFF, TATIANA

1955. *Bonampak, Chiapas, Mexico* (Publication 602, Carnegie Institution of Washington).

SAENZ, CESAR A.

1959. 'El Ceremonial' (*Esplendor del México Antiguo*, Vol. 2, pp. 789–818, Mexico).

DE SAHAGUN, BERNARDINO

1829. *Historia General de las Cosas de Nueva España* (3 vols., Mexico).

1905. *Codex Florentino: Illustrations for Sahagun's Historia General de las Cosas de Nueva España* (edited by Francisco del Paso y Troncoso, Vol. 5, Marid).

1932. *Historia General de las Cosas de Nueva España* Books 1–4 (translated by Fanny Bandelier. Nashville).

1938. *Historia General de las Cosas de Nueva España* (5 vols., Mexico).

1956. *Historia General de las Cosas de Nueva España* (4 vols., Angel M. Garibay K., ed. and translator of part, Mexico).

1957, 1959. *See* Dibble.

SANDERS, W. T.

1956. 'The Central Mexican Symbiotic Region: A Study in Prehistoric Settlement Patterns' (in *Prehistoric Settlement Patterns in the New World*, G. R. Willey, ed., Viking Fund Publications in Anthropology, No. 23, pp. 115–27, New York).

SATTERTHWAITE, LINTON, AND RALPH, ELIZABETH K.

1960. 'New Radiocarbon Dates and the Maya Correlation Problem' (*American Antiquity*, Vol. 26, No. 2, pp. 165–84, Salt Lake City).

SAUER, CARL ORTWIN

1932. 'The Road to Cibola' (*Ibero-Americana*, 3, Berkeley).

1936. 'American Agricultural Origins: A Consideration of Nature and Culture' (*Essays in Anthropology in Honor of Alfred Louis Kroeber*, pp. 279–97, Berkeley).

SAUER, CARL, AND BRAND, DONALD

1932. 'Aztatlan, Prehistoric Mexican Frontier on the Pacific Coast' (*Ibero-Americana*, 1, Berkeley).

SAVILLE, MARSHALL H.

1896. 'The Temple of Tepoztlan, Mexico' (*Bulletin, American Museum of Natural History*, Vol. 8, pp. 221–6, New York).

1899. 'Exploration of Zapotecan Tombs in Southern Mexico' (*American Anthropologist*, n.s., Vol. 1, pp. 350–62, New York).

1900a. 'A Shell Gorget from the Huasteca, Mexico' (*Bulletin, American Museum of Natural History*, Vol. 13, pp. 99–103, New York).

1900b. 'An Onyx Jar from Mexico in Process of Manufacture' (*Bulletin, American Museum of Natural History*, Vol. 13, Art. 11, pp. 105–7, New York).

1901. 'Mexican Codices, a List of Recent Reproductions' (*American Anthropologist*, n.s., Vol. 3, pp. 532–41, New York).

1909. 'The Cruciform Structures of Mitla and Vicinity' (*Putnam, Anniversary Volume*, pp. 151–90, New York).

1916. 'Monolithic Axes and Their Distribution in Ancient America' (*Contributions*, Museum of the American Indian, Heye Foundation, Vol. 2, no. 5, New York).

1917. *See* Anonymous Conqueror.

1920. 'The Goldsmith's Art in Ancient Mexico' (*Indian Notes and Monographs*, Museum of the American Indian, Heye Foundation, New York).

1922. 'Turquois Mosaic Art in Ancient Mexico' (*Contributions*, Museum of the American Indian, Heye Foundation, Vol. 6, New York).

1925. 'The Wood-Carver's Art in Ancient Mexico' (*Contributions*, Museum of the American Indian, Heye Foundation, Vol. 9, New York).

1928. 'Ceremonial Axes from Western Mexico' (*Indian Notes*, Museum of the American Indian, Heye Foundation, Vol. 5, pp. 280–93, New York).

1929a. 'Votive Axes from Ancient Mexico' (*Indian Notes*, Museum of the American Indian, Heye Foundation, Vol. 6, pp. 266–99, 335–42, New York).

1929b. 'Tizoc, Great Lord of the Aztecs, 1481–86' (*Contributions*, Museum of the American Indian, Heye Foundation, Vol. 7, no. 4, New York).

SAYLES, E. B.

    1935. 'An Archaeological Survey of Texas' (*Medallion Papers*, Gila Pueblo, No. 17, Globe).

    1936. 'An Archaeological Survey of Chihuahua, Mexico' (*Medallion Papers*, Gila Pueblo, No. 22, Globe).

    1937. *See* Gladwin, Gladwin, Haury, and Sayles.

SEARS, PAUL B.

    1951. 'Pollen Profiles and Culture Horizons in the Basin of Mexico' (*Selected Papers of the International Congress of Americanists*, Vol. 1, No. 29).

    1953. 'Interdependence of Archaeology and Ecology' (*Transactions of the New York Academy of Sciences*, Series 2, Vol. 15, pp. 113–17).

    1958. 'Environment and Culture in Retrospect' (in *Climate and Man in the Southwest*, ed. by T. L. Smiley. University of Arizona Bulletin, Vol. 28, No. 4, Nov. 1957, pp. 77–84, Tucson).

SÉJOURNÉ, LAURETTE

    1957. *Burning Water: Thought and Religion in Ancient Mexico* (Evergreen Edition, Grove Press, New York; and Thames and Hudson, London).

    1959. 'Un Palacio en la Ciudad de los Dioses' (*Exploraciones en Teotihuacan, 1955–56*, Instituto Nacional de Antropológia e Historia, Mexico).

SELER, CAECILLIE

    1900. *Auf Alten Wegen in Mexiko und Guatemala*. Berlin.

    1922. 'Alterthümer des Kanton Tuxtla im Staate Veracruz' (*Festschrift Eduard Seler*, pp. 543–56, Stuttgart).

SELER, EDUARD

    1901. *The Tonalamatl of the Aubin Collection*. Commentary (translated by A. H. Keane, London).

    1902. *Codex Fejervary-Mayer*. Commentary (translated by A. H. Keane, London).

    1902–23. *Gesammelte Abhandlungen zur Amerikanischen Sprach- und Alterthumskunde* (Vols. 1–5, Berlin).

    1903. *Codex Vaticanus 3773*. Commentary (translated by A. H. Keane, London).

    1904a. 'Ancient Mexican Feather Ornaments' (*Bureau of American Ethnology, Bulletin 28*, pp. 57–74, Washington).

    1904b. 'The Temple Pyramid of Tepoztlan' (*Bureau of American Ethnology, Bulletin 28*, pp. 339–52, Washington).

    1904c. 'The Venus Period in the Borgian Codex Group' (*Bureau of American Ethnology, Bulletin 28*, pp. 353–92, Washington).

    1904d. Altmexikanischer Schmuck und Soziale und Militärische

Rangabzeichen (*Gesammelte Abhandlungen*, Vol. 2, pp. 509–619, Berlin).

1904–9. *Codex Borgia. Eine Altmexikanische Bilderschrift der Bibliothek der Congregatio de Propaganda Fide.* 3 vols., Berlin.

1915. 'Die Teotiuacan-Kultur des Hochlands von Mexico' (*Gesammelte Abhandlungen zur Amerikanischen Sprach- und Alterthumskunde*, Vol. 5, pp. 405–585, Berlin).

SHEPARD, ANNA

1948. 'Plumbate, a Mesoamerican Trade Ware' (*Publication No. 573*, Carnegie Institution of Washington).

SHOOK, E. M.

1951. 'The Present Status of Research on the Preclassic Horizon in Guatemala' (*Selected Papers*, 29th International Congress of Americanists, Vol. 1, *The Civilizations of Ancient America*, S. Tax, ed., pp. 93–100, University of Chicago Press).

1957. 'Olmec Sculpture from Guatemala' (*Archaeology*, Vol. 9, No. 4, pp. 260–2, Cincinnati).

SHOOK, EDWIN M., AND KIDDER, A. V.

1952. 'Excavations at Kaminaljuyú' (*Publication 596*, Vol. 11, Nos. 52–56, Carnegie Institution of Washington).

SHOOK, EDWIN M.; COE, WILLIAM R.; BROMAN, VIVIAN L.; AND SATTERTHWAITE, LINTON

1958. *Tikal Reports*, Nos. 1–4 (University Museum, University of Pennsylvania, Philadelphia).

SMITH, MARIAN W.

1953. 'Asia and North America; Transpacific Contacts' (*Society for American Archaeology, Memoir 9*).

SMITH, ROBERT E.

1958. 'The Place of Fine Orange Pottery in Mesoamerican Archaeology' (*American Antiquity*, Vol. 24, No. 2, pp. 151–60).

SOLÍS ALCALÁ, E.

1949. *Codice Pérez. Traducción libre del Maya al Castellano Merida de Yucatan, Imprenta Oriente.*

SORENSON, JOHN L.

1955. 'Chronological Ordering of the Mesoamerican Preclassic' (*Middle American Research Records*, Vol. 2, No. 3, New Orleans).

SOUSTELLE, JACQUES

1937. *La Famille Otomi-Pame du Mexique Central* (Institut d'Ethnologie, No. 26, Paris).

1955. *La Vie quotidienne des Azteques.* Paris.

1961. *The Daily Life of the Aztecs* (translated by Patrick O'Brian, Weidenfeld and Nicolson, London; and Penguin Books, 1964).

SPENCE, LEWIS

    1923. *The Gods of Mexico*. London.

SPINDEN, E. S.

    1933. 'The Place of Tajin in Totonac Archaeology' (*American Anthropologist*, n.s., Vol. 35, pp. 271–87, Menasha).

SPINDEN, HERBERT J.

    1913. *A Study of Maya Art* (Memoirs, Peabody Museum of American Archaeology and Ethnology, Harvard University, Vol. 6, Cambridge).

    1916. *See* Wissler and Spinden.

    1924. *The Reduction of Mayan Dates* (Papers, Peabody Museum of American Archaeology and Ethnology, Harvard University, Vol. 6, no. 4, Cambridge).

    1928. *Ancient Civilizations of Mexico and Central America* (Handbook Series, American Museum of Natural History, No. 3, 3rd edition, New York).

    1933. 'Indian Manuscripts of Southern Mexico' (*Annual Report of the Smithsonian Institution for 1933*, pp. 429–51, Washington).

    1940. 'Diffusion of Maya Astronomy' (in *The Maya and Their Neighbors*, pp. 162–78, New York).

    1957. *Maya Art and Civilization*. Indian Hills, Colorado.

SPRATLING, WILLIAM

    1960. *Mas Humano Que Divino* (Universidad Autónoma de México).

STARR, F.

    1908. *In Indian Mexico*. Chicago.

STAUB, WALTER

    1933. 'Zur Uebereinanderschichtung der Völker und Kulturen an der Ostküste von Mexiko' (*Mitteilungen der Geographisch-Ethnographischen Gesellschaft in Zürich*, Vol. 33, pp. 3–26, Zurich).

STIRLING, M. W.

    1939. 'Discovering the New World's Oldest Dated Work of Man' (the *National Geographic Magazine*, Vol. 76, no. 2, Washington).

    1940a. 'Great Stone Faces of the Mexican Jungle' (the *National Geographic Magazine*, Vol. 78, no. 3, pp. 309–34, Washington).

    1940b. 'An Initial Series from Tres Zapotes, Vera Cruz, Mexico' (National Geographic Society, *Contributed Technical Papers, Mexican Archaeology Series*, Vol. 1, no. 1, Washington).

    1943. *Stone Monuments of Southern Mexico* (Publication 138, Bureau of American Ethnology, Washington).

    1955. *Stone Monuments of the Rio Chiquito Veracruz, Mexico* (Bureau of American Ethnology, Bulletin 157, Washington).

STREBEL, H.
1885–9. *Alt Mexiko* (2 vols., Hamburg and Leipzig).

STRONG, WILLIAM DUNCAN
1935a. *An Introduction to Nebraska Archaeology* (Smithsonian Miscellaneous Collections, Vol. 93, no. 10, Washington).

STUDLEY, CORNELIA
1887. 'Notes upon Human Remains from Caves in Coahuila' (*Reports*, Peabody Museum of American Archaeology and Ethnology, Vol. 3, 1880–6, pp. 233–59; cf. also pp. 10, 21, 32, Cambridge).

SWANTON, JOHN R.
1911. *Indian Tribes of the Lower Mississippi and Adjacent Coasts of the Gulf of Mexico* (Bureau of American Ethnology, Bulletin 43, Washington).
1911b. See Thomas, Cyrus, and Swanton, John R.

SWANTON ESSAYS
1940. See Emmart, Emily W.

TAX, SOL; EISELEY, L. C.; ROUSE, IRVING; AND VOEGELIN, C. F., EDITORS
1953. *An Appraisal of Anthropology Today* (University of Chicago Press, Chicago).

TEEPLE, JOHN E.
1931. 'Maya Astronomy' (Carnegie Institution of Washington, pub. no. 403, *Contributions to American Archaeology*, Vol. 1, no. 2, pp. 29–115, Washington).
1935. *Tenayuca* (Departamento de Monumentos, Mexico).

TEZOZOMOC, H.
1878. *Crónica Mexicana* (XVI Century) (in Biblioteca Mexicana, Mexico).
1944. *Crónica Mexicana*. Mexico.

THOMAS, CYRUS, AND SWANTON, JOHN R.
1911. *Indian Languages of Mexico and Central America and Their Geographical Distribution* (Bureau of American Ethnology, Bulletin 44, Washington).

THOMPSON, J. ERIC
1927. *A Correlation of the Mayan and European Calendars* (Field Museum of Natural History, Anthropological Series, Vol. 17, no. 1, Chicago).
1932. *Civilization of the Mayas* (Anthropology Leaflet 25, 2nd edition, Field Museum of Natural History, Chicago).
1933. *Mexico before Cortés*. New York.
1934. 'Sky Bearers, Colors and Directions in Maya and Mexican Religion' (*Carnegie Institution of Washington, pub. no. 436*, pp. 209–42, Washington).

1935. 'Maya Chronology: the Correlation Question' (*Carnegie Institution of Washington, pub. no. 456*, contribution no. 14, Washington).

1935. *See* Gann, Thomas, and Thompson, J. Eric.

1939. 'Excavations at San José, British Honduras' (*Carnegie Institution of Washington, pub. no. 506*, Washington).

1943. 'Some Sculptures from Southeast Quetzaltenango, Guatemala' (*Carnegie Institution of Washington, Vol. 1, pub. no. 17*, pp. 100–12, Cambridge).

1954. *The Rise and Fall of Maya Civilization* (University of Oklahoma Press, Norman).

1958. *Civilization of the Mayas* (Hatchards, London).

1960. *Maya Hieroglyphic Writing – An Introduction*, Second Edition (University of Oklahoma Press, Norman).

TOLSTOY, PAUL

1958. 'Surface Survey of the Northern Valley of Mexico' (*Transactions of the American Philosophical Society*, n.s., Vol. 48, Pt 5, Philadelphia).

TONALAMATL AUBIN

1900. *A Pre-Columbian Codex Preserved in the National Library, Paris* (published by le Duc de Loubat, Paris).

See Orozco y Berra, 'El Tonalamatl', 1887 (*Anales del Museo Nacional*, 1a Época, Vol. 4, pp. 30–44 and end of book, Mexico).

TORQUEMADA, JUAN DE

1723. *Los Veinte i un Libros Rituales i Monarchía Indiana* (3 vols., Madrid).

1943. *Los Veinte y un Libros Rituales: Monarquía Indiana* (3 vols., Mexico).

TOSCANO, SALVADOR

1944. *El Arte y la Historia de Occidente de México* (Instituto de Investigaciones Esteticas. Universidad Nacional Autónoma de Mexico. 2nd edition aumentada, Mexico).

1946. 'El Arte Antiguo' (*México y la Cultura*, Mexico).

TOTTEN, GEORGE OAKLEY

1926. *Maya Architecture*. Washington.

TOZZER, ALFRED M.

1912. 'The Value of Ancient Mexican Manuscripts in the Study of the General Development of Writing' (*The Smithsonian Institution, Annual Report for 1911*, pp. 493–506, Washington).

1918. 'The Domain of the Aztecs and their Relation to the Prehistoric Cultures of Mexico' (*Holmes Anniversary Volume*, pp. 464–8, Lancaster).

1921. *Excavation of a Site at Santiago Ahuitzotla, D. F. Mexico* (Bureau of American Ethnology, Bulletin 74, Washington).

1927. 'Time and American Archaeology' (*Natural History*, Vol. 27, pp. 210–21, New York).

1930. 'Maya and Toltec Figures at Chichen Itza' (*Proceedings, XXIII International Congress of Americanists*, New York, 1928, pp. 155–64, New York).

1933. *Tres Siglos de Arquitectura Colonial* (Departamento de Monumentos, Secretaría de Educación Pública, Mexico).

1937. 'Prehistory in Middle America' (*The Hispanic American Historical Review*, Vol. 17, pp. 151–9, Durham).

1957. 'Chichen Itza and its Cenote of Sacrifice' (*Memoirs of the Peabody Museum*, Harvard University, Vols. 11, 12, Cambridge).

TRIBUTE ROLL OF MONTEZUMA (See CODEX MENDOZA)
   A Pre-Columbian Codex Preserved in the Museo Nacional, Mexico.
   See Peñafiel, *Monumentos*, 1890, Vol. 2, Pls. 228–59; *Transactions of the American Philosophical Society*, Philadelphia, 1892, n.s., Vol. 17, Pt 2, Philadelphia.

VAILLANT, GEORGE C.
   1929. 'On the Threshold of Native American Civilization' (*Natural History*, Vol. 29, pp. 530–42, New York).

   1930a. 'Excavations at Zacatenco' (*Anthropological Papers*, American Museum of Natural History, Vol. 32, Pt 1, New York).

   1930b. 'Reconstructing the Beginning of a History' (*Natural History*, Vol. 30, pp. 606–16, New York).

   1931a. 'A Bearded Mystery' (*Natural History*, Vol. 31, pp. 243–52, New York).

   1931b. 'Excavations at Ticoman' (*Anthropological Papers*, American Museum of Natural History, Vol. 32, Pt 2, New York).

   1932a. 'A Pre-Columbian Jade' (*Natural History*, Vol. 32, pp. 512–20, 557–8, New York).

   1932b. See Merwin and Vaillant.

   1934. See Vaillant and Vaillant.

   1935a. 'Excavations at El Arbolillo' (*Anthropological Papers*, American Museum of Natural History, Vol. 35, Pt 2, New York).

   1935b. 'Early Cultures of the Valley of Mexico: Results of the Stratigraphical Project of the American Museum of Natural History in the Valley of Mexico, 1928–33' (*Anthropological Papers*, American Museum of Natural History, Vol. 35, Pt 3, New York).

   1935c. 'Chronology and Stratigraphy in the Maya Area' (*Maya Research*, Vol. 2, pp. 119–43, New York).

   1935d. *Artists and Craftsmen in Ancient Central America* (American

Museum of Natural History, Guide Leaflet Series, No. 88, New York. Supplement: Chart in Vaillant, 1936, Guide Leaflet No. 103).

1936. 'The History of the Valley of Mexico' (*Natural History*, Vol. 38, pp. 324–40, New York. Accompanying chart reprinted as *Guide Leaflet No. 103*, American Museum of Natural History).

1937a. 'History and Stratigraphy in the Valley of Mexico' (*The Scientific Monthly*, Vol. 44, pp. 307–24, New York).

1937b. 'The Death Throes of the Aztec Nation' (*Natural History*, Vol. 39, pp. 185–95, New York).

1938. 'A Correlation of Archaeological and Historical Sequences in the Valley of Mexico' (*American Anthropologist*, n.s., Vol. 40, pp. 535–73, Menasha).

1939a. 'The Twilight of Aztec Civilization' (*Natural History*, Vol. 43, pp. 38–46, New York).

1939b. *Indian Arts in North America*. New York.

1939c. 'An Early Occurrence of Cotton in Mexico' (*American Anthropologist*, n.s., Vol. 41, p. 170, Menasha).

1940. 'Patterns in Middle American Archaeology' (in *The Maya and Their Neighbors*, pp. 295–305, New York).

1957. *La Civilta Azteca* (Giulio Einaudi, Rome).

1962. *The Aztecs of Mexico* (Doubleday & Company, New York).

VAILLANT, GEORGE C., EDITOR

1940. *A Sacred Almanac of the Aztecs* (*Tonalamatl of the Codex Borbonicus*) (American Museum of Natural History, Limited Edition, New York).

VAILLANT, S. B., AND VAILLANT, G. C.

1934. 'Excavations at Gualupita' (*Anthropological Papers*, American Museum of Natural History, Vol. 35, no. 1, New York).

VILLAGRA CALETI, AGUSTÍN

1949. *Bonampak: La Ciudad de los Muros Pintados. Nota preliminar por Salvador Toscano* (Supplemento al Tomo 3, 1947–8 de los Anales, Instituto Nacional de Antropología e Historia, Mexico).

1952. 'Teotihuacan: sus Pinturas Murales' (*Anales del Instituto Nacional de Antropología e Historia*, Vol. 5, pp. 67–74).

1954. 'Las Pinturas de Tetitla, Atetelco e Ixtapantongo' (*Artes de México*, No. 3, Mexico).

1956–7. 'Las Pinturas Murales de Atetelco, Teotihuacan' (*Revista Mexicana de Estudios Antropológicos*, Vol. 14, Pt 2, pp. 9–14, Mexico).

1959. 'La Pintura Mural' (*Esplendor del México Antiguo*, Vol. 2, pp. 651–70, Mexico).

VEYTIA, MARIANO
1836. *Historia Antigua de México* (3 vols., Mexico).

VIOLLET-LE-DUC, E. E.
1863. *See* Charnay and Viollet-le-Duc.

WAUCHOPE, ROBERT
1947. 'An Approach to the Maya Correlation Problem through Guatemala Highland Archaeology and Native Annals' (*American Antiquity* Vol. 13, pp. 59–66, Menasha).

1950. 'Tentative Sequence of Preclassic Ceramics' (*Middle American Research Records*, Vol. 1, No. 14, Tulane University, New Orleans).

1954. 'Implications of Radiocarbon Dates from Middle and South America' (*Middle American Research Records*, Vol. 2, No. 2, Tulane University, New Orleans).

WATERMAN, T. T.
1917. 'Bandelier's Contribution to the Study of Ancient Mexican Social Organization' (*University of California Publications in American Archaeology and Ethnology*, Vol. 12, no. 7, pp. 249–82, Berkeley).

1924. 'On Certain Antiquities in Western Guatemala' (*Bulletin of the Pan-American Union*, April, 1924, pp. 1–21, Washington).

WEIANT, C. W.
1943. *Introduction to the Ceramics of Tres Zapotes, Veracruz, Mexico* (Bureau of American Ethnology, Bulletin 139, Washington).

WEITLANER, ROBERTO, AND LEONARD, JUAN
1959. 'De la Cueva al Palacio' (*Esplendor del México Antiguo*, Vol. 2, pp. 933–56).

WEYERSTALL, A.
1932. 'Some Observations on Indian Mounds, Idols and Pottery in the Lower Papaloapam Basin, State of Vera Cruz, Mexico' (*Middle American Research Series*, pub. no. 4, pp. 23–69, Tulane University, New Orleans).

WICKE, CHARLES
1959. 'Así Comían los Aztecas' (*Esplendor del Mexico Antiguo*, pp. 983–94, Mexico, D. F.).

WILLEY, GORDON R.
1955. 'The Interrelated Rise of the Native Cultures of Middle and South America' (in *New Interpretations of Aboriginal American Culture History*, 75th Anniversary Volume of the Anthropological Society of Washington, pp. 28–45, Washington).

1955. 'Prehistoric Civilizations of Nuclear America' (*American Anthropologist*, Vol. 57, pp. 571–93, Menasha).

1960. 'New World Prehistory' (*Science*, Vol. 131, No. 3393, pp. 73–86, Washington).

WINNING, HASSO VON
  1959. 'El Sacerdocio' (*Esplendor del México Antiguo*, Vol. 1, pp. 141–8).

WISSLER, CLARK
  1938. *The American Indian* (3rd edition, New York).

WISSLER, CLARK, AND SPINDEN, HERBERT J.
  1916. 'The Pawnee Human Sacrifice to the Morning Star' (*American Museum Journal*, Vol. 16, no. 1, pp. 49–55, New York).

WOLF, ERIC R.
  1959. *Sons of the Shaking Earth*. Chicago.

WORMINGTON, H. M.
  1957. *Ancient Man in North America* (Denver Museum of Natural History, Popular Series, No. 4).

YANEZ RUIZ, MANUEL
  1959. 'Los Tributos en los Aztecas' (*Esplendor del México Antiguo*, Vol. 2, pp. 777–88, Mexico, D. F.).

YANOVSKI, E.
  1936. *Food Plants of the North American Indians* (U. S. Department of Agriculture, Miscellaneous Publications, No. 237, Washington).

ZINGG, R. M.
  1935. *See* Bennett and Zingg.

ZURITA, A.
  1891. 'Breve y Sumaria Relación de los Señores de la Nueva España' (García Icazbalceta, *Nueva Colección de Documentos para la Historia de México*, Vol. 3, pp. 71–227, Mexico).

Index

The rules for the pronunciation of Aztec names are simple despite the horrifying assemblage of consonants and vowels. X in general has a Sh sound; Qu has a K value; Hu and Gu have a W sound when preceding a vowel. All consonants and vowels are sounded as in Spanish. Rough English phonetic equivalents have been provided in the index to guide the errant tongue.

Index

Index

Index

Index

Index

Index

Index

*Some other Pelican books are described
on the following pages*

THE HITTITES   *O. R. Gurney*

The Hittites as a legendary Palestinian tribe are familiar to us from our schooldays. In this book the story is told of the rediscovery of the historical Hittites during the last eighty years, as the result of excavation and the decipherment of cuneiform and hieroglyphic documents. The Hittites of history were a great nation of Asia Minor, whose kings treated on equal terms with those of Egypt, Babylon, and Assyria, during a period of about two hundred years in the second millennium B.C. There was an Indo-European strain in them which is revealed in their language and perhaps in the physical types of some of the Hittite prisoners represented on Egyptian monuments. Their earliest social organization also shows some points of resemblance to that of the heroic age of Greece. Their religion on the other hand seems to have been largely that of the indigenous population, who must be supposed to have inhabited the country before the Indo-European reached it. They developed a rupestrian art, which has its roots in the soil of Mesopotamia, but exhibits a strong and independent style of its own.

This is an attempt to present a balanced picture of what is known of the Hittites and in the chapter on literature to give some impression of the more important types of documents found among their archives.

THE ANCIENT CIVILIZATIONS OF PERU

J. Alden Mason

Our detailed knowledge of the people of pre-Columbian Peru has grown enormously since 1940. Many expeditions have made excavations and published their reports. Regions archaeologically unknown hitherto have yielded their secrets, and far more is known of all of them. Especially is this true of the cultures that preceded the Inca whom Pizarro found and conquered in one of the great adventures of history. Four thousand years before his day, radiocarbon analyses now permit us to state with confidence that simple fishermen-hunters on the coast were beginning the long climb towards the extraordinary blend of communism and monarchy that was the Inca empire. Our concepts of the latter and of its history also have been altered somewhat by recent studies. This book presents a summary of our present knowledge and point of view regarding the development and nature of these past civilizations and their fascinating and diversified country. There are 64 pages of plates.

*For a complete list of books available
please write to Penguin Books
whose address can be found on the
back of the title page*